YOUTH IDENTITY, POLITICS AND CHANGE IN CONTEMPORARY KURDISTAN

To my nieces and nephews, I hope they grow up in a more just, prosperous, and democratic Kurdistan.

Shivan Fazil

To Mari Toivanen and Dzeneta Karabegovic, the two strong women who have inspired me and surrounded me with love and wisdom since the day I met them…

Bahar Baser

This work has been part of a research project (2018-2023) called "Youth, Violence and Conflict Transformation: Exploring Mobilisation into Violence and the Role of Peacebuilding", funded by the Allan and Nesta Ferguson Trust and supported by the Centre for Trust, Peace and Social Relations, Coventry University.

The authors would like to thank Daniel Metz for his editorial assistance and Tobias Schreiner for the cover photo and Olivia Blinn for the cover design.

YOUTH IDENTITY, POLITICS AND CHANGE IN CONTEMPORARY KURDISTAN

Editors:
Shivan Fazil and Bahar Baser

TRANSNATIONAL PRESS LONDON

2021

Youth Identity, Politics and Change in Contemporary Kurdistan
Editors: Shivan Fazil and Bahar Baser

PEACE, CONFLICT AND VIOLENCE SERIES: 1
Series Editors: Bahar Baser, Marcos S. Scauso, Elena B. Stavrevska

Copyright © 2021 Transnational Press London

All rights reserved. This book or any portion thereof may not be reproduced or used in any manner whatsoever without the express written permission of the publisher except for the use of brief quotations in a book review or scholarly journal.

First published in 2021 by Transnational Press London in the United Kingdom. 13 Stamford Place, Sale, M33 3BT, UK.
www.tplondon.com

Transnational Press London® and the logo and its affiliated brands are registered trademarks.

Requests for permission to reproduce material from this work should be sent to: sales@tplondon.com

Paperback
ISBN: 978-1-80135-078-5
Digital
ISBN: 978-1-80135-079-2

Cover Photo by Tobias Schreiner, www.tobias-schreiner.com
Cover Design: Olivia Blinn, www.oliviablinn.com

Transnational Press London Ltd. is a company registered in England and Wales No. 8771684

CONTENTS

Foreword: Youth in the Kurdistan Region and Their Past and Present Roles 1

Karwan Jamal Tahir

Kurdish Youth as Agents of Change: Political Participation, Looming Challenges, and Future Predictions 13

Shivan Fazil and Bahar Baser

CHAPTER 1. Youth Political Participation and Prospects for Democratic Reform in Iraqi Kurdistan 25

Munir H. Mohammad

CHAPTER 2. Social Media, Youth Organization, and Public Order in the Kurdistan Region of Iraq 47

Megan Connelly

CHAPTER 3. Constructing Their Own Liberation: Youth's Reimagining of Gender and Queer Sexuality in Iraqi Kurdistan 75

Hawzhin Azeez

CHAPTER 4. Kurdish Youth and Civic Culture: Support for Democracy Among Kurdish and non-Kurdish Youth in Iraq 97

Dastan Jasim

CHAPTER 5. Youth and Nationalism in the Kurdistan Region of Iraq 125

Sofia Barbarani

CHAPTER 6. An Elitist Interpretation of KRG Governance: How Self-Serving Kurdish Elites Govern Under the Guise of Democracy and the Subsequent Implications for Representation and Change 139

Bamo Nouri

CHAPTER 7. Educational Policy in the Kurdistan Region: A Critical Democratic Response 163

Abdurrahman Ahmad Wahab

CHAPTER 8. Making Heaven in a Shithole: Changing Political Engagement in the Aftermath of the Islamic State 185

Lana Askari

CHAPTER 9. Kurdish Youth and Religious Identity: Between Religious and National Tensions 201

Ibrahim Sadiq

CHAPTER 10. Youth Radicalization in Kurdistan: The Government Response 223

Kamaran Palani

AUTHORS

Karwan Jamal Tahir is the Kurdistan Regional Government's High Representative to the UK. He has previously served as the Deputy Minister at the Department of Foreign Relations where he has promoted the Kurdistan region's relations with the international community on political and cultural levels through his engagements in numerous conferences around the world. From 2005-2007 he also served as an Advisor at the Council of Ministers and a Senior Advisor at the KRG's Ministry of Natural Resources. He played a pivotal role in the Ministry of Natural Resources' strategic plans and relations with the IOCs.

Shivan Fazil is a Researcher with the Middle East and North Africa Programme at Stockholm International Peace Research Institute. His work focuses on drivers of conflict, peacebuilding, and governance in Iraq. Shivan holds an MSc in Middle Eastern Politics from the School of Oriental and African Studies, University of London. He is the recipient of the Chevening Scholarship, a prestigious award by the UK Foreign, Commonwealth and Development Office.

Bahar Baser is Associate Professor in Middle Eastern Studies at Durham University. Previously, she was Associate Professor at the Centre for Trust, Peace and Social Relations at Coventry University. She is also a research associate at the Security Institute for Leadership in Africa, Stellenbosch University and visiting researcher at the Tampere Peace Research Institute, Finland. Her expertise lies in diaspora studies and peace and conflict studies with a regional focus on the Middle East.

Munir Hasan Mohammad holds a PhD in Politics and International Studies from University of Warwick, United Kingdom. Previously he was Lecturer at Salahaddin University-Erbil. He also worked as a trainer with several International NGOs to promote democracy in the Kurdistan region. His research interests include international politics of the Middle East with particular focus in democracy and democratization politics. He is the author of a book on Social Media and Democratization in Iraqi Kurdistan.

Megan Connelly is Non-Resident Fellow at the American University of

Iraq-Sulaimani, Institute of Regional and International Studies. She is focusing on the politics of the Kurdistan Region – Iraq and she has published articles for the Middle East Institute, Sada, and the Arab Center for Research and Policy Studies. She received her BA from Buffalo State College in 2014 and her JD from SUNY University at Buffalo in 2020.

Hawzhin Azeez is a Kurdish academic, activist, and poet. She holds a Ph.D. in Political Science and International Relations specializing in post-conflict nation building and democratization. She has worked with local and international NGOs in the field of post-war reconstruction in Syria for three years. She is researching and teaching as a visiting scholar at the American University's Centre for Gender and Development Studies in Sulaimani, Iraq.

Dastan Jasim is a doctoral candidate at the German Institute for Global and Area Studies in Hamburg. Her dissertation project covers the Civic Culture of Statelessness of Kurds in Iraq, Iran, Syria and Turkey. She is also a researcher at the Heidelberg Institute for International Conflict Research, focusing on violent conflicts of Kurdish areas in Syria and Iraq. In 2019, she was a visiting scholar at the Center of Gender Development and Studies at the American University of Iraq - Sulaimani, where she coordinated a project analyzing gender depictions in Iraqi TV.

Sofia Barbarani is a freelance journalist covering the Middle East. Her work focuses on the impact of conflict on civilian populations, as well as gender, security, politics and women's issues. She was based in the Kurdistan Region from 2013 to 2016, during which she reported on the rise and fall of ISIS in Iraq and Syria for leading publications including The Telegraph, The Economist and Thomson Reuters Foundation.

Bamo Nouri is Lecturer in International Relations at the School of Human and Social Sciences, University of West London. He is an independent investigative journalist and writer with interests in American foreign policy and the international and domestic politics of the Middle East. He is currently an Honorary Research Fellow at City, University of London.

Abdurrahman Wahab is a Policy Researcher at Institute of Regional and International Studies (IRIS) at the American university of Iraq-Sulaimani.Previously, he was a Lecturer in the Faculty of Education at Tishk International University, in Erbil. Dr Wahab has a Ph.D. in Social Justice Education and Educational Policy from the University of Toronto. He is also a Fulbright alumnus from Iraq to the United States where he received his MA in

English. His research focuses on democratic education and pedagogy, educational policy and program evaluation, sociology of ethnic and national identities and nation-state building, teacher education, literary and cultural studies, curriculum design and program development.

Lana Askari has a PhD in Social Anthropology with Visual Media from the University of Manchester. She studied political science and anthropology at University College Utrecht and Cambridge University, and was trained in documentary filmmaking at the Granada Centre for Visual Anthropology Manchester. Lana is interested in the anthropology of the Middle East, the Kurdistan Region and issues of migration, youth, future and (urban) planning and ethnographic documentary film. Her PhD research focused on how people in Iraqi Kurdistan imagine and plan their future in times of crisis, for which she produced the films "Bridge to Kobane" (2016) and "Future Factory" (2018). She currently works for the Dutch Ministry of Foreign affairs and researches the human rights and security situation in countries in the Middle East.

Ibrahim Sadiq is a researcher and writer who has worked as a lecturer in sociology at Soran University in Iraqi Kurdistan. He is also a visiting fellow at Coventry University. He has decades of experience working with a variety of Kurdish newspapers and TV channels in Iraq and Europe and advising humanitarian organizations in the Middle East and Europe on social integration and intercultural relations.

Kamaran Palani is a Research Fellow at the Middle East Research Institute and a Lecturer in International Relations at Salahaddin University-Erbil. Palani is also an Associate Fellow at Al Sharq Strategic Research. He defended his PhD thesis on Fluidity and Dynamics of De Facto Statehood: The Case of Iraqi Kurdistan (Leiden University, 2021). His research interests include Iraqi politics, regional Kurdish politics, de facto statehood in the international system, and violent extremism in the Middle East.

FOREWORD

YOUTH IN THE KURDISTAN REGION AND THEIR PAST AND PRESENT ROLES

Karwan Jamal Tahir

Youth are an essential part of any nation's social, political, cultural, and economic capital. Nations and countries have defined this capital differently, and while there is no universally agreed international definition of the youth age group, the United Nations, for statistical purposes, describes "youth" as persons between the ages of fifteen and twenty-four.

The World Bank shares this definition of the youth and, as an international institution, aims to empower young people to help in its ambitious objectives of "ending poverty and boosting shared prosperity."

However, Kurds, especially in the Kurdistan Region of Iraq, define youth as between the ages of sixteen and thirty-five. The Ministry of Planning and the Regional Statistics Authority have conducted numerous surveys and considerable research, and some of which is referred to here to help illustrate the debates.

To understand the Kurdish youth, we have to reflect back on the history of the Kurdish nation and the environment in which its youth have been raised.

Throughout its history, the Kurdish nation has lived off its land and soil, always been peaceful, and believed in coexistence among the different peoples and nations of the wider region. From the era of the emirates in the Ottoman Empire, Kurdistan was a recognized entity that maintained considerable influence. Many historical maps that include Kurdistan as a unified entity and historical research corroborate this fact.

After the collapse of the Ottoman Empire at the end of World War I, the victors—Britain and France—reordered the region and the world to preserve peace and, no doubt, to bolster their own interests.

The contribution of the United States began with President Woodrow Wilson's support for national self-determination, but the country then opted for isolation until the end of World War II, therefore weakening Anglo-French and

German imperialism and granting it a much bigger role, including on the Kurdish questions.

Previously, however, the secret Sykes-Picot treaty of 1916 between Britain and France impacted the Middle East to the greatest extent. The original plan of Britain and France was to demarcate the Middle East to make it fit into the orbits of each respective power based on their existing interests and pursuits for greater power. Regrettably, the rights of these nations and those "who lived there" were not considered, and the agreement was implemented not in law but more in spirit. If the principle of the treaty was to be peacebuilding, then, without a doubt, peace was bestowed upon many, but it was misery that befell the Kurdish nation, which suffered the greatest impacts from the agreement later on.

This situation was changed by the emergence of the Turkish Republic, whose first nationalist leader, Kemal Ataturk, convinced the Greek Empire to block the Treaty of Sèvres, which promised an independent Kurdistan.

The Treaty of Sevres was succeeded by the Treaty of Lausanne, an agreement that denied nationhood to the Kurds and further divided them against their will between the new Turkish Republic, Iran, and the two nascent states of Iraq and Syria. The primary focus here is on what is now known formally as the Kurdistan Region of Iraq, whose status and rights are formally recognized in the landmark Iraqi constitution of 2005, although these are far from being fulfilled in law and in spirit.

From the moment of Iraq's creation as a British dominion in 1920 and as an independent republic in 1932, the Kurdish nation has struggled and fought politically to attain national rights. But throughout the history of modern Iraq, whether during the early days of the monarchy or the subsequent eras republicanism and dictatorship, the Kurds were deprived of rights and subjugated to numerous forms of oppression. This injustice and oppression led to the rise of nationalism and a spirit of resistance, which, in turn, resulted in the birth of "Kurdayeti," a concept meaning Kurdishness.

From this point, we must consider the role of youth in the Kurdish struggle for liberty and democracy, which encompassed a host of ideologies including leftism and communism, and its impact on various periods of Kurdish history.

Continued oppression and persecution have created an environment in which Kurdish youth have enlightened and educated themselves on various philosophies of struggle and liberalism. And it has also allowed them to become a driving force in revolutions, clashes of political organizations, labor rights battles, and subsequent armed conflicts.

Kurdish history has proven that youth in Kurdistan have played an influential role and have been crucial in developing the path of democracy and a sense of national responsibility as well as in building leadership and role models. They became inspiring history makers, and it is therefore essential to illuminate the different stages of the struggle and the domestic and international roles of youth in Kurdish society.

Youth in the Age of Dictatorship and Isolation

The era of dictatorship was the most tumultuous period for youth in Kurdistan, representing a time during which they were oppressed, denied their identity, isolated from the world, and prevented from participating in society. But the chauvinist Arab Ba'athist Party failed to extinguish the spark of the struggle instilled in the hearts and minds of youth and their desire to liberate the nation. They resisted the Ba'ath regime and learned from other nations' struggles for liberty, democracy, and justice.

Youth have mobilized themselves through the creation of various organization and unions, the most important of which being the Students Union of Kurdistan. Through these organizations, they labored for the nation's identity and stressed the Kurdish nation's existence, right to self-determination, and equality with other nations. The youth movement has strived for these principles, seeking to restore the long-lost rights of the Kurdish people.

Youth in Kurdistan during that period, in addition to organizing themselves, encouraged other groups and classes—workers, peasants, and women—to define the right path for struggle and to demand rights to collectively constitute a productive role in the revolution and the mass movement of progress.

Additionally, youth have an enduring belief in establishing relations with the regional and international youth organizations in order to understand the struggles of other nations and to familiarize themselves with leftist theories and ideologies. The veins of Marxist and Leninist philosophies constitute elements of a common struggle against imperialism throughout the world and within this bloc.

Oppressive Iraqi regimes have always feared youth and have sought to isolate them from the outside world to suppress the vigor of the Kurdish cause and restrict their rights within Iraq.

However, archives reveal the secret actions of Kurdish youth, who collaborated with youth groups in other nations in order to amplify the Kurdish cause on the international stage. This was in spite of the constant attempts to silence their civil, political, and organizational struggles.

I am reminded, here, of the immense contributions of these Kurdish youth leaders, figures such as Mam Jalal Talabani, who later became the first Kurdish president of Iraq, with whom I had the privilege of working as a young man myself in nineties. He stood at the forefront of the Kurdish struggle for freedom and democracy and was a prominent figure in the Socialist International organization. He was joined by others such as Ghassemlou and those who put the Kurdish questions on the agenda for notable statesman of the time, including Schmidt, Brandt, Jim Callaghan, and Francois Mitterrand. The contributions in these international forums made a real difference as we can see in the continuing contributions of prominent intellectuals in France, Germany, and the United Kingdom to this day.

Such international networking helps explain why Halabja in 1988 was a cause célèbre for previous generations of Western leaders. And a link can be made between this incident and the introduction of the no-fly zone in 1991, albeit through an initiative pioneered by the Conservative Prime Minister, John Major. It was also the result of lobbying effort by young Kurds in the United Kingdom, a significant victory for our diaspora that I will explore later.

It all illustrates how the networking in which youth engaged in was ultimately impactful, something that should be remembered by youth today who may otherwise despair over being neglected.

Youth and the Revolt

As the Ba'ath regime consolidated its power in Iraq, spheres of freedom and political activities gradually narrowed and finally diminished. Almost all forms of liberal freedom and movement have been banned with the imprisonment and execution of thousands of youth. The revolt constituted the response that created an environment in which many Kurdish youth were inspired to engage in political activities and fuel party vigor. Youth were central to the eruption of the revolution and formed its leadership and military commanders. While it normally takes years to become an effective military commander, many young Kurds were allowed no such luxury, as they were vital to securing the partial freedom of Iraqi Kurdistan in 1991.

As Winston Churchill said of the RAF pilots who beat the German air force in the Battle of Britain eighty years ago, "Never in the field of human conflict has so much been owed by so many to so few." The average British fighter pilot was just twenty years old, meaning that, at the time, they could not even vote in elections.

The active participation of youth during these periods of history was derived from a sense of national responsibility and desire to liberate the country. Their role was prime, and this illustrated that the Kurdish youth could be political leaders, enlightening the society and contributing to the creation of a democratic society and a nation-state. For that, they made enormous sacrifices.

Youth in the Era of Democracy and Openness

The progress of youth is directly linked to the environment in which they grow up such that it guides their political, economic, and social trajectories.

It is evident in this era of adaptation to political, social, and economic atmospheres that the vision, perceptions, and demands of Kurdistan's youth have changed substantially. Kurdish youth learned about the outside world, globalization, equality, human rights, civil struggle, and also the wellbeing and the way of life of other nations. All these have heightened the desire of Kurdistan's youth to engage more significantly in politics and to moderate a political system with their distinct flare, whether by participating in elections to voice their opinions or assuming roles in the country's political processes. Surveys have shown that voter turnout among Kurdish youth is 69.7 percent and that they contribute to democracy-building initiatives through civil society and democratic organizations.

Kurdistan's youth also played a key role in developing the economy by contributing to the public and private sectors. The Kurdistan Region Statistics Office and Ministry of Planning reported in 2019 that the Kurdistan Region is, in fact, a young society, with individuals aged fifteen to thirty-five constituting 62 percent of the population and 43.5 percent of the workforce.

However, the political and economic turmoil stemming from the war with ISIS has resulted in a rise in the unemployment rate—now at 23 percent—for those between the ages of fifteen and twenty-four. This rate was 9 percent until 2019, according to a section on population and the workforce in a survey conducted by the Kurdistan Region Statistics Office.

This is a stark contrast to Kurdistan's golden age of economic prosperity, which lasted from 2005 to 2014 and in which the youth played a prominent role in building the public and private sector.

Furthermore, the Kurdistan Regional Government made education one of its key priorities to overcome the isolation that Kurdish generations had endured under successive dictatorial and chauvinist regimes in Iraq. Hence, the provision of higher standards of education and the opening of many universities, colleges, and vocational institutions for youth resulted in high levels of education among the youth. A survey conducted by the KRG found that 78 percent of the youth population has educational qualifications.

Education at all levels is free in the Kurdistan Region, including at vocational institutions, colleges, and universities. Education is compulsory until the age of nine, and denying a child the right to an education is a violation of the law.

According to the Kurdistan Statistics Office survey, 92.4 percent of students receive free public education, and 6 percent receive a private education. The rate of primary school attendance is 95.53 percent, and these figures are 92 percent for lower secondary and 86 percent for upper secondary school. The KRG also provides a scholarship program to foster capacity building of the Kurdish youth, thus improving the quality of education and enhancing its relevance for broader economic and social development.

Accordingly, an overwhelming proportion of youth in the Kurdistan Region is educated and has been actively participating in the political process and contributing to the region's economic progress.

Another attribute of Kurdish youth is their proclivity for critical thinking with the objectives of problem-solving, progressiveness, and improving their wellbeing. These are the goals they fought for during the revolution.

After the liberation of the Kurdistan Region in the spring of 1991, youth built oppositional structures and supported trends of continuous progress in addition to establishing hundreds of civil society groups to strengthen the foundation of democracy, human rights, and the rule of law while maintaining critical views of deficiencies in governance. These actions are considered the main elements of progress in democracy. Within this context, youth are vital contributors to the securing the freedoms of speech and the press, which have become essential pillars of the Kurdistan Region.

According to statistics from the Kurdistan Region's Ministry of Culture and Youth, there are 894 daily, monthly, quarterly, and annual newspapers and magazines as well as 284 local and satellite radio channels. It is worth noting that the youth represent the largest group of workers in the media.

Youth and Authority

For the Kurdistan Region and its government, youth constitute an immense source of wealth and are the leading source of energy fueling societal progress.

The Kurdistan Regional Government understands and values the role and impacts of youth. Accordingly, the government designs strategies and policies to encourage youth to be a positive force and to actively participate in processes of politics and governance.

An understanding of the need for comprehensive reform at all levels resulted in the lowering of the age qualification for standing for parliament from thirty-five to twenty-five—an example of the KRG's push for increased youth participation in politics. Hence, economic reform and the government's endeavors to expand the private sector in order to encourage youth involvement is a testament to the government's belief in the strength that youth can provide.

But such reform has been stalled by both the Kurdistan Region's political and economic circumstances and the destabilizing crisis in the relationship between the federal and regional governments. This volatile relationship often causes political, social, and economic instability. The budget crisis and national wealth inequality have also inhibited natural economic growth and have increased unemployment. Youth have suffered the most from such crises at a time when young people have different hopes and aspirations. Failures to meet their expectations and demands have led to criticisms and calls for reform.

Youth and the Search for Identity

For the Kurdish youth, identity is a two-fold concept with national identity and self-identity, both of which are intertwined and interrelated.

Kurdish youth have fought throughout history to establish the national identity alongside other segments of society, similar to the struggles of youth in other nations. Psychologically, this lack of ownership over the national identity has caused a degree of tension in the hearts of Kurds that will persist until it is ameliorated and all Kurdish people, including the youth, are enabled to uphold their Kurdish national identity as well as a recognized and respected cultural identity.

Moreover, from a theoretical perspective, the Kurds have not yet been able to answer the question of "Who am I?" A Kurd would indeed say, "I am Kurd," but this answer has often been challenged by responses identifying with Iraqis, Syrians, Turks, or Iranians. They may be a part of those countries but should have the right to describe themselves as Kurds, speak their own language, and have democratic rights.

This is one of the most profound problems in the Middle East. The continued suppression of myriad identities has prevented the Middle East from achieving its potential of cultural, political, and economic success. But this is unlikely to happen unless dominant state actors recognize the Middle East as a mosaic of Arabs, Persians, Turks, Christians, Jews, and, of course, Kurds. There are approximately forty million Kurds, and they should be embraced rather than ignored and oppressed.

The other element is youth self-identity, which evolves together with the natural progression through the stages of life. Youth identity in the Kurdistan Region is perceived positively due to the role that youth play in the stages of its construction. Behaviors, ideas, courage, revolution, and resistance are all attributes of the Kurdish youth identity. It is a label that has been emphasized by different civil society organizations, media outlets, public opinion surveys, and politicians. These attributes of self-identity are affixed to the majority of Kurdish youth in Kurdistan.

At the same time, there is another group whose identity is viewed as listless, unproductive, and negligent, but these characteristics describe a minority of individuals.

The rates of crime and drug addiction among the youth population, according to statistics published annually by the Kurdistan Region's Ministry of Interior, are the lowest recorded and, in some instances, are nonexistent.

Even under the cruel circumstances that have plagued Kurds and Kurdistan in which oppressor regimes have attempted to alienate, ethnically cleanse the Kurdish nation, and conduct genocide against them, ideologies of extremism and terrorism have, still, never become a characteristic inherent to the Kurdish identity. This is why the efforts to achieve a national identity have placed significant importance on favorably constituting self-identity.

Youth and Diplomacy

The Kurdistan Region's welcoming policy toward foreigners and foreign investment has created an environment in which many opportunities have emerged for youth to explore and benefit from. Many young people are playing a pivotal role in our efforts at diplomacy and good governance after studying international relations and other disciplines both in Kurdistan and abroad.

The previous priority of revolutionary struggle has transformed into one of academic endeavor, to study our history and conduct research to prove the "Kurd is a Nation" and inform the world diplomatically, politically, and culturally about Kurdistan's history and legitimacy. This will raise awareness among foreign nations of culture and values in which the Kurdish nation believes so strongly. Kurdish youth have actively progressed in this field and have contributed to the shaping of Kurdistan.

Youth in the Diaspora

The Kurdish diaspora, including youth, is an integral component and vital asset of the Kurdistan Region. The youth in the diaspora fall into two categories. The first group represents youth from families who emigrated from Kurdistan and were either born abroad or arrived at an early age. The second group comprises those who emigrated from or fled Kurdistan for various reasons and motivations.

Some are keen on self-development, gaining experience, and lobbying for their nation. Others can assist their nation economically. Others yet can promote Kurdish culture, from cuisine to music. All can create political, cultural, and social benefits for the Kurdistan Region.

Conclusion and Comparison

Have the Kurdish youth at home and abroad been able to incorporate these events and developments into their own experiences and struggles? Does the Kurdistan government offer an environment in which they can voice their demands and ambitions? Are youth presently educated about progressive concepts and democracy? Have youth been able to fill the expected pivotal role in helping the economy prosper and becoming a force of productivity? Are we doing enough? The answers are not so simple.

Empowering youth in society depends partly on their own actions and behaviors as well as on the functions of government and the circumstances and climate in which they come of age.

Youth often boycott politics despite the centrality of politics in daily life. Through political participation, they can maintain and secure their future along with that of their nation. We must convince youth not to ignore politics but, instead, to become more involved in these issues.

Apart from positive arguments, we must also consider some criticism to offer a fair analysis and identify obstacles in order to provide solutions.

In the end, if we analytically compare the roles of youth at different stages, it becomes clear that during the fascist rule, the youth of Kurdistan, like the other elements of society, faced threats and persecution, were deprived of education, and were isolated from the world.

The only permissible party then was the Ba'ath party, which was not a popular entity. All other parties and political activities were banned, and work opportunities were extremely limited.

But the obstacles and aggressions of that era created a dedicated and revolutionary generation defined by a form of patriotism blended with nationalism, freedom and democracy. These tenets became a core of the revolutionary struggle and led to the liberation of part of the Kurdistan Region of Iraq and ushered in a new age for the Kurdish cause.

This era—the stage following liberation, freedom, consolidation of the democratic pillars, globalization, and social media—brought transformations in which a new generation emerged, different from previous, that touted grander and more ambitious desires.

Although the role of youth in the Kurdistan Region is prominent and straightforward, it is too early to conduct a distinctive assessment of youth in the new globalized world. The impacts of social media and other obstacles are largely responsible for hindering the development of youth.

As an older generation, we must remember the obstacles we faced and understand that for our children and grandchildren, new obstacles have appeared. This is how the world has functioned for thousands of generations.

Kurdish youth are not biologically distinct from the youth of any of the advanced countries in which they have a stable and established democratic state and a steadfast economy and culture. But Kurdish youth are from a divided nation and unstable region, politically and economically, due to dictatorial rule and a prevalence of undemocratic and neglectful authorities.

Had they been in similar circumstances, they would have performed similarly. Still, we must acknowledge that Kurdish youth, despite the challenges they have faced historically and the absence of opportunities to pursue endeavors more creatively, have still played a significant role in developing Kurdistan and its democratic processes.

There is a pressing need for youth movements, political parties, government authorities, and civil organizations to collectively and comprehensively cooperate to set the youth on the right path and encourage them to assume both constructive and productive roles. The alternative is the adherence of some youth to following populist movements, which represents one of the greatest threats in global politics today, and such inclinations would directly impact the functions and trajectory of governance and national security. It would also have directly influence youth, and Kurdistan is certainly not immune from the rise of populism.

Political thinkers always cite the importance of youth. Although this notion may be obvious, any country that fails to support its youth will lose the opportunity to gain from the potential of a young generation, even if older generations cannot always immediately understand.

We are, in every sense, a young country. My hope is that the historical importance of youth in general—and our youth in particular—is understood.

KURDISH YOUTH AS AGENTS OF CHANGE: POLITICAL PARTICIPATION, LOOMING CHALLENGES, AND FUTURE PREDICTIONS

Shivan Fazil and Bahar Baser

Scholars who research peacebuilding and post-conflict reconstruction repeatedly warn policymakers and practitioners that youth should be an indispensable component of peacebuilding strategies from the very start of peace negotiations that seek the reconstruction and development phases in conflict settings. The body of scholarly work on the role of youth in building sustainable peace has emerged rapidly in recent years, focusing on a wide range of topics, from deradicalization to youth employment as a peacebuilding strategy (Berents and Mollica 2020; Borer, Darby, and McEvoy 2006; Izzi, 2013). However, as Berents and McEvoy-Levy (2015, 115) rightly assert, "Youth voices and experiences are still far from integrated or understood in critical security or other scholarly deliberations about peace praxis." The literature often presents young people as a combative or destabilizing force within post-conflict communities (Ozerdem and Podder 2011) or as victims and passive recipients of conflict (Del Felice and Wisler 2007). But more recent studies suggest that they also work on the frontlines of peacebuilding, contributing to the rebuilding of civil society and the local economy (Ozerdem and Podder 2015). Berents and Mollica (2020) also underline that "youth are active peacebuilders who negotiate systems of insecurity and risk to work for peace in their communities and countries and on the international stage." The academic literature is slowly catching up, yet policymakers and practitioners are still slow to consider the potential of youth. Policymakers must better tailor economic, socio-cultural, and political approaches toward youth engagement in order to enhance their agency in political processes. Therefore, we must ask what positive role youth can play in peacebuilding and development in post-conflict societies and what can be done to enhance their positive contribution. To find answers to these questions, it becomes imperative that we "study further how youth think and feel about war and peace, peace processes, conflict and conflict resolution, politics and violence, themselves, the 'other,' and the 'future'" (McEvoy-Levy 2006, 285).

Research suggests that youth are still given little room to influence political processes and overcome hurdles in terms of finding space to engage with existing networks and structures. Young people's lack of political representation and their ostracization from decision-making in many conflict-affected societies explains why their positive contributions go unrecognized (Ozerdem and Podder 2015). Young people, whether they experience war and trauma directly or indirectly, are still vulnerable, as they often face "additional barriers of a lack of sufficient education, health care, protection, livelihood opportunities, recreational activities, friendship, and family support" (Pandey 2016, 153), even after a conflict ends. The disparities that youth face in accessing economic, political, and socio-cultural resources explain why the impact of youth peacebuilding activities is sometimes limited. Many young people also experience a "double" marginalization due to gender, disability, religion, or ethnic status, yet the current literature and programming often fail to consider this when seeking to understand barriers to youth participation. Youth must be included in political processes in order to feel that they are a part of the solution in peacebuilding rather than feeling sidelined by an older generation making decisions on their behalf. Youth also must better engage with each other to create bottom-up perspectives in order to influence such political processes. As Ungerleider succinctly argues, "Youth dialogue is part of a holistic, programmatic approach to building relationships and a sense of empowerment, particularly for teens from communities in conflict" (2012, 381–82).

There are many ways in which youth can engage with political mechanisms in post-conflict settings. Some youth segments might opt for becoming part of the system —a cog in the wheel —and therefore do not challenge existing structures but, to the contrary, enforce them. Others still might choose to become bystanders and refrain from action even though current conditions that are the remnants of myriad conflicts also affect their lives and future prospects. Some might even choose to protest either peacefully or violently. As McEvoy-Levy states, "When mainstream or establishment politics are barred, children will still engage in political activity, often violent and structured by confrontation and brinkmanship rather than dialogue and cooperation" (2001, 24).

How can we ensure that young people's voices are heard and acted upon in societies in which youth have inherited traumas from a violent past or where marginalization has previously been a factor that has facilitated their violent mobilization? In what ways does this create a duty or responsibility for policymakers to create spaces for youth participation?

Today's youth are challenging the older political class around the world and are forming "new political generations" (Roberts 2015). Examples from South Africa and elsewhere where peace processes were deemed to be successful show signs of youth disapproval of the current post-conflict conditions. Moreover, the Arab Spring witnessed numerous youth movements emerge in authoritarian and illiberal contexts (Schwartz 2010). This book was prepared in light of these discussions and aims to contribute to these ongoing debates by presenting as a case study for the situation of youth in the Kurdistan Region of Iraq (KRI). Youth involvement in efforts for peace, democratization, and development in the KRI and beyond is crucial to foster sustainable peace in the region, in the short and long term. In the KRI today, youth are involved in both violent conflict and in peacebuilding initiatives. As these young people represent the future of the region, their participation in political processes is vital for constructing a genuinely democratic country where structural inequalities are eliminated, rule of law is restored, and basic freedoms are protected by the governing bodies. The youth therefore continue to face important decisions about how they will respond to the existing divisions and what impact they can have on the future developments (Pruitt 2011).

This edited volume is the first book that specifically focuses on the Iraqi Kurdish youth and their political, social, and economic participation in Kurdistan, situating the youth within these contexts in the KRI. It brings together a variety of authors who are specialized in diverse aspects of youth politics and Kurdish studies and offer a comprehensive understanding of youth's role in social change and reform in Kurdistan. We shed light on the positive areas through which youth can contribute to Kurdistan's future, and we present the political, social, and economic hurdles that youth confront in pursuit of active participation in nation- and state-building process in Kurdistan. The contributors come from academic and nonacademic backgrounds, and each author focuses on a different aspect of Kurdish youth at home and abroad. Our approach is interdisciplinary, and we aim to create a fruitful source for those wishing to better understand contemporary youth politics in a de facto state that aspires for independence after having survived wars, massacres, and genocides.

Youth Participation and Politics in the Kurdistan Region of Iraq: A Bumpy Road Ahead

The contemporary history of the KRI is marked by conflict, war, and ethnic cleansing under Saddam Hussein and the tyranny of the Ba'ath regime, significantly affecting the political situation of the Kurds in the Middle East. Most of the recent academic literature has focused on the broader picture or, in other words, the macro politics of the Kurdish conundrum within Iraq and beyond. The sociological issues that concern the everyday lives of Kurdish people and their concerns for the future have been, to some extent, ignored in the Western academic literature. There is little scholarship about the Kurdish population and their socio-economic conditions after 2003, and almost none about the younger generation of Kurds who came of age during autonomous Kurdish rule. This is a generation that, unlike their forebears, has no direct memory of the decades-long campaigns of repression. Studying and examining the rise of this generation of Kurdish young millennials—"Generation 2000"— who came of age in the aftermath of the United States invasion of Iraq offers a unique approach to understand the dynamics in a region that underwent substantial socio-political transformation after 2003 as well as the impact of these developments on the youth population. Pursuing different themes and lines of inquiry —from youth identity and political participation to education reform policies and social media —the contributors analyze the challenges and opportunities for young men and women to fulfill their needs and desire and contribute to the ongoing quest for nationhood and nation-building.

Similar to federal Iraq, the demographic characteristics of the KRI suggest a historically youthful society. There are 1.8 million people aged fifteen to twenty-nine, constituting nearly 28.5 percent of the population. The KRI also has a significant share of the population aged ten to fourteen, corresponding to 11 percent of the population (UNDP 2014). This youthful population indicates a considerable number of adolescents with a high dependency ratio that challenges the government to implement certain programs and projects to meet their specific needs in education and health. The needs of the older age group are different but no less challenging as they attempt to start a new phase in life focused on completing their education, finding employment, and forming families.

Having a young population is indeed a positive characteristic of a developing country. It provides opportunities as youth reach working age rebalances the population inside and outside of the job market in order to reduce the dependency ratio, increase national income, and improve productivity. This positive phenomenon, known as "demographic dividend," is, in essence, a change in the population structure brought about by decreased fertility while the working-age population is still high. Its successful management depends on timely and responsive social and economic policies. The threat of the demographic youth bulge lies in the assumption that youth, particularly young men facing "political disenfranchisement" and a lack of outlets for formal socio-economic participation, will likely resort to some combination of apathy, violence, radicalization, or emigration (Herrera 2009). Furthermore, a large youthful population, apart from constituting a burden on resources, could threaten social stability, especially if accompanied by "ethnic and sectarian" divisions, real or perceived. Recent studies suggest a strong correlation between countries prone to conflict and those with burgeoning youth populations (Beehner 2007).

The above-mentioned population transition will last for more than a generation in Iraq due to slowly declining fertility rates and increasing life expectancy. Furthermore, federal Iraq, including the KRI, must wait until at least 2030 for the proportion of children and youth under fifteen to fall below 30 percent and the proportion of people aged sixty-five and older to dip below 15 percent (UNDP 2014). This projected population growth is dangerous as long as the KRI, similar to federal Iraq, lacks the social infrastructure necessary to integrate them. While the KRI has remained less susceptible to sectarian divisions, its ongoing revenue sharing and territorial disputes with Iraq and the contentious nature of internal Kurdish politics coupled with economic crises and corruption continue to thwart opportunities for its large youthful population. Such a stagnant socio-economic situation could potentially prompt a radical response by the youth.

The exclusion of youth has clear implications, with a profound impact on "youth belonging," as 22.2 percent of Iraqis aged fifteen to twenty-nine wish to emigrate. This rate increases to 35.5 percent in the KRI. However, motivations for emigration are complex and should not be reduced merely to insecurity and livelihood, as the KRI has until recently been relatively more stable and prosperous than the rest of Iraq. The key motivations identified as prompting emigration for Iraqis, including young men from the KRI, are a lack of access to employment (30 percent), higher incomes (12 percent), and education (18 percent) (UNDP 2014). But those who remain, by choice or circumstance, seek more than earning a living. They have fostered an increase in youth activism, largely outside formal political structures such as established political parties. Youth groups established in the KRI all represent broad segments of youth who believe their interests are not represented—or even overlooked—by the all-powerful ruling parties and are yet to be swayed by the opposition parties. Hence, they set themselves apart from the older generations by rejecting their institutions and practices as unrepresentative and inadequate.

The role of youth in post-conflict societies in terms of political participation and peacebuilding is also frequently overlooked. As we mentioned above, international and peacebuilding actors are increasingly aware of the need to include young people more substantively in shaping society. It is imperative to address the question of how the peacebuilding actors might be enabled to fully integrate young people into activities geared toward political change and to ensure that young people's voices are heard and acted upon in societies where youth marginalization has previously been a factor facilitating their mobilization into violence. This places a responsibility on others to create spaces for youth participation. What, then, can KRI policymakers, international actors, and civil society do to make this happen?

Pressing Issues Related to Youth in Kurdistan Today

As we were putting the final touches on the first manuscript of this book, violent protests flared up across the PUK-controlled areas (Sulaymaniya, Halabja, Garmian, and Raparin) of the KRI. The initial protests were organized by teachers and civil servants demanding the payment of their delayed salaries. In the ensuing days, however, largely youth-led protests spread throughout the entire eastern part of the KRI with far-flung and mid-sized towns witnessing some of the greatest levels of violence. For almost a week, young protestors took to the street to demonstrate against high unemployment, lack of public services, and widespread corruption. Their rhetoric reflected a growing disillusionment and despair with the ruling establishment along with demands for complete political overhaul. The protests did not reach the KDP-controlled areas due, in part, to the deep territorial and political divisions within the KRI and to the particular challenges inherent to mobilization in the KDP-controlled provinces of Erbil and Duhok. The KRI is heavily reliant on direct oil sales and on budget transfers from the federal government of Iraq, but revenue sharing has been an issue of contention between the central and regional governments in recent years. At the end of December 2020, the KRG had already amassed several months of unpaid debts and become unable to pay the salaries of its 1.2 million employees after Baghdad had halted budget transfers, thus reigniting the oil-for-budget dispute between the two governments. With COVID-19 leading to lockdowns and restrictions and poverty and unemployment on the rise, many blame the ruling elite for neglect and marginalization by prioritizing their own interests before those of the Kurdish public (O'Driscoll et al. 2020).

A majority of the protesters were young, born in the early 2000s, and were protesting against mismanagement that has lingered since the KRI was founded.

They were protesting a broken social contract in which the ruling parties had previously used the newfound oil wealth to offer jobs and services for its constituents in return for loyalty and acquiescence. They extended patronage to consolidate their grip on power instead of diversifying the economy and creating jobs for its youthful population. In doing so, the same KRI ruling parties that had previously delivered a short-lived peace and prosperity subsequently failed to maintain it. The KRI, once hailed as "the other Iraq" for its relative peace, stability, and economic prosperity, seemed to be a distant memory due to widespread corruption and crippling economic crisis stifling the middle and lower classes. The KRI's failure to provide economic security to its citizens has, accordingly, reduced its "democracy" to procedural characteristics such as elections, political freedoms, and fundamental rights that were already under scrutiny—not unimportant, but insufficient.

These protests were another indication that the KRI's fraught political scene is further aggravated by the divide between the youth and the political class, yet another fault line—the youth pitted against the ruling elite—beyond partisan squabbles as well as territorial, social, and urban -versus -peripheral divisions. The number of voters has shrunk in recent elections, as stagnant politics, unpaid salaries, and corruption have undermined the public's faith in politics. Apathy among the youth contributed significantly to the low voter turnout in the 2018 parliamentary election; out of 3.08 million eligible voters, an estimated 1.78 million people (58 percent) turned out to the polls, a sharp decline from 74 percent in 2013 and the lowest in the KRI's history. Furthermore, the election was clouded by allegations of vote rigging and fraud, reinforcing a widely held view among disillusioned voters, especially the youth, that they cannot bring about change through ballot boxes or through peaceful democratic means. Subsequent investigations into electoral fraud were also tainted by political interests, all of which served only to further undermine the democratic process (Bogos 2019).

In order to create a sustainable peaceful environment for all generations in the KRI and beyond, young people should be listened to and the issues that are troubling them must be addressed properly. The findings of the authors included in this book demonstrate the essential nature of this idea for several reasons. First is to reach out to the youth, a substantial segment of voters, in order to encourage them to reconcile with the state of elections and to offer them a participatory political space to realize their potential and assist them in addressing their grievances. Second is to strengthen electoral integrity, empower citizens, and educate voters before the elections. It takes an engaged citizenry and civic education for the KRI's nascent democracy to thrive. And third is to engage with youth in order to counteract their waning interest in politics and increase their political participation. It is also important to avoid condescending language while reaching out to youth, otherwise these efforts will fall flat. The young generation in the KRI deserves a vision for the future and a participatory political space in which to realize their potential or that will offer them solutions to their problems. Finally, despite the severe challenges that the KRI faces, youth must be prioritized, lest Kurdistan's most important resource—the youth dividend— may become a major security threat. Kurdish youth often state that they desire increased visibility and opportunity to make an impact and contribute to society through community initiative, with women in particular expressing adamant opinions on this matter. Hence, they demand employment, which is essential for raising a family, progression in life, and a genuine political space for participation.

The current conditions due to COVID-19 do not promise an optimistic picture with regards to employment and prosperity in the short term. The pandemic-related economic crises will have a tremendous impact on the KRI's economy as well as its domestic and foreign politics. This means that youth will need to be more proactive while trying to carve out a space for their voice and that policymakers should be open to more challenges by grassroots organizations in times of uncertainty and ever-evolving crisis at home and abroad.

Scope of the Book

In this book, our aim is to bring together a variety of perspectives from local and foreign academics who have been working on pressing issues in Kurdistan and beyond. The chapters focus on an array of themes, particularly including political participation, political situation and change, religiosity, and extremism. The book starts with Munir H. Mohammad's chapter on youth political participation and the prospects for democratic reform in the KRI. The author specifically focuses on the formal and informal modes of participation in order to demonstrate how the KRI responds to demands from the youth and how policymakers find formal ways to engage with the young Kurds. The chapter presents an insightful background about why reforms have fallen short in constructively bringing together youth and the older generation in political processes and shaping the future. The following chapter, penned by Megan Connelly, discusses social media, youth organization, and public order in the

KRI. The author elegantly argues that social media platforms have opened new spaces for young Kurds to mobilize politically, especially in situations in which civil society organizations are otherwise controlled by and contained within the dominant ruling parties in the KRI. Considering "how politics and media are locked in an embrace" (Taha 2020) in the KRI, Connelly's research demonstrates that social media enabled Kurdish society as a whole to organize opposition and exchange communication outside the controlled networks of the ruling parties. Hawzhin Azeez's chapter on the youth's reimagining of gender and queer sexuality is one of the first academic articles to focus specifically on these aspects of Kurdish society. Building on what Mohammad and Connelly argue, the author illustrates how youth are largely excluded from political participation and representation in formal politics in the KRI and how they search for alternative means of self-expression. She uses the LGBTQIA+ community's efforts to attain visibility and demand political spaces with a specific focus on their socio-political, ethno-religious, and economic concerns and insightfully examines how they challenge the established patriarchal notions of *Kurdayeti*.

The following chapter by Dastan Jasim focuses on the youth identity from a quantitative perspective. She explains how millennials experience different situations in the KRI and elsewhere in Iraq by showing how a generational divide, gender, and Kurdish citizenship in the KRI influences the civic culture of Iraq's citizenry. Following Jasim's analysis is a journalistic opinion piece by Sofia Barbarani, who has spent a considerable amount of time in the KRI watching nationalism unfold at critical junctures and beyond. Her observations revealed that despite the considerable size of the young generation in the KRI, the region's system has for decades catered primarily to the old and established elite, creating numerous hurdles for the young men and women who lack significant connections or privileged status. After Barbarani's first-hand observations comes Bamo Nouri's excellent chapter, which presents a critical opinion of the elite rule in the KRI and explains how it represents a barrier to further democratization in the region. More importantly, Nouri opens a whole new debate in Kurdish politics by arguing that a dysfunctional elitist political system has contributed to a disillusioned youth who have lost faith in the KRI's political system. Abdurrahman Ahmad Wahab zeroes in on the educational policies in the KRI as a vital concern for the youth. He scrutinizes the major educational policy directives that the Kurdistan Regional Government (KRG) has upheld since its establishment in 1992. Lana Askari takes a more anthropological approach and looks at the impacts of youth disillusionment and disappointment with the current ruling parties at the micro level. By narrating individual stories in detail, she elucidates the perspectives and hopes of Kurdish youth through political engagement.

Ibrahim Sadiq's chapter is based on a recent research project on Kurdish youth and religious identity. He presents how Kurdish young people juggle their identity between religious and nationalist tensions. The chapter's findings are all the more valuable as they reflect on the recent pressing issues in the region including ISIS and the impact of the pandemic. And finally, the book ends with an excellent chapter by Kamaran Palani, who presents an essential and accurate picture of youth radicalization in Kurdistan with a specific focus on the KRG's response to this phenomenon. He specifically examines the diminishing sense of *Kurdayati* among youth as a cultural concept that has long been perceived as an element preventing religiously motivated extremism and violence in the KRI. His analysis of the current situation clarifies the motives for radicalization, emphasizes the pitfalls of government policies, and explains why they fail to prevent violent and nonviolent extremism.

Taken together, the chapters provide us with an introduction to youth politics in Kurdistan. This book is just the first attempt to open academic and nonacademic debate on this subject at a time when protests around youth-related issues are becoming a more prevalent method of political engagement in the region. Our hope is that more research follows and supplements what has not been addressed in this book, especially through the introduction of first-hand youth perspectives to the core of this analysis and giving them a voice in nonviolent platforms.

References

Beehner, Lionel. 2007. "The Effects of 'Youth Bulge' on Civil Conflicts." Council on Foreign Relations, February 3. https://www.cfr.org/backgrounder/effects-youth-bulge-civil-conflicts

Berents, Helen and Caitlin Mollica. 2020. "Youth and peacebuilding." *The Palgrave Encyclopedia of Peace and Conflict Studies*.

Berents, Helen and Siobhan McEvoy-Levy. 2015. "Theorising youth and everyday peace (building)." *Peacebuilding* 3 (2): 115–25.

Bogos, Kristina. 2019. "Analysis: Looking Back on the 2018 Kurdish Elections." American University of Iraq, Sulaimani. Institute of Regional and International Studies.

Borer, Tristan Anne, John Darby, and Siobhán McEvoy-Levy. 2006. *Peacebuilding After Peace Accords: The Challenges of Violence, Truth, and Youth*. Notre Dame, IN: University of Notre Dame Press.

Del Felice, Celina and Andria Wisler. 2007. "The Unexplored Power and Potential of Youth as Peace-builders." *Journal of Peace Conflict & Development* 11, available from www.peacestudiesjournal.org.uk.

Herrera, Linda. 2009. "Youth and Generational Renewal in the Middle East." *International Journal of Middle East Studies* 41 (3): 368–71.

Izzi, Valeria. 2013. "Just keeping them busy? Youth employment projects as a peacebuilding tool." *International Development Planning Review* 35 (2): 103–18.

McEvoy-Levy, Siobhán. 2001. *Youth as social and political agents: Issues in post-settlement peace building*. Joan B. Kroc Institute for International Peace Studies, University of Notre Dame.

McEvoy-Levy, Siobhán, 2006. ed. *Troublemakers or peacemakers?: Youth and post-accord peace building*. University of Notre Dame Press.

O'Driscoll, Dylan, Amal Bourhrous, Meray Maddah, and Shivan Fazil. 2020. "Protest and State–Society Relations in the Middle East and North Africa." Stockholm International Peace Research Institute.

Özerdem, Alpaslan and Sukanya Podder. 2011. "Disarming Youth Combatants: Mitigating Youth Radicalization and Violent Extremism." *Journal of Strategic Security* 4 (4): 63–80.

———. 2015. *Youth in Conflict and Peacebuilding: Mobilization, Reintegration and Reconciliation*. London: Palgrave Macmillan.

Pandey, Kshama and Pratibha Upadhyay, eds. 2016. *Promoting Global Peace and Civic Engagement through Education*. IGI Global.

Pruitt, Lesley J. 2011. "Music, youth, and peacebuilding in Northern Ireland." *Global Change, Peace & Security* 23 (2): 207–22.

Roberts, Ken. 2015. "Youth mobilisations and political generations: Young activists in political change movements during and since the twentieth century." *Journal of Youth Studies* 18 (8): 950–66.

Schwartz, Stephanie. 2010. *Youth and Post-conflict Reconstruction: Agents of Change*. US Institute of Peace Press.

UNDP (United Nations Development Program). 2014. "Iraqi Youth, Challenges and Opportunities." Iraq Human Development Report.

Taha, Mohammedali Yasee. 2020. *Media and Politics in Kurdistan: How Politics and Media are Locked in an Embrace*. London: Lexington Books.

Ungerleider, John. 2012. "Structured Youth Dialogue to Empower Peacebuilding and Leadership." *Conflict Resolution Quarterly* 29 (4): 381–402.

CHAPTER 1

YOUTH POLITICAL PARTICIPATION AND PROSPECTS FOR DEMOCRATIC REFORM IN IRAQI KURDISTAN

Munir H. Mohammad

Since the establishment of Kurdistan Regional Government (KRG) in 1991, political participation among youth has generally been an unseparated reality in the region's political space. In the last three decades, Kurdish youth in the KRG have participated in three main activities: voting in local and national elections; participating in decision making institutions such as parliament, political parties, and civil society groups; and participating in informal politics such as demonstrations and protests. Despite youth participation in these three types of political activities, democratic reform in Iraqi Kurdistan (IK) remains weak and largely unsuccessful. Presently, the KRG faces serious challenges in consolidating its nascent democracy. This chapter asks why Kurdish youth participation has had limited impact in producing democratic reform and consolidating democracy in IK. It addresses this issue and aims to assess democratic reform in the Kurdistan region in regard to youth political participation. More specifically, it attempts to shed light on the current political situation of youth in IK, with a particular focus on their formal and informal participation in politics and the implications of their participation for democratic reform in Iraqi Kurdistan.

This chapter benefits from the conceptualization of political participation as discussed in the academic literature on democracy, democratization, and social movement theories. The academic literature divides political participation into formal and informal. Formal political participation includes political activities that occur within the political system and are permitted, to varying degrees, by political authorities, and this category includes participation in elections, membership in political parties, and establishing political groups. Informal political participation refers to political activities that are performed outside the political system, such as protests, demonstrations, writing petitions, and even participating in violent armed groups. The chapter also builds upon analysis advanced by social movement theories regarding the state's positioning toward the political participation of its citizens and how states respond to this development. It concentrates on these analyses to understand the relationship between youth political participation and democratic reform in the context of IK.

Hence, this chapter consists of several sections. The second section aims to conceptualize political participation in relation to democratization and the state's strategies in response to this political participation. The third section attempts to understand the KRG's democratic reform as they relate to the formal participation of Kurdish youth. The fourth section explains the prospects of informal political participation for democratic reform, especially to scrutinize why demonstrations in IK have remained ineffective in bringing about real change to Kurdish nascent democracy. And lastly, the chapter discusses the major findings of the study.

Studying Youth Political Participation and Democratic Reform

There has been a growing scholarly attention to the theme of youth participation and democracy on a global scale. Youth in different countries have invented various methods of political participation and expressing grievances in efforts to influence political processes and improve their lives (Özerdem and Podder 2015; Yom, Lynch, and al-Khatib 2019; Pickard 2019; Sloam and Henn 2019). In 2011, youth in many Arab countries poured into the streets to protest the most recalcitrant dictators in the region and force them to implement comprehensive reforms in every aspect of state and society (Larémont 2014; Sadiki, Wimmen, and Al-Zubaidi 2013; Howard and Hussain 2013).

Scholars of democracy do not dispute the notions that political participation is a critical element of democratic system and that discussions of democracy or democratization are impossible without considering the real, active, equal, and effective participation of citizens in political life. However, due to variations in engagement with politics, the occurrence of political participation in assorted political contexts, and the disparate intensity with which political participation emerges in terms of time, resources, and the types and forms of political participation, it is difficult to propose a straightforward formulation for this concept. Political participation can be formal in contexts such as elections, political parties, and other recognized institutions, engagement with parliament, and communication with representatives. And it can be informal through participation in demonstrations, protests, social movements, riots, and even armed resistance groups and rebellion. But the common theme among scholars of democracy regarding political participation is in regard to the type of participation that ultimately aims to effect change in the composition of government, behavior of politicians, incumbent officeholders, and government policies (Pateman 1970; Verba and Nie 1987; Verba, Schlozman, and Brady 1995; Verba, Schlozman, and Brady 1995; Kitschelt and Rehm 2011; Hague, Harrop, and McCormick 2016).

Scholars of democracy have developed several theories that provide explanations for who may perform political participation and how it will affect political settings. Early theorists of democracy, also known as micro-level theorists, emphasize that political participation is a privilege for individuals who possess skills, time, and money, who are interested in politics, and who possess political orientation. These individual resources will enable individuals to easily participate in politics. Participation, according to this perspective, tends to be higher among individuals with a higher socio-economic status (SES). Additionally, citizens with greater political interests and orientation, who feel a sense of social trust as well as a civic duty to participate, and who believe in political efficacy are more likely to partake in politics (Verba and Nie 1987; Verba, Nie, and Kim 1978; Dalton 2014). Although micro-level theories can explain which type of individual may participate, they have been criticized for falling short in clarifying the timing and geography of individual political participation. Moreover, the characteristics and skills emphasized by micro-level theories—social-economic status and political orientation—are, to a great extent, not permanent attributes (Vráblíková and Císar 2015; Leighley 1995). Micro-level theories also ignore the social character of political participation, consider individuals to be isolated from their social environment, and suggest that political participation is only performed by those with privilege. But it is notable that participants of politics do not make decisions in a vacuum. Their choices are shaped by numerous influences arising from their socio-political environment. Therefore, every type of political participation should be considered a social behavior (Leighley 1995; Rosenstone and Hansen 2003).

Contrary to micro-level understandings, scholars of comparative politics emphasize macro-level understandings when explaining individual incentives to participate in politics. This school of theorists argue that political institutions and national culture are important elements for the development of political participation and social networks. They further argue that individuals' political activities and behaviors are shaped by a variety of contexts and are influenced by the political atmosphere created by three contextual determinants: formal political institutions, economic development, and political culture (Vráblíková and Císar 2015).

Political participation is not an activity without purpose. According to Hague, Harrop, and McCormick (2016), citizens' participation in political life can bring various expectations for the political process and system of the state. The first expectation views political participation as both a commitment of community and a performance for personal development, expanding citizens' horizons and creating political culture for society. From this perspective, individuals' needs and the operation of political systems alike are necessary for political participation. The second expectation has a foundation in practical realities, suggesting that, naturally, citizens are not political animals and are not inclined toward politics. While extensive participation in politics denotes a crisis within the political system, high voter turnout, demonstrations, and protests are signs that the political system suffers from crisis and partial or total dysfunction. Surprisingly, limited participation can be interpreted to mean that the political system enjoys a measure of success in responding to the public's demands and needs, compelling citizens to follow more fulfilling activities. In this situation, citizens participate on a necessary basis and will observe political events through available channels. The third expectation states that those who fail to participate normally feel neglected or marginalized or believe that their participation has no value in making a politically tangible difference due to the dominance a set of government institutions and elites maintains over politics. Moreover, those non-participants may normally make cost-benefit considerations and a rational decision that participation in politics is not worth the effort. Alternatively, they may choose different paths through which to be heard such as engaging in violence and extremism (Hague, Harrop, and McCormick 2016).

Scholars of democracy and political participation notably position youth among other societal groups as the most prominent population category that is involved with politics. However, it is important to note that it is a difficult feat to produce a comprehensive framework to understand how youth participate in politics and produce a possible application of that framework in different contexts (Yom, Lynch, and al-Khatib 2019). One issue relates to the conceptualization, classification, and categorization of youth. Scholars face two challenges pertaining to the specification of who is considered a "youth" and the manner in which they partake in politics. First, being classified as a youth does not imply that all youth share common characteristics, nor that young people are unequal in their political participation. Youth have various interests, backgrounds, political orientations, levels of political participation, and political attitudes. Second, there are variations in the domestic and international jurisdiction for categorization when considering whether a person is a child, youth, or adult, as different jurisdictions recognize this categorization based on social, cultural, and political accounts that influence the status of youth in particular society. In recent decades, the incentives for sustained democratic participation have altered. The changes in economic, social, cultural, and political circumstances are all strongly intertwined (Pickard 2019; Sloam and Henn 2019).

Many studies on Western democracies revealed that the contemporary democracies suffer from the alienation of citizens, particularly youth, from formal participation in politics. The symptoms of this malady appeared in declining youth membership in political parties, voter turnout, and trust in politicians and political institutions (Putnam 2000; Norris 2002; Coleman and Blumler 2009). Additionally, young people appear to be disappointed with the efforts of the political system and classic politicians in their societies to work on behalf of youth. Conversely, the interests of youth have increased in informal forms of political participation such as boycotts, petitions, and demonstrations (Amnå and Ekman 2013; Spannring, Ogris, and Gaiser 2008). Several possible causes of this declining participation in formal politics arise in this context. It is indisputable that youth perspectives and modes for political participation have evolved recently. Political participation is considered to be an individual action of citizens, while formal institutions are losing their control over individuals, and social networks have become an active and alternative form of connecting young citizens with politics. These social networks, empowered with globalization trends and technological developments, transmitted to youth a culture of individualization, which seems to be more appropriate and suitable for their preferences and can generate horizontal participation. Moreover, young citizens are inclined toward issue-based engagement with politics, especially when politicians and candidates address youth interests in their political program. Research suggests that many young voters will engage actively with politics and support politicians or political parties that identify issues important for young people. This is a serious challenge for political parties and politicians, because connecting with youth requires policies and political objectives that are designed to respond to the demands of youth and capture their attention (Bennett and Segerberg 2012; Sloam and Henn 2019).

It is important to note that the disillusionment of youth with formal participation in politics does not mean that the young generations are completely separated from politics. With the advancement of digital technologies, especially social media, youth have globally benefitted from these platforms to rejuvenate their interest in and reengage with politics. Social media platforms, especially Facebook, Twitter, and YouTube, have expedited political engagement worldwide and provide real-time opportunities for political mobilization, facilitate political communication, and gather individuals around common grievances and political objectives (Howard and Hussain 2013; Dencik and Leistert 2015; Anduiza, Jensen, and Jorba 2012; Castells 2012; Mohammad 2020).

Practically, the power of youth political participation in consolidating democratic reform depends, to a great extent, on how political elites and government officials address it. Governments are unequal in their responses to youth political participation. Based on understandings from social movement theories and elite studies, it is possible to identify a number of strategies that governments pursue in order to regulate youth political participation in a way that serves the government's interests. Governments may respond to youth political participation through the process of political incorporation, which includes many steps such as expending state resources to integrate young citizens into political and economic structures, employing state institutions to control youth activities, formulating public policies, and disseminating legitimation rhetoric. Incorporation into political and economic structures can be in forms of partisan incorporation, meaning that governments tend to mobilize youth who are already politicized in an attempt to politically activate and establish an alliance with them. This strategy aims to increase the government's bargaining power vis-à-vis other competing political groups, or to further consolidate its power. Incorporation can also be in forms of depoliticization and control, which enables the government to alienate youth from politics, expedite the political disengagement of youth, and, eventually, prevent the establishment or rejuvenation of youth movements against the state. Governments sometimes rely on both strategies concurrently to regulate youth political participation in what is known as hybrid incorporation. This strategy includes the implementation of pluralist and limited-pluralist policies and material incentives. Finally, states may simply resort to coercive measures and formally and informally institutionalized mechanisms such as selective repression as a way to incorporate youth who have remained outside the incorporation process. Under these circumstances, governments crack down on youth participation and consider it a threat to national security—a common discourse and practice (Uzun 2019).

The study of youth political participation and democratic reform can guide and direct the trajectory of analysis in addressing the central question of the chapter: Why was youth political participation unsuccessful in effecting democratic reform in Iraqi Kurdistan? The framework is particularly useful in helping readers understand how Kurdish youth participate in political life and to identify the challenges confronting their participation. This framework also allows us to realize how the KRG designed its corporation strategy to control youth political participation and how the KRG shaped youth political participation, and to understand the implications for democratic reform.

The KRG, Youth Participation, and Democratic Reform

Youth constitute an important population sector in Kurdish society and their number is constantly rising. Official statistics of the KRG and NGOs indicate that 35 percent of the population is younger than fifteen, 61 percent is older than fifteen, and 4 percent is sixty-five or older (IOM 2018). Politically, since the establishment of KRG in the 1990s, youth have engaged in a variety of formal and informal modes of political participation, such as voting, membership in political parties and political institutions, involvement in civil society organizations, campaigning for political and social issues, demonstrations, and signing petitions. By using the above framework, this section aims to assess youth political participation and its consequences for enhancing democratic change in IK. To do so, this chapter attempts to scrutinize democratic reform, regarding formal and informal political participation as separate phenomena.

Democratic Reform Through Formal Youth Political Participation

The establishment of the KRG and IK in 1990s was a new and promising development in the history of the Kurds. Residents of IK experienced for the first time the emergence of democratic traditions such as elections, the establishment of new political parties, parliament, media, civil society organization, and nongovernment organizations. Numerous elections have been held in IK since 1991 at varying levels of government, including Kurdistan parliamentary elections, local elections, and Iraqi parliamentary elections. The first elections were held in 1992, but the KRG subsequently did not hold parliamentary elections until 2005 due to civil war and the fragmentation of IK. In these political events, Kurdish youth established considerable levels of participation.

There are fundamental structural problems in the political system of IK that render formal political participation weak and, to a great extent, ineffective at generating democratic reform. One of these structural problems is the politicization of KRG institutions and public life, a development that is a result of an inadequate constitution. Because IK had not yet written a democratic constitution, this created a space for two main political parties, the Kurdistan Democratic Party (KDP) and Patriotic Union of Kurdistan (PUK), which dominated the political institutions that are responsible for implementing democratic changes, such as the parliament, executive government, and judicial apparatus (Kadir 2007). In 2009 and 2013, for example, parliamentary elections witnessed relatively high levels of voter turnout, and the opposition parties—Change Movement (Bzwtnaway Goran), the Kurdistan Islamic Union (KIU), and the Kurdistan Islamic Group (KIG)—won nearly forty-five of the 111 parliamentary seats (Knights 2009; MacQueen 2015). The rise of opposition parties was an important development for the political process, as it was enhanced by the participation of citizens. The opposition parties coordinated on various levels and began to pressure the KDP-PUK ruling duopoly in order to force comprehensive reform (MacQueen 2015). However, due to the politicization of other government institutions, these opposition parties remained unsuccessful in bringing substantial reform to life.

Moreover, youth in IK have limited access to decision-making institutions. It is clear that political parties in well-established democracies represent channels for the generation of new political leaders who will be able to effect meaningful changes for society and constituencies (Hazan and Rahat 2010). An examination of most Kurdish political parties illustrates that the nature of political parties and their organizational structures create barriers for youth to rise to top leadership positions. It does not mean that young leaders are absent from party leadership, but the problem is that certain families dominate the major Kurdish parties. For example, the KDP is dominated by the Barzani family, and the PUK is dominated by the Talabani family. These families wield overwhelming influence and reserve the final decision over how the party operates. And the KDP and the PUK behave as more than traditional political parties; they converted government institutions into patronage and parochial networks in service of the Barzani and Talabani families' businesses (Khalil 2009; Wahab 2019). Notably, there are relatively young leaders within both families. For example, former Prime Minister Nechirvan Barzani, current Prime Minister Masrour Barzani, and Deputy Prime Minister Qubad Talabani are all young, but the problem lies in the fact that these leaders still govern in a style that resembles that of their fathers and grandfathers. These leaders so far have not presented a modern political project and vision for improving the democratic governance of IK. Youth, therefore, exists in the political process, but they do not possess power to make decisions. If they exist, they do not possess a modern political vision or way of thinking. The young members of the party can only reach the leadership council of the party, but they cannot be members of the family. The only way for a young member to promote to leadership level is through the support of members of one of the two families (Chomani 2020; Shahin 2020). This problem is not limited solely to the KDP and the PUK, as other parties such as Goran are dominated by certain family members. After the death of Nawshirwan Mustafa, who was Goran's general coordinator, his sons dominated the party, though they did not hold official positions in the party's leadership (Abdullah and Hama 2019; Hama 2020). More dangerously, Himdad Shahin (2020) posited that the role of the political party as a political institution is fading gradually, and individuals inside the party are taking control over the entire party. Kurdish political parties cannot play an important role in consolidating democracy, but certain individuals who possess financial resources, investments, militias, and media outlets are designing the policies of the party. Youth members of political parties gather mainly around individuals rather than the party's platform or ideology (Shahin 2020).

Additionally, the KDP and the PUK suffer from internal rivalry and factionalist groupings. For example, after the death of former PUK Secretary General Jalal Talabani, the party faced a crisis of leadership, and internal rivalry peaked. This became evident when the PUK failed to elect a new leader to replace Talabani and instead adopted a co-leadership model in which the party has two leaders. Accordingly, the party elected Jalal Talabani's eldest son Pavel Talabani and nephew Lahur Shekh Jangi as the co-leaders (*Rudaw* 2019). There is also undeclared rivalry inside the KDP between Nechirvan Barzani and Masrour Barzani over control of the party. Therefore, for young members to fill top leadership positions, they must be supported by certain groups inside the party. Even if a young member reaches leadership level, it is arduous to work against the interests of the group that supported that leader.

Moreover, it is difficult for youth to access political institutions without the support of political parties. For example, the minimum age of candidacy for membership of parliament was reduced in 2005 to twenty-five, but, in reality, youth cannot be members of parliament if they are not nominated through political parties. Even if young individuals are able to reach parliament through political parties, they cannot be independent and must work in congruence with the party's policies. As KIU leader Abubakir Sleman (2020) noted, political parties turned youth in Kurdistan parliament into a tool for misleading the public and became part of detrimental political struggles. It is difficult to see an active and independent young member of parliament, as such members merely support the actions of political parties (Sleman 2020).

The KDP and the PUK are also working systematically on weakening other means that enable youth capacity to challenge the power of both parties such as civil society organizations (CSOs), syndicates, and associations. These organizations normally strive to occupy the middle ground between the state and civil life. This middle ground covers public-serving organizations, member-serving organizations, and political organizations. CSOs, syndicates, and associations play an important role in monitoring government's performance, expanding political participation, enhancing and consolidating collaborative spirit and democratic practice, and publicizing and disseminating information to the public (Edwards 2011).

After the establishment of the KRG in the 1990s, CSOs started to gradually be established and operate in various sectors (Al-Salehi 2002). However, CSOs in IK face myriad challenges that ultimately undermine their capacity to direct youth toward political issues. According to (Kadir 2007), with the establishment of CSOs and syndicates, the KDP and PUK intervened in their internal affairs and placed them under tight control. CSO founders were representing political parties rather than their own members. CSOs were registered at the Ministry of Interior (MOI) and security apparatus (Asayish). The MOI, like other government institutions, was under the tight control of the KDP and PUK. Consequently, the MOI and security apparatuses were monitoring and investigating the political background and orientation of the founders of CSOs. And due to the problem of politicization, it was extremely difficult to establish a CSO in IK without the support of either party. This policy enabled the KRG to place a tight control over the work and operation of civil society groups, limiting the space available to establish an independent CSO (Kadir 2007; Hakeem 2017). The KRG has made some progress in terms of registering CSOs and NGOs. This progress is illustrated in NGO legislation and the establishment of the Department of Nongovernmental Organizations (DNO), which facilitated the registration and financial support of NGOs. The new law also created some degree of transparency and more independence from KRG control and diversified areas of working and interest (Chantizi 2017).

Conversely, and due to possessing huge financial resources, both parties have used the DNO to establish many party-supported CSOs, youth unions, and women's unions. These CSOs provided services in various fields such as training and educational courses. But both parties likely attempted to restrict youth and their capacity and redirect them in line with their political interests. They also benefit from these CSOs in their further consolidation of power. According to (Hakeem 2017, 151),"

All political parties in Kurdistan have organizations such as student's unions, youth's union and women's union. These organizations alongside the parties are attempting to conquer their own strata. They get their budget from their respective parties, and in the name of serving, they carry out political work and attempt to secure more votes for their parties. High-ranking members of these organizations are given similar positions and ranks once they finish their work in the organizations; hence, these organizations can be thought of as the extension of the parties."

The political division among Kurdish youth is a substantial challenge. According to Sleman (2020), the current political situation is dividing youth and pushing them in different political directions, rendering them fragmented and unable to present long-term, democratic demands to the KRG. Therefore, the political perspectives of youth have developed under the influence of political parties .

Another problem relates to youth activism and the structure of civil society groups. The culture of civil society activism in IK still is in its infancy, and it has not become a common practice for youth to organize themselves through civic organization and to pressure the KRG to implement comprehensive reforms. Kurdish youth still hope that the KDP and PUK implement reforms on their behalf, while, in reality, these two parties are responsible for side-lining democracy in IK. Civil organization requires volunteers and the voluntary work of members of society, but it seems that youth Kurdish are not keen to engage voluntarily with civil organizations. There is a common perception that civic organization is a method of making money for businesses. The challenges of civil society demonstrate fundamental issues of power allocation and similar structure problems within broader Kurdish society, sharply hindering their capacity to gain political power and escape from the constraints of the KRG (Chantizi 2017).

Additionally, the KDP and PUK have used state resources and public funds to buy the political loyalties of citizens—including youth—through employment in the bloated public sector. Most of these appointees will likely never work and are colloquially referred to as "ghost employees" (*farmanbari bndiwar*). According to former President of the Kurdistan Region Masoud Barzani (2017), the political competition between the KDP and PUK starting in 2007 compelled both parties to appoint a huge number of citizens in government sectors. Those appointees were used by both parties during election times to secure the votes of appointees in favor of their parties. In Michael Robin's (2019) estimation, the number of employees in the KRGs public sector is 1.4 million servants, and 80 percent of the KRGs budget in 2008 went to pay salaries in this saturated civil service (Rubin 2019). These employees are not normal civil servants, as they sold their political loyalty in exchange for money and employment. It is unlikely that young ghost employees will turn against the KDP or PUK and demand political reform.

The discussions presented here demonstrate that the main problem of political parties and civil society in IK in relation to youth political participation is politicization and independence. Political parties developed systematic mechanisms to control youth political participation and consolidate power. They succeeded in weakening youth capacities in reaching the senior leadership of the party and decision-making positions. Therefore, political parties are curbing and redirecting youth's political participation in favor of strengthening the power and popularity of both parties. With respect to civil society groups, syndicates, and associations, they are largely controlled by political parties, rendering them incapable of improving the lives of youth. Political parties are administering those organizations in a way that serves to further the consolidation of power. Organizations with these characteristics are definitely restricting youth participation rather than empowering it. It seems that the KRG mainly opted to implement mixed strategies to incorporate youth activities. These mixed strategies restricted the formal political participation of youth as well as their influence in achieving democratic reform.

Democratic Reform Through Informal Youth Political Participation

Informal modes of political participation such as demonstration, contacting politicians, and writing petitions have existed since 1992, but demonstration is the most enduring political activity. Many demonstrations have been organized over the past three decades for various causes: the Halabja demonstration in 2006, the February 17, 2011 demonstrations in Slemani, and the civil servants' demonstration in 2016, 2017, and 2018 in various cities and districts of IK.

These protests and other civic activities focused on a diversity of issues. The civil activities pursued by Kurdish youth after 2003 include seminars, political debates, gatherings, and TV shows. With the rise of social media platforms, these activities have proliferated in the virtual world (Mohammad 2020).

Like formal political participation, informal political participation seems to be weak and ineffective in bringing democratic reform in the KRG politics. Many reasons can explain this weakness and ineffectiveness. Internally, the KDP and PUK did not attempt to understand the objectives of the youth movement and, instead of listening to youth demands, sought to suppress dissent. For example, the PUK cracked down on demonstrations in Halabja province in 2006 when hundreds of young students protested the lack of services for their city, resulting in the destruction of Halabja Monument of Martyrs (Watts 2012). In the February 17 demonstration in 2011, youth protestors presented numerous demands and proposals for reform, but the KRG cracked down on the demonstrations and ignored the movement's demands (Mohammad 2020). Similarly, in the protests that erupted between 2015 and 2018, the KRG police and security apparatus responded with violence, killing and injuring a number of protestors (Petkova 2019).

Moreover, the KDP and PUK have, through legal means, limited the organization of informal political participation. For example, demonstrations in IK are organized under the "Regulation of Demonstrations Bill 11 of 2010." According to Paragraphs 2 and 3 of the bill, "Demonstration will not be permitted unless a written request is submitted to the Ministry of Interior or head of local administration 'Qaem Maqam' and written permission is obtained from the government. Ministers and heads of local administration have the power to reject and ban any unauthorized demonstration if the demonstration aims to harm the public order in IK" (Bill No. 11 2010). The law, on the one hand, is a positive step toward preventing demonstrations from turning violent but, on the other hand, is legislated under the domination of the KDP and PUK. The problem is not that permission must be obtained for demonstrations but, rather, who approves the requests for demonstrations. Because government institutions in IK are heavily politicized, demonstrations that target KDP and PUK policies will not be permitted. Many CSOs demanded the parliament and president of Kurdistan region to amend the bill because it is considered a great threat to basic human rights and freedom of speech (*Ekurd Daily* 2011). More dangerously, according to *Awena* digital news, the Kurdistan parliament recently held a first reading of a draft bill called the "Regulation of Digital Media." Some of the draft bill's content was leaked to the media, and it indicated that this law would enable the KRG to crack down on online dissent and criticism of KRG officials, and severely narrow the scope of freedom and liberty for Kurdish citizens. The draft bill gives power to police and the security apparatus to prosecute individuals in regard to any social media accounts, pages and personal accounts, posts, comments, and online content that is critical of government officials. If this bill is enacted by the parliament, it will create a dangerous environment for youth participation, as the majority of social media users in IK are young individuals (*Awena* 2020).

Another challenge for informal youth political participation comes from the position of political parties other than the KDP and PUK in supporting the Kurdish youth movement. Previously, the opposition forces in IK did not present a clear strategy in supporting, embracing, or rejecting youth activism. But the formation of Goran in 2009 by former PUK leader Nawshirwan Mustafa was a symbol of hope for many young citizens. Goran somewhat created spaces for youth to fill roles in political processes, and in a short time, many youth appeared in the party's leadership. In 2011, the Arab Spring reached IK, and youth activism began to flourish, culminating with the February 17 demonstrations in 2011. The demonstrations were not initially supported by the opposition parties at the time—Goran, the KIU, and the KIG. The parties prioritized their own policies and interests before the demonstrations. Even Goran General Coordinator Nawshirwan Mustafa issued a statement describing the demonstrations as a "chaotic movement" (Mohammad 2020). The high-ranking leaders of opposition neglected to join the protests or legitimate their demands, nor did they provide effective media coverage to the protest activities. This ambiguity in the opposition's position regarding the demonstrations engendered negative sentiments among young protesters. They felt alone in their struggle with the KDP and PUK. The opposition parties ultimately did challenge and condemn the KRG's actions when force was used to suppress the protests. These parties dealt with other demonstrations, such as teachers and civil servants' demonstrations in 2017, 2018, and 2020 in much the same way (Shahin 2020; Lucente 2020).

Moreover, the former opposition parties in IK lacked a political strategy for reform, and their political activities were frequently detrimental for political reform and youth enthusiasm for reform. In 2009 when Goran was formed, the main political slogan that was used by the party for the election campaign and its political discourse was corruption and the mismanagement of the KRG.

Consequently, the party succeeded in gaining twenty-four parliamentary seats in the 2009 and 2013 parliamentary elections. Together with the KIU and KIG, the opposition gained forty-five parliamentary seats (Saleem and Skelton 2019). But in 2013, the opposition parties changed direction. They modified their strategy, no longer challenging the KDP and PUK and, instead, partnering with them. Their justification was that partnership is meant to bring about comprehensive reform in the KRG. But this was the biggest mistake committed by Goran, the KIU, and the KIG, as they changed their revolutionary rhetoric into discourse that prescribed accommodationist reform and the implementation of its reform agenda from within, concentrating on tackling corruption, finishing party domination over government institutions, and unifying Peshmerga units in a modern, nationalized force. Unfortunately, this move by the opposition parties damaged their reputation and credibility. They failed to gain real partnership with the KDP and PUK. And their leaders frequently complained that their parties are only participants in government and not real partners. They also failed to effect real reform and tackle corruption as they had promised to their Kurdish constituencies. The KDP and PUK did not share power in decision-making processes. The opposition's failure in IK was not theirs alone, as it ultimately spoiled the trust of their constituents in any claims for reform and generated feelings of frustration among Kurdish citizens with both the parties and, more generally, the political process. This frustration peaked in the 2018 parliamentary election, which a majority of voters boycotted (Saleem and Skelton 2019; Aljazeera 2018; Bakr 2019).

Alongside the internal challenges obstructing informal youth political participation, a range of external challenges undermine the impact of demonstrations and other forms of informal political participation. One of these challenges is linked to regional political dynamics and the security environment surrounding IK. For example, the United States withdrew its combat forces from Iraq in 2011 in accordance with the States of Force Agreement (SOFA) it signed with Iraq. The withdrawal of the US forces left Iraq's nascent democracy and state -building process in unsafe hands, ultimately creating a political and security vacuum and allowing anti-democratic leaders such as Nouri al-Maliki to exploit the Iraqi state's fragile political institutions and to consolidate power. Against these attempts, Sunni areas witnessed protests and demonstrations criticizing al-Maliki's government practices. These demonstrations were suppressed with an extreme use of force, and hundreds of people were killed as a result. These practices created an environment suitable for the eruption of war and the rise of extremism with the Islamic State in Iraq and Syria (ISIS), which occupied key Iraqi cities (Mannina 2018). ISIS's attack on IK, as Kamal Chomani (2020) noted, became a significant threat for the wider region and, in particular, for the survival of Kurdish society. Because of ISIS' war with IK, Kurdish political forces did not engage seriously with political and economic reform, as the focus was on saving IK and defeating ISIS (Chomani 2020). The ISIS war also sidelined democratic processes. For example, Masoud Barzani did not leave his position as president of the Kurdistan Region when his term legally ended in 2015. He maintained control over parliament until 2017 and remained in power without any legal authority. Barzani's behavior damaged the democratic process in Kurdistan, as it devalued the rule of law and peaceful transition of power in the mind of Kurdish political parties and citizens. More influentially, youth activism in regional states, such as the Green Movement in Iran in 2009, Gezi Park protests in Turkey in 2013, and other Arab Spring protests in Syria and Yemen in 2011, was unsuccessful in producing change that had implications for Kurdish youth activism.

The KRG's democratic process and efforts for reform are also shaped by the rivalry of regional states —especially between Turkey and Iran —and wider regional dynamics. It is obvious that in the post-Saddam era, the influence of regional states significantly increased in Iraqi and KRG politics. Since 2003, Turkey and Iran have developed security, political, and economic ties with the KDP and the PUK. These strategic ties are mainly intended to maintain the balance of power between the two main parties. Turkey developed a strategy that was predominantly framed as a Turkey-KDP project to strengthen the KDP's position as a dominant party in IK's politics against the PUK, its main rival. The PUK, which is believed to be close to Iran and other militia forces in Iraq and Syria, has relied on Iran to challenge the KDP. The regional dynamics could further destabilize the KRG (Alaadin 2016; Wahab 2017). In this situation, youth political activism would be unable to alter the course of KRG politics, as regional politics would not permit such a change. Ultimately, youth activism cannot challenge the KDP or PUK as long as they are supported by these prominent regional powers.

The analysis in this chapter illustrates how informal youth political participation in IK suffers from many internal and external challenges. KRG authorities used mixed strategies to place informal political participation under tight control such as monitoring activists, establishing pro-party CSOs, and using force and state resources to suppress youth movements. Externally, KRG politics are inseparable from the impact of the regional rivalry and political dynamics of Iran and Turkey. Therefore, Kurdish youth must consider these challenges; otherwise, their chance of a successful movement remains exceedingly constrained.

Conclusion

Recently, youth political participation has become an attractive political theme among scholars of democratization. This chapter aimed to assess the impact of youth political participation on democratic reform in IK. With the spark of the Arab Spring, the Middle East broadly witnessed a multitude of examples illustrating youth activism in favor of democratic change. The wave of youth activism across the Middle East resulted in the overthrow of many authoritarian regimes and set the country's political future on an unknown trajectory. Some succeeded in establishing a basis for democratic governance, while others became entangled in civil war and political unrest.

The findings of this chapter indicate that since the establishment of the IK in the 1990s, Kurdish youth have become an important part of Kurdish politics. This youth have certainly pursued various modes of participation in political processes and political activities, including voting, membership in and support of political parties, establishing CSOs and other political groups, and participation in demonstrations and protests. Nevertheless, the nascent Kurdish democracy suffers from serious challenges, and prospects for consolidating democracy in IK remain discouraging in the foreseeable future.

The findings also conclude that there are some structural problems that weaken the impact of youth political participation. Most important among these is the politicization of Kurdish society and dominance of the two ruling parties over public life. Politicization is a result of the lack of a democratic constitution, which paved the way for the KDP and PUK to gain control over government institutions and weaken political participation through the use of state resources to establish a network of patronage and clientelism. Even the rise of opposition parties in 2009 failed to bring about real change in Kurdish politics due to this politicization and clientelism.

With respect to political parties, the findings reveal that Kurdish youth have limited opportunities to effect democratic change through involvement with political parties. Young members of political parties, especially in the KDP and PUK, struggle to rise to the leadership level of the party. Youth are physically present in politics, but they do not possess decision-making powers. Additionally, young members who have managed to enter the party leadership do not possess a modern political vision or project aiming to achieve democratic reform. These young leaders are the sons of grandsons of previous leaders, and they espouse the same political vision as their forebears. There are sharp divisions among political parties in the form of rising smaller groupings, and each group attempts to increase its capacity to shape the party's policies. Young leaders cannot rise to leadership circles without the support of a specific group.

With respect to the role of opposition parties in enabling youth political participation, the findings of the chapter indicate that former opposition parties —Goran, the KIU, and the KIG —enabled Kurdish youth to participate actively in political life and offered hope for youth to influence politics. Many youth appeared as leaders in these parties and applied considerable pressure on the ruling parties to implement comprehensive reform. However, the lack of a strategic vision, limited state resources available for opposition parties, and, more consequentially, the lack of direct support for youth activism and the establishment of a partnership with the KDP and PUK in the name of reform have gradually weakened the opposition parties, especially as they failed to reform the KRG. The opposition's move toward partnership rather than transforming the KRG damaged the credibility of the opposition parties and reduced public's trust in their ability to lead democratic reform.

The findings indicate that the KRG systematically limited and restricted youth participation in favor of consolidating power. The KDP and PUK attempted to limit demonstrations through legal means such as passing legislation that restricted rather than regulated demonstrations. Moreover, the IK security apparatus is not unified or nationalized professionally, as it is still under the control of both ruling parties. Like other state resources, the security apparatus is a tool utilized to guarantee party patronage and suppress dissent, and it has frequently been used to deal with youth activism.

The chapter's findings also reveal that Kurdish youth face challenges in using CSOs as channels for informal political participation. Similar to other state institutions, both parties have great influence over the regulation of CSOs. Before establishing a department of NGOs, the KDP and PUK placed CSO affairs, such as financing and registration, under the authority of the Ministry of Interior and the Asayish. Therefore, youth were unable to establish independent CSOs because the security apparatus monitored the political background of organizations' founders. Ultimately, the Ministry of Interior and security apparatus did not permit independent CSOs to emerge. After establishing the Department of Nongovernmental Organizations—a positive step toward improving CSO affairs in IK —the ruling parties indirectly politicized this civil sphere through the establishment of countless pro-party CSOs. These politicized CSOs were financially backed by the ruling parties, presented various youth programs and projects, and engaged with youth activities. But their goal was to incorporate youth rather than empower them politically.

Finally, the regional dynamics surrounding the KRG in general also impacted Kurdish youth political participation. The KRG politics cannot be understood without the impact of regional states particularly Iran and Turkey. From this perspective, youth activism alone cannot produce reform in the KRG away from the impact of regional states. Due to the geopolitical position of IK, regional dynamics will certainly affect issues of youth activism and reform.

References

Abdullah, Farhad Hassan, and Hawre Hasan Hama. 2020. "The Nature of the Political System in the Kurdistan Region of Iraq." *Asian Journal of Comparative Politics* 5 (3): 300–15.

Alaadin, Ranj. 2016. "Why the Turkey-KRG alliance works, for now." Brookings Institute, November 8. https://www.brookings.edu/articles/why-the-turkey-krg-alliance-works-for-now/

Aljazeera. 2018. "Polls close in Kurdish parliamentary election." September 30. https://www.aljazeera.com/news/2018/09/iraq-kurds-vote-parliamentary-election-180930053256161.html

Al-Salehi, Kareem. 2002. *Democracy and Civil Society*. Erbil: Mukiryani Center for Research and Publication.

Amnå, Erik, and Joakim Ekman. 2013. "Standby Citizens: Diverse Faces of Political Passivity." *European Political Science Review* 6 (2): 261–81.

Anduiza, Eva, Eva Anduiza Perea, Michael James Jensen, and Laia Jorba, eds. 2012. *Digital Media and Political Engagement Worldwide: A Comparative Study*. New York: Cambridge University Press.

Awena. 2020. "میدیای ئەلیکترۆنی" ژمارەیەك کەسایەتی هۆشداری لە هەوڵی تێپەڕاندنی پڕۆژە یاسای "ڕێکخستنی" دەدەن [A number of figures warning against passing regulation of digital media draft bill]. August 2020 https://www.awene.com/detail?article=32259&fbclid=IwAR1G5xfGHRKmssEA-CMMoEjGBMxP8EtqxZ69VQOQrk5ae0H9RUaTtD8j1x8

Bakr, Mera Jasm. 2019. "Gorran and the End of Populism in the Kurdistan Region of Iraq." Washington Institute, July 8. https://www.washingtoninstitute.org/fikraforum/view/gorran-and-the-end-of-populism-in-the-kurdistan-region-of-iraq

Barzani, Masoud. 2017. "دەقی وتاری سەرۆك بارزانی لە کۆبوونەوەی لەگەڵ سەندیكا و رێکخراوەکاندا" [Speech of President Barzani with syndicates and organizations]. YouTube video, August 21. https://www.youtube.com/watch?v=gTCo4SFkReI

Bennett, W. Lance, and Alexandra Segerberg. 2012. "The Logic of Connective Action: Digital Media and the Personalization of Contentious Politics." *Information, Communication & Society* 15 (5): 739–68.

Bill No. 11. 2010. An act for the organization of demonstrations in the Kurdistan Region – Iraq https://www.parliament.krd/media/2337/

Castells, Manuel. 2012. *Networks of Outrage and Hope Social Movements in the Internet Age*. Cambridge: Polity Press.

Chantizi, Frini. 2017. "Iraqi Kurdistan: Civil Society at the Crossroads." National Endowment for Democracy, June 29. https://www.demdigest.org/iraqi-kurdistan-civil-society-crossroads/

Chomani, Kamal. 2020. Interview by the author.
Coleman, Stephen, and Jay G. Blumler. 2009. *The Internet and Democratic Citizenship: Theory, Practice and Policy*. New York: Cambridge University Press.
Dalton, Russell J. 2014. *Citizen Politics: Public Opinion and Political Parties in Advanced Industrial Democracies*. Los Angeles: SAGE.
Dencik, Lina, and Oliver Leistert, eds. 2015. *Critical Perspectives on Social Media and Protest Between Control and Emancipation*. London: Rowman & Littlefield International.
Edwards, Micahel, ed. 2011. *The Oxford Handbook of Civil Society*. New York: Oxford University Press.
Ekurd Daily. 2011. "The law on demonstrations in Iraqi Kurdistan to be amended." October 21. https://ekurd.net/mismas/articles/misc2011/10/state5513.htm
Hague, Rod, Martin Harrop, and John McCormick. 2016. *Comparative Government and Politics an Introduction*. New York: Palgrave Macmillan.
Hakeem, Murad. 2017. "The Reality of Civil Society in Kurdistan Region." In *Between State and Non-State Politics and Society in Kurdistan-Iraq and Palestine*, edited by Gülistan Gürbey, Sabine Hofmann, Ferhad Ibrahim Seyder, 143–57. New York: Palgrave Macmillan.
Hama, Hawre Hasan. 2020. "The Rise and Fall of Movement for Change in the Kurdistan Region of Iraq (2009–2018)." *Asian Journal of Comparative Politics*.
Hazan, Reuven Y., and Gideon Rahat. 2010. *Democracy within Parties: Candidate Selection Methods and Their Political Consequences*. New York: Oxford University Press.
Howard, Philip N., and Muzammil M. Hussain. 2013. *Democracy's Fourth Wave? Digital Media and the Arab Spring*. New York: Oxford University Press.
IOM (International Organization for Migration). 2018. *Demographic Survey: Kurdistan Region of Iraq*. https://iraq.unfpa.org/sites/default/files/pub-pdf/KRSO%20IOM%20UNFPA%20Demographic%20Survey%20Kurdistan%20Region%20of%20Iraq_0.pdf
Kadir, Rizgar. Mohamed. 2007. *La penaw Kurdistaneki Nweda* [For the sake of a new Kurdistan]. Erbil: Mnara.
Khalil, Lydia. 2009. "Stability in Iraqi Kurdistan: Reality or Mirage?" Brookings Institution, June 3. https://www.brookings.edu/research/stability-in-iraqi-kurdistan-reality-or-mirage/
Kitschelt, Herbert, and Philipp Rehm. 2011. "Political Participation." In *Comparative Politics*, edited by Daniele Caramani: 310–26. New York: Oxford University Press.
Knights, Michael. 2009. "National Implications of the Kurdish Elections in Iraq." Carnegie Endowment for International Peace, September 09. https://carnegieendowment.org/sada/23804
Larémont, Ricardo R. 2014. *Revolution, Revolt, and Reform in North Africa: The Arab Spring and Beyond*. New York: Routledge.
Leighley, Jan E. 1995. "Attitudes, Opportunities and Incentives: A Field Essay on Political Participation." *Political Research Quarterly* 48 (1): 181–209.
Lucente, Adam. 2020. "Criticism mounts in Iraqi Kurdistan over unpaid teacher salaries." *Al Monitor*, May 22. https://www.al-monitor.com/pulse/originals/2020/05/criticism-kurdistan-iraq-teacher-salaries.html#ixzz6VIQQvqo6
MacQueen, Benjamin. 2015. "Democratization, Elections, and the 'de facto state dilemma': Iraq's Kurdistan Regional Government." *Cooperation and Conflict* 50 (4): 423–39.
Mannina, Ryan N. 2018. "How the 2011 US Troop Withdrawal from Iraq Led to the Rise of ISIS." *Small Wars Journal*, December 23. https://smallwarsjournal.com/jrnl/art/how-2011-us-troop-withdrawal-iraq-led-rise-isis
Mohammad, Munir. 2020. *Social Media and Democratization in Iraqi Kurdistan*. Lanham, MD: Lexington Books.
Norris, Pippa. 2002. *Democratic Phoenix: Reinventing Political Activism*. Cambridge: Cambridge University Press.
Özerdem, Alpaslan, and Sukanya Podder. 2015. *Youth in Conflict and Peacebuilding: Mobilization, Reintegration and Reconciliation*. New York: Palgrave Macmillan.
Pateman, Carole. 1970. *Participation and Democratic Theory*. Cambridge: Cambridge University Press.
Petkova, Mariya. 2019. "Why are Iraqi Kurds not taking part in protests?" *Aljazeera*, November

11 https://www.aljazeera.com/news/2019/11/iraqi-kurds-part-protests-191111125744569.html

Pickard, Sarah. 2019. *Politics, Protest and Young People: Political Participation and Dissent in 21st Century Britain*. London: Palgrave Macmillan.

Putnam, Robert D. 2000. *Bowling Alone: The Collapse and Revival of American Community*. New York: Simon & Schuster.

Rosenstone, Steven J., and John Mark Hansen. 2003. *Mobilization, Participation, and Democracy in America*. New York: Longman.

Rubin, Michael. 2019. "The continuing problem of KRG corruption." In *Routledge Handbook on the Kurds*, edited by Michael M. Gunter, 329–40. New York: Routledge.

Rudaw. 2019. "4th PUK congress kicks off after years of delay." December 21. https://www.rudaw.net/english/kurdistan/21122019

Sadiki, Larbi, Heiko Wimmen, and Layla Al-Zubaidi. 2013. *Democratic Transition in the Middle East Unmaking Power*. New York: Routledge.

Saleem, Zmkan Ali, and Mac Skelton. 2019. "Protests and Power: Lessons from Iraqi Kurdistan's Opposition Movement." LSE Middle East Centre, November 10. https://blogs.lse.ac.uk/mec/2019/11/10/protests-and-power-lessons-from-iraqi-kurdistans-opposition-movement/

Shahin, Himdad. 2020. Interview by the author.

Sleman, Abubakir. 2020. Interview by the author.

Sloam, James, and Henn, Matt. 2019. *Youthquake 2017: The Rise of Young Cosmopolitans in Britain*. Cham: Springer International Publishing AG.

Spannring, Reingard, Günther Ogris, and Wolfgang Gaiser. 2008. *Youth and Political Participation in Europe: Results of the Comparative Study EUYOUPART*. Opladen: Verlag Barbara Budrich.

Uzun, Begum. 2019. "Youth Politics in Contemporary Turkey: Political Hegemony, Hybrid Incorporation, and Youth (De-)Mobilization (2010–2016)." In *Youth Politics in the Middle East and North Africa*, edited by Sean Yom, Marc Lynch, and Wael al-Khatib, 7–13. George Washington University, Project on Middle East Political Science.

Verba, Sidney, and Norman H. Nie. 1987. *Participation in America: Political Democracy and Social Equality*. University of Chicago Press.

Verba, Sidney, Norman H. Nie, and Jae-on Kim. 1978. *Participation and Political Equality: A Seven-Nation Comparison*. Cambridge: Cambridge University Press.

Verba, Sidney, Kay Lehman Schlozman, and Henry E. Brady. 1995. *Voice and Equality: Civic Voluntarism in American Politics*. Harvard University Press.

Vráblíková, Kateřina, and Ondřej Císař. 2015. "Individual Political Participation and Macro Contextual Determinants." In *Political and Civic Engagement: Multidisciplinary Perspectives*, edited by Martyn Barrett and Bruna Zani, 55–75. New York: Routledge.

Wahab, Bilal. 2017. "Iran's Warming Relations with the PKK Could Destabilize the KRG." Washington Institute, February 6. https://www.washingtoninstitute.org/policy-analysis/view/irans-warming-relations-with-the-pkk-could-destabilize-the-krg

Wahab, Bilal. 2019. "Iraqi Kurdistan Chooses a New President, But Internal Rifts Deepen." Washington Institute, May 30. https://www.washingtoninstitute.org/policy-analysis/view/iraqi-kurdistan-chooses-a-new-president-but-internal-rifts-deepen

Watts, Nicole F. 2012. "The Role of Symbolic Capital in Protest: State-Society Relations and the Destruction of the Halabja Martyrs Monument in the Kurdistan Region of Iraq." *Comparative Studies of South Asia, Africa and the Middle East* 32 (1): 70–85.

Yom, Sean, Marc Lynch, and Wael al-Khatib. 2019. *Youth Politics in the Middle East and North Africa*. George Washington University, Project on Middle East Political Science.

CHAPTER 2

SOCIAL MEDIA, YOUTH ORGANIZATION, AND PUBLIC ORDER IN THE KURDISTAN REGION OF IRAQ

Megan Connelly

The advent of social media opened new spaces for the Kurdistan Region of Iraq (KRI)'s youth to mobilize politically in a region where civil society organizations are otherwise controlled by and contained within the political bureaus of the Kurdistan Democratic Party (KDP) and the Patriotic Union of Kurdistan (PUK).

Social media has enabled Kurdish society to transcend the barriers to communication throughout the region imposed during the civil war, to establish informal associations on the periphery of the partisan network of unions and syndicates, and to organize opposition activity against the government. Yet while participation in social networks, particularly by the youth, has challenged the hegemony of the KDP and PUK, the parties have also become less tolerant of dissent. As economic instability continues to stoke popular discontent, the parties have begun to adjust their approach to managing the media. While the Kurdistan Regional Government (KRG) continues to employ traditional tactics to monitor and suppress online activity, the government and dominant parties have increasingly embraced legal means to intimidate dissidents and strategies to repurpose social media platforms as instruments of control over their constituencies.

Through analysis of statutory law and legislative history as well as interviews with journalists, members of parliament, and attorneys, this chapter examines the trajectory of the KRG's application of legal and extralegal means to adapt to changes in global media and regulate political expression. First, it surveys the phenomenon of hybrid regimes and their development of new strategies to respond to the emergence of social media. Second, it examines the development of Kurdish media and the regulatory framework that contains political speech within permissible bounds. Third, it describes the emergence of social media in the KRI as a platform utilized primarily by the youth as an alternative to party-controlled media. Fourth, it analyzes the legal and extralegal methods applied by the KRG to suppress subversive speech and dictate the content of conversations in social networks.

Hybrid Regimes and Networked Authoritarianism

The number of democracies has increased significantly since the 1990s, but many of these states, which adopted procedurally democratic political systems, did not consolidate them in substance. Such regimes have been referred to as "hybrid regimes," "delegative democracy" or "competitive," "democratic," or "stealth" authoritarian states (Bracanti 2014; Gibson 2005; Levitsky and Way 2002; O'Donnell 1994; Svolik 2008; Varol 2014). In this chapter, all are referred to as "hybrid regimes."

The promotion of this model in the past twenty years has typically been in response to international pressure for states to adopt democratic institutions as a condition to military support, humanitarian and development aid, and even external legitimacy (Broers 2013; Kolstø and Blakkisrud 2012; O'Loughlin et al. 2011; Richards and Smith 2015; Varol 2014). Thus, elites in these states have implemented democratic procedures, such as elections, and even have active legislatures in which opposition parties participate (Gandhi and Przeworski 2006; Reuter and Robertson 2015). And their laws are often facially liberal to such an extent that they are nearly indistinguishable from those observed in liberal democracies (Varol 2014).

Varol (2014, 1673) argues that the difference between "authoritarian" and "liberal" democracies is in the methods through which they apply the law. Incumbents that have no intention of relinquishing control over the state or exchanging power to manipulate the electoral rules, exploit loopholes, and limit judicial independence in order to reduce the probability that they will lose power. They are more likely to use libel and terrorism legislation—the latter of which address security goals that have coincided with American "democratization" efforts after 2001—to chill free speech and induce self-censorship rather than to expend the effort to censor media themselves or assassinate journalists. While raising the cost of engaging in subversive forms of expression, authoritarians also increase the value of support by conditioning employment opportunities, welfare benefits, and housing on loyalty (Bracanti 2014; Hermann 2010). Force is often a last resort, when procedural barriers to the expression of dissent have failed and the benefits of cooptation are insufficient to induce cooperation or acquiescence (Sika 2019; Svolik 2012).

The pretense of democracy becomes a powerful instrument of the hybrid regime's legitimizing narrative, both internally and externally. Authoritarians can claim to embrace dissent and plausibly deny being repressive while erecting legal and economic barriers to independence from the party and critical speech. Yet the proliferation of the internet and social media have posed new challenges to authoritarians. Traditional hybrid regime tactics focus on channeling dissent through platforms that they can easily regulate or distort, such as state-sponsored media and elections (Bracanti 2014). Conversely, the internet and social networking platforms allow users to circumvent these institutions altogether and interact on a platform that is unregulated or relatively less regulated than TV, radio, print publications, or the voting booth (Carpentier, Dahlgren, and Pasquali 2013). The anonymity and relative freedom of these networks reduces the cost of accessing and publishing information and allows users to express opinions or react to them in a way that disrupts and discredits the authoritarian's legitimizing narrative—even to organize collectively against the government (Cottle 2011; Reuter and Szakonyi 2015; Shirky 2011). To manage these new challenges to their incumbency, authoritarians have developed a mixture of repressive, legal, and cooptative tactics.

The accompanying challenge is the youth bulge experienced by many of the authoritarian states in which social media has been a significant platform for mobilizing protests and holding governments accountable through the publication of critical posts and comments (Tucker et al. 2017). Scholars have pointed to the rise of a third generation of hybrid regime tactics: "networked authoritarianism" (Pearce and Kendzior 2012), which refers to the methods employed by hybrid regimes in response to the rise of social media. Networked authoritarians filter, censor, and monitor, but they increasingly rely on the liberal application of libel laws and instrumentalize social media as a space in which it can advance its own platform to crowd out, distract, defame, demoralize, and demobilize critics (Tucker et al. 2017).

The application of these networked authoritarian tactics has been successful, particularly in the post-Soviet Commonwealth of Independent States (CIS) and in the Middle East (Akgül and Kırlıdoğ 2015; Reuter and Szakonyi 2015; Warf 2011). Many of these countries, in addition to monitoring and censorship, have employed registration requirements for websites and website curators, libel and defamation laws to punish dissent and the publication of "propaganda," as well as national security and counterterrorism laws carrying heavy penalties for subversive content (Deibert, et al. 2010, 634). Finally, they have sought to change the content of the online conversation much in the same way they have distorted the purpose of elections and legislatures—from being forums of open expression to a support system for hegemonic elites.

The Kurdistan Region of Iraq

The Kurdistan Region of Iraq has responded to international inducements—primarily those created by the United States' occupation of Iraq from 2003 to 2011—to establish a democratic legal and institutional order. The KRG sought international support in its bid for greater autonomy from Baghdad; support that was ostensibly conditioned upon the achievement of democratic benchmarks such as holding free and fair elections and protecting press freedom (Natali 2010, 77–82). In particular, the KRG often capitalized on contrasting its own political system's democratic attributes favorably with those of the Government of Iraq (GoI) and modeled its institutions to advance this goal.

Yet while constructing a pretense of democracy, the institutional structure of the KRG is designed to maintain the incumbency of its dominant parties, the KDP and PUK. To that end, authority is concentrated in a power-sharing coalition in which both participate while subordinating all other formal and informal institutions to their coalition (Jüde 2017). Parliamentary elections have been held with a fair degree of regularity, but particularly sensitive elections, such as those for provincial councils and the presidency, have been adjourned, sometimes for years, and are marred by fraud (Mansour and van den Toorn 2018). The 7 percent threshold for representation was eliminated in 2004 to facilitate the representation of smaller parties (Third Amendment to Law No. 1 2004), and even opposition and ethno-religious minority parties have achieved electoral victories. However, elected representatives have far less influence than the unelected politburo elites, and they are cast out from the government when they violate the norms of political participation (i.e., deference to the KDP and PUK). Minority parties tend to be dependent on the major Kurdish parties (namely, the KDP) for financial and political support, leading to complaints that they merely serve the interests of the KDP as proxy parties.[1] Democratic institutions are also easily "suspended" or subverted. After efforts by an opposition bloc to unseat him, President Barzani dissolved parliament in 2015 and it remained dormant until 2017 (Hama 2020).

The contradictions between authoritarian and democratic impulses are most apparent in the KRG's treatment of the press. The KRG has been credited for

---

[1] For additional information on the function of religious minority parties as proxies of dominant Kurdish parties in the Kurdistan Region, see Hanna and Barber (2017) and Abdullah and Hama (2020).

its high degree of press freedom, but as Taha (2020, 58) notes, the media in Kurdistan have historically been controlled by the KDP and PUK as a means to advance nationalist and patriotic narratives throughout the armed struggle against the Ba'ath regime rather than to serve as a forum for free and open debate. In the KRI, nationalism and partisanship are intertwined and mutually constitutive. By extension, questioning the parties' legitimacy is a threat to the nation itself; the result of "foreign interference." To mitigate the threat of critical voices eroding the sacred myths of the parties' defense of Kurdish nationhood and also to maintain the façade of democracy, the parties have primarily relied upon what Taha (2020, 73) refers to as the "semi-party media." These are high-production television news and radio networks which purport to be independent but for which there is a "clear and distinct link with official party media."

But criticism that does not rise to this level of subversion has been tolerated and even welcomed by the parties to reinforce their image as credible democrats.[2] Furthermore, the media may engage in criticism of rival parties. As the PUK and KDP still hold effective control over separate territorial zones of influence—the PUK in Sulaimaniyah and Halabja (the "Green Zone") and the KDP in Erbil and Duhok (the "Yellow Zone") opposition to authority is permitted, so long as it is directed against the dominant party in the other zone (*Draw Media* 2020).[3] After the reunification of the KRG, a number of independent media outlets that were critical of the KDP and PUK became influential in the political arena. These included the newspapers *Hawlati*, *Awene*, and *Lvin* and the independent television news channel *NRT*. However, the audience for these sources was primarily based in Sulaimaniyah, where the PUK had more permissive attitudes toward political expression than the KDP did in Duhok and Erbil. Journalists continued to face intimidation, arrest, torture, prosecution, and occasionally assassination for broadcasting or publishing information that opened the legitimacy of the political parties to scrutiny. Yet violence was largely targeted, and in the worst cases, such as the assassinations of Kawa Germiyani, Sardasht Osman, and Soran Mama Hama, the political

---

[2] For example, Jalal Talabani (2012), responding to a commentator who complained in *Kurdistani Nwe* about certain PUK officials' interference in the judiciary wrote: "Please, to all my brothers who work in the courts, inform my secretariat of those who are engaged in corruption . . . It is necessary for every comrade of the PUK to help us in exposing corruption in the courts in order to advance the policy of the PUK and ensure judicial independence" (37–38).

[3] Journalist Rebwar Karim Wali illustrated this dynamic with a joke about a conversation between a Russian and an American: "The American says, 'we are free because we can criticize our president in front of the White House.' The Russian man responds, 'we are free because we can condemn the American president in front of the Kremlin!'" (Draw Media, 2020).

parties denied their involvement, even launching investigations into the murders and prosecuting suspects (*Kirkuk Now* 2020b). The parties have primarily relied on their monopolization of the media market, bureaucratization, and the dependence of the media on the government to regulate dissent. This will be described in greater detail later in the chapter.

The Emergence of Social Media in the KRI

With the US invasion came an influx of technology, including mobile phones and internet that became widely accessible to consumers. The expansion of internet and social media access brought with it new opportunities to transcend barriers to free expression and collective action, and to create a new civil society outside the party bureaucracy.

While less than 10 percent of households had internet access in 2013 (Invest in Group 2013), that figure increased to 45.9 percent by 2018, and over 80 percent of Iraqi Kurds had at least one smartphone in their household (IOM 2018, 55). Most Kurds access the internet from their cell phones (Rashid, Faraj, and Shareef 2016), and the proliferation of these devices has resulted in a corresponding rapid development of data networks. Mobile providers Asiacell and Korek have made the biggest gains in this sector, with 10 million and 4.8 million subscribers, respectively, in 2013 (Invest in Group 2013). In addition, some twenty-six internet service providers sprang up throughout the region after 2005 (Rashid, Faraj, and Shareef 2016).

The emergence of this relatively ungoverned platform coincided with the onset of a generational malaise as the youth of the Kurdistan Region have become increasingly disillusioned with the narrative of national struggle that justified the rule of the KDP and PUK, and to which the older generation was emotionally attached. This generation did not witness the horrors of the Ba'ath regime but has suffered most acutely from the region's economic collapse in 2014—a crisis triggered largely by policies enacted by the KRG. Forging loyalty through patronage had for decades shored up popular support for the KRG's dominant parties (Ali Saleem and Skelton 2020; Hassan 2015). However, the region's fiscal paralysis bankrupted the parties' patronage network. By 2018, 25 percent of youth aged fifteen to thirty-five were unemployed, a figure that stands well above the region's average of 10.2 percent, and most of them have abandoned their search for employment (IOM 2018). Another fifty-five thousand left Kurdistan between 2015 and 2017 in search of work in Europe or North America (*Rudaw* 2017).

Politicians and their media have not communicated viable solutions to the crises and have even responded to youth demands for work with scorn and condescension (Connelly 2018). At other times, they have attempted to regain the confidence of their constituents and allay criticism by emphasizing external threats and exploiting popular support for Kurdish independence (O'Driscoll and Baser 2019). However, the fallout from the 2017 independence referendum has reinforced the belief of many, particularly the youth, that the government and its political parties are irredeemably corrupt, exploitative, and do not have their best interests at heart (Salih and Fantappie 2019).

Therefore, it is unsurprising that the youth have lost trust in, and eschewed traditional media dominated by the KDP or PUK for independent news sources and for posts on Facebook published by freelance journalists, politicians, or online social groups (Jiyad, Küçükkeleş, and Schillings 2020, 49). Iraqi Kurds age fifteen to thirty-four—over half of the population—are more likely than other segments of the population to use social media for news (Gallup 2014). These networks have provided new avenues through which this generation of dissidents could connect with one another and exchange ideas that were critical of governing elites.

The preference for social media as a source of information also coincides with the decline of independent newspapers and websites, which suffered from a lack of financial and marketing resources. "Semi-party media" such as *Rudaw*, *Kurdistan24*, *Kurdsat*, and *GKSat*, which are funded by the KDP and PUK, have crowded out the market because the political parties are the only organizations able to support such an expensive and profitless endeavor (Taha 2020, 73). Furthermore, party-backed media offered journalists gainful employment and benefits, with which independent platforms could not compete. Particularly in times of financial crisis, few writers can pursue journalism as a profession with independent media (Chomani 2020; Taha 2020, 83). Yet unlike opening a newspaper or a television station, posting on Facebook requires few resources, and the content attracts more attention. Kamal Chomani (2020), the editor-in-chief of the *Kurdistan Times*, an online platform for political analysis, described how Facebook has overtaken traditional news media in Kurdistan:

> On my Facebook, I have forty thousand followers and five thousand friends, but if I write the same thing for *Rudaw*, *Kurdistan 24*, or *Kurdistan Times*, it will not get as many readers as my Facebook posts. There is also, because the majority of the youth are using Facebook, even if they are not your followers, sometimes

your article will be shared . . . Also, there are some media outlets like *Draw, Zhyan, Sharpress,* and *Standard.* When I write something on my Facebook, they are also sharing . . . they are republishing what I am writing. It is not only with me but with other journalists who are known in Kurdistan. So it is very fast . . . But if I write for *Rudaw,* then no one will share or no one will read.

Social media's ability to evade censorship and bureaucratic barriers to organizing has become the youth's most important tool in mobilizing protests (Mohammad 2019, 88–91). Organizers such as the Disgruntled Teachers used the platform to circumvent the control of party-backed unions by essentially creating an alternative, non-partisan union to advocate for their interests. Through their Facebook group, members brought awareness to their cause and published information related to the location and time of demonstrations.

Furthermore, the ubiquity of mobile phones gave the average internet user access to events as they unfolded on the ground that even journalists did not have: Where journalists were barred from filming social unrest, youth with their mobile phones supplied live feeds identifying the location of the protest and revealing the size of crowds, the anti-government chants, and even violent unrest that party-owned TV stations would have concealed from the public. According to "Huner," a journalist[4] who reported on the protests in Raniya in December 2017, "If the broadcasters couldn't report, then by live feed on Facebook, the people broadcast their own videos . . . so that way the journalists knew where the protests were happening. The teachers always, through the groups, informed one another that there was a protest."

Social media also had a powerful, persuasive effect by distributing viral videos of the kidnappings, beatings, shootings, and harassment of protestors faced at the hands of local security forces (Mohammad 2019). For example, a cell phone video of plain clothes *asayish* officers kicking an elderly teacher during the Erbil protests in March 2018 was widely circulated on Facebook and Twitter and became a powerful visual symbol of the abuse that many Kurdish citizens felt the regional government had inflicted on them by cutting salaries and then suppressing protests.

Finally, social media has made progress in overcoming long-standing social divisions that were reinforced under the so-called *du idara* (parallel

---

[4] A pseudonym is used here to protect his identity

administration) era and that have remained long after the unification of the KRG. One of the primary mechanisms of social control during *du idara* was the interruption of channels of communication between citizens of the PUK and KDP's Green and Yellow Zones, respectively, through journalistic censorship and the monopolization of print and electronic media within their areas of influence (Invest in Group 2013). Today, social media users are able to communicate across the ceasefire line (Mohammad 2019, 92). Campaigns originating from Sulaimaniyah for the release of protestors detained in Erbil and Duhok have had success in bringing to light the repression faced by their compatriots in the Yellow Zone and in some cases, securing the release of detainees or a reduction of criminal charges.

The opposition movement Gorran was the first party to capitalize on the trend toward social media and online organizing, particularly in the landmark protests of 2011, and its social media savvy can be credited with propelling the party to electoral victories (Mohammad 2019; Rauf 2014). The dominant parties were slower to adjust to the transition, even ridiculing politicians who used social media to criticize the government and one another (Jiyad, Küçükkeleş, and Schillings 2020, 49). As the KRG and its political parties suffered a crisis in public confidence, particularly after the failure of the independence referendum, regulating the content of speech on social media platforms has become a top priority of the KDP and PUK.

As political crises mounted following the withdrawal of Kurdish forces from the disputed territories, there was a spike in demonstrations throughout the KRI in December 2017 and March 2018, including in areas where protests had previously been successfully prevented like Erbil and Duhok. In Sulaimaniyah, rioting triggered a massive crackdown by PUK security forces, wearing the same gear and carrying the same weapons that they had used to fight the Islamic State (Niqash 2018). The protests signaled a changing tenor in the political discourse, one of increasing frustration among the youth and, among the parties, a desperate need to control political expression in a society that had withdrawn confidence from the system. While the parties continued to use force to suppress protests and coerce dissidents, the main battles would be fought in the courts and online.

The Law and Public Order

To advance the goal of maintaining the pretense of democracy that satisfies international benefactors while supporting the incumbency of the KDP and

PUK, the Kurdistan Region Parliament has passed legislation addressing topics of interest to international observers such as domestic violence, minority rights, press freedom, and the right to access information. In some cases, these laws amount to declarations of support for the *idea* of rights without developing an institutional undergirding to substantiate them. In others, such laws are prefaced with human rights platitudes that are qualified by exceptions or loopholes that undermine the substance of the right. In this section, we explore this phenomenon with regards to legislation addressing speech and association.

Iraq's 2005 constitution guarantees freedom of expression, media, and assembly "in a way that does not violate public order and morality" and is "regulated by law." This leaves the Kurdistan Region, as a federated region of Iraq, to define the legal bounds of expression and assembly. In this regard, Kurdistan Region laws have been widely credited as being some of the most liberal in the Middle East in removing critical obstacles to free speech, reducing the severity of penalties for violations, and advancing the rights of minorities. However, these laws contain attributes that permit the parties to apply them selectively to inhibit free expression.

First, in general, KRI legislation is replete with ambiguous and overly broad language, catch-all phrases, and delegations of discretion to ministries or other executive agencies to define and interpret them. Terms such as "Damage to public order and morality," "slander," "false claims," and "propaganda" are never defined by the law but nevertheless constitute elements of criminal or tort violations. The ambiguity of this language gives prosecutors and judges—themselves appointed by the ruling parties in exchange for loyalty—broad discretion to construe the laws' provisions in ways that are inclusive of most types of critical speech.

Second, Kurdistan Region laws regulate conduct by bureaucratizing civil society and annexing it to the political bureaus. Non-governmental organizations such as the Journalists Syndicate, Teachers Union, and Bar Association are formed by statute and regulated by the Council of Ministers.[5] These organizations are dominated by the KDP and PUK, which distribute their leadership positions and benefits on the basis of parity (Sheikh Mohammad 2020; Taha 2020, 85).[6] Registration in all cases requires petitioners to divulge

---

[5] See the Law of the Journalists Syndicate of the Kurdistan Region – Iraq No. 4 of 1998. The establishment of other non-governmental organizations is governed by statute and regulated by the Council of Ministers ("Law of Non-Governmental Organizations in the Kurdistan Region – Iraq" 2011)

[6] In a conversation about proposals to appoint heads of non-governmental organizations and unions to municipal councils, Barzan Sheikh Mohammad (2020), Deputy Speaker of the Sulaimaniyah Provincial

the names, locations, contact information, and identifying information about organizers and members. As a result, the only recognized organizations advocating for professionals are those that are unlikely to be critical of the government (*VOA Kurdish* 2013).

Third, litigation under these statutes is decided by a judiciary dominated by partisan interests. As with other government posts, the KDP and PUK exercise a veto over the selection of judges in courts with jurisdiction over their areas of administration (Chomani 2019) and the judiciary is, in fact, widely regarded as an arm of the party system.

In 2007, the Kurdistan Region Parliament passed Law 35/2007, the Journalism Law, to "provide what is necessary for a free, professional press and the expression of opinions for meaningful participation in the institutions of civil society, and to promote the principles of democracy and human rights." The law declares that journalists are immune from arrest and that the press is free of censorship within the ethical bounds set forth by the International Federation of Journalists and removes the requirement under the 1993 Publication Law that journalists seek accreditation with the Ministry of Culture (Taha 2020, 85).[7] Civil remedies are offered to plaintiffs alleging slander or other violations of journalistic ethics. Specifically, the complainant has the right to demand a clarification in the publication and the editor and writers have an obligation to issue a correction or to defend the story as published. A journalist may be fined one million IQD for a first offense to twenty million IQD for inciting hatred against social components,[8] insulting religious rites or symbols, defamation, or the publication of information that interferes with litigation. Journalists and editors alike can be held liable for violations.

Yet, while Law 35/2007 is more liberal than federal laws regulating media, it conditions the rights of journalists on their adherence to the International Federation of Journalists Charter of Ethics. Thus, it implies that journalists can still face criminal liability for activities that are outside the scope of their ethical responsibilities. The general public is also not covered under the law, thus leaving open the possibility of being prosecuted under the Iraqi Penal Code (IPC). The IPC, a federal law remains in effect in the KRI unless amended or annulled by the Kurdistan Region Parliament. Commonly cited sections of the

---

Council: "Those [non-governmental] organizations are political party syndicates."
[7] Under Article 3(3) of Law 35/2007, owners of media organizations are required to register with the Journalists' Syndicate.
[8] A term used to refer to ethnic or religious communities in Iraq and the Kurdistan Region

law by KRI officials include calling for unauthorized gatherings (Art. 221), contravening the orders of a public official (Art. 240), and defamation (Art. 433).

Another statute that the parties have relied upon is the Misuse of Electronic Communication Devices Law (Law 6/2008), which is currently the only law designed to regulate the internet and other forms of electronic communications. Like Law 35/2007, it purports to protect the rights of vulnerable individuals. In this case, as the legislative history reveals, the overriding concern was with the protection of women from harassment and blackmail amid a disturbing trend in femicide (Mufti, 2008, 403–08). This increase in honor killings—or, at least, in their visibility—was regarded as being directly related to the proliferation of mobile phones and the more widespread use of internet and text messaging to distribute indecent images of women as slander or blackmail. Specifically, the law punishes

> any person who misuses mobile phones or telecommunication devices, wireless or otherwise, or internet or email for the purpose of threatening or making false claims or insulting or publishing fabricated news in such a way that it induces fear, or intercepts conversations or distributes images or video or messages that are inconsistent with public morality, or if photographs are taken without permission and the situation is such that one's honor would be harmed, or if it motivates crime or other bad acts or the publication of information pertaining to one's personal or family life.

Violations are punishable by a prison sentence of three months to five years, a fine of between 750,000 and five million IQD, or both, with a more severe sentence to be imposed if the defendant is a member of the armed forces or *asayish*, or a civil servant acting in an official capacity. The law requires telecommunications firms operating in the Kurdistan Region to surrender cell phone user data in response to a court order. At the time the law was being debated in parliament, much of the debate centered around the severity of the penalties, not the possibility that the law could be used to suppress speech (Mufti 2008, 403–408).

Many feminists have considered the law a step forward in the fight against harassment and honor-based violence against women and girls by addressing a "gap in the penal code" that men exploited with impunity (Hardi 2013, 52). However, as described in later sections, the law has increasingly been applied against journalists and citizens who are critical of the government.

Defendants may also be tried under the Law to Combat Terrorism in the Kurdistan Region of Iraq (3/2006) for participation in "committing . . . threatening, inciting, or condoning" acts of terrorism, which the law defines as an act targeting an individual or group with the intent to "intimidate, cause fear, anxiety, or chaos in the public to do harm to the public order, and the peace, security, and health of society and the region . . . to achieve a some political, [or] ideological . . . purpose." In addition to prescribing penalties for acts of violence, the legislation also criminalizes "propaganda" or published content on the internet that "directly inspires the commission of terrorist crimes such that public security is put in jeopardy, citizens are made fearful, and that existentially threaten the Kurdistan Region's system." Lawyers and human rights observers claim that those arrested on terrorism charges, most of whom are sympathetic to Islamic parties or movements, are held in detention for extended periods without access to an attorney and that the proceedings of the special *asayish* courts are difficult to gain access to or information about (Human Rights Watch 2007). Government attorneys do not disclose the evidence against the accused and attorneys claim that their clients are targeted and tried in the *asayish* investigation courts—courts within the jurisdiction of the Kurdistan Region Security Council—for political reasons rather than for the commission of crimes that truly threaten the security of the region (Nouri 2020).

Networked Authoritarianism

Dr. Shayan Askary,[9] an oncologist at Nanakali Hospital, had gathered with hundreds of her colleagues on the streets of Erbil on March 25, 2018—just six months after the streets were filled with revelers in anticipation of the independence referendum—to protest salary cuts for civil servants and corruption in the KRG. In the course of the protest, she witnessed plain clothes *asayish* agents, Sangar Balaki and Nasih Mahmoud, assaulting another protestor and began capturing it on video with her cell phone. A confrontation ensued when the men insulted Dr. Askary and demanded she stop filming. When she refused, Mahmoud struck her, knocking the phone out of her hand. The video went viral on Kurdish social media after Askary posted it on her personal Facebook page. While a clear example of abuse of authority and excessive use of force, Balaki and Mahmoud later sued Dr. Askary for defamation—and won. Her counterclaim for assault went unanswered and she was ordered to pay a

---

[9] Dr Askary is currently a member of parliament representing Gorran

sum of fourteen million IQD for the plaintiffs and the men's attorneys (*Draw Media* 2019). In addition, Dr. Askary was docked four days of pay, she received threatening phone calls, and there were attempts to remove her from her shift as a result of her participation in the protests and her distribution of the video (*NRT* 2018).

The case of Dr. Askary is a clear example of the economic hardship that social media users face when they criticize the government on these platforms. It is also illustrative of the hybrid of traditional authoritarian and networked authoritarian practices employed by the KRG's political parties to silence and control dissent. In the following section, we examine how surveillance and litigation, or threats of litigation have been increasingly deployed to manage the organization of protests and the expression of dissent on online platforms. We also examine how the parties have attempted to control the narrative of online discourse surrounding protests.

Monitoring and Coercion

To respond to the potential threats posed by increased engagement with social media, the KDP and PUK have deployed extensive surveillance efforts to identify, coerce, or otherwise dissuade internet users from associating with groups or disseminating media that would undermine their legitimacy (Mohammad 2019, 117). The KRG and its political parties have committed officers of the party branches, *asayish* forces, and mukhtars (community leaders typically of tribal lineage) to the task of reviewing social media content and reporting violations (Chomani 2020).

Occasionally, when monitors identify a violation, they engage in repressive tactics, including the mass arrests of users posting Facebook live feeds during protests, or kidnapping and/or beating users for posts on social media platforms (Huner 2020; Sirwan 2020). The penalties for posting criticism on the internet can be tragic: Sardasht Osman, a blogger from Erbil, was assassinated in 2010 for posting an article critical of the Barzani family. In a video posted after his abduction, beating, and release from *asayish* custody, Amanj Hassan, the brother of Disgruntled Teachers organizer Awat Hassan (2020), urged followers to be cognizant of their online activity so as not to give the appearance of support for violent protests and provide *asayish* with a pretext for arrest or retaliatory violence: "This is most important: Your struggle should under no circumstances, under no pressure, turn to violence. Not by speech or writing or a Facebook post, under no circumstances. Do not even like a post that advocates for violence."

In most other cases, the parties and their security forces use threats of litigation to persuade social media users to regulate their own online behavior. Kamal Chomani (2020) recounted several instances in which users were contacted by party offices and asked to delete comments or "unlike" Facebook posts that they have reacted to: "There are people who have liked one of my Facebook posts. The head of the [party] office had called him and talked to the guy, and they said, 'Look, you have liked Kamal's post and you should unlike [it].' One of my friends—he's a teacher—and he called me and said, 'Kamal, I had liked one of you posts and I didn't know which one, and I was looking for a way to unlike.'"

A Raparin-based journalist, "Sirwan" (2020), added that "many, many people" have been arrested or detained for posting, reacting to, or commenting on Facebook posts throughout the protests in Raparin in the summer and fall of 2020 during a resurgence of protests against the government: "Most of the television stations use [internet users'] live feeds in their broadcasts of the protests and the [identifying] data from those pages is restored. Once the administrator is found out, that person is arrested."

In many cases, social media users and journalists have been forced to sign waivers, promising to refrain from writing "defamatory" articles or comments and acknowledging that they would be subject to liability under KRI law if they persisted in these activities (Chomani 2020; Human Rights Watch 2018; Euro-Mediterranean Human Rights Monitor 2020, 13).

Lawfare

Litigation has become the KRG's go-to strategy in regulating social media. Court proceedings, in the most direct way, give authoritarian politics a veneer of legitimacy, and without judicial independence or procedures in place to ensure the fairness of the proceedings, the KDP and PUK have been able to selectively apply the law in a way that both serves their interests and supports their claims to advance "law and order" (Ginsburg and Moustafa 2008). Although it is difficult to identify and close online accounts or to censor internet content, prosecuting some users can chill speech and promote self-censorship.

In some cases, journalists are charged under federal law for their online publications. Surkew Mohammad, editor-in-chief of *Peregraf*, an independent news website, was sued by former Deputy Speaker of the Iraqi Council of

Representatives Aram Sheikh Mohammad (a member of Gorran) under Article 236 of the IPC (*Shan Press* 2020) for publishing an article documenting the latter's alleged misappropriation of government property. The charge was later reduced to a complaint under Law 35/2007 (*Kirkuk Now* 2020a). More recently, Iraqi President Barham Salih filed suit against Bahrooz Jaafar under Article 433 for defamation for writing an article in which he accuses Salih of corruption (*NRT* 2020b). Conviction may lead to detention for up to two years.

But the most frequently used statute is Law 6/2008. The ambiguous language of Article 2 has been construed as a catch-all to prosecute internet users and journalists for posting politically sensitive or subversive content online. The law is versatile, applying to both journalists who act outside the bounds of journalistic ethics and non-professional commentators on social media. Furthermore, when prosecuting journalists, Law 6/2008 prescribes incarceration for defamatory publications and, thus, is theoretically a more effective deterrent to the publication of defamatory content than Law 35/2007 which provides only for fines.

In May 2020, KDP *asayish* arrested journalists and other participants in a teachers' demonstration in Duhok protesting the non-payment of their wages. Several detainees were charged under Article 2 of Law 6/2008 and IPC Article 240 (punishing the "contravention of an order issued by a public official"). Dindar Zebari (2020), Coordinator for International Advocacy, responded to international human rights reports critical of the government response (Human Rights Watch, 2020b) by claiming that the Teachers Union had not submitted a formal request to organize, and thus the gathering was illegal. Moreover, the journalists arrested had acted "outside of their capacity" as responsible reporters and were therefore not protected under Law 35/2007:

> Practicing journalism in the Kurdistan Region is guaranteed and organized by law. In instances of maligning, spreading violence, vandalism, libel, however, Iraqi Penal Code No. 111 of 1969 will be executed. An instance that involves libel often will be subjected to the Law of Misuse of Telecommunication Devices. An instance that involves libel often will be subjected to the Law of Misuse of Telecommunication Devices. These exceptions should not be perceived as erratic, because journalists will face these laws when they violate law while they are not in their journalistic career capacity, or if the violations involve legal procedures prescribed by other laws.

Zebari added that dissidents engaged in criminal activities when they participated in demonstrations "driven by political aims": "The protest in Duhok was mainly driven by political aims, unfortunately... the majority of the protesters came from outside Duhok. Moreover, senior members of political bureau of some opposition parties were directly involved, in addition to political cadres of some parties. Furthermore, on the basis of some information from the security apparatus, PKK affiliates influenced the protest in the phase of its preparation."

Thus, it is fair to say that while KRG officials declare "journalism" and "protest" to be protected activities, they define the scope of these activities so narrowly that the meaningful exercise of the right is extinguished. According to Zebari's interpretation of Law 35/2007 and Law 6/2008, political speech is not protected and is indeed criminal, if it aligns with the platforms of opposition parties. The message is thus that almost anyone can anticipate litigation if they participate in protests or criticism of the government.

Chomani (2020) noted that litigation threats are now the most powerful weapons in the parties' arsenal for silencing dissent. He described how the parties would threaten contributors to his news platform with prosecution. Prospective contributors are sometimes reluctant to write articles for fear of economic loss (particularly in the midst of a financial crisis), or from fear that the editor may disclose confidential information to *asayish*. The result, Chomani says, is self-censorship:

> Over the past two, three years, [writers] are also very, very cautious because the KDP and PUK are using Article 2 of the [Misuse of Electronic Communication Devices] Law against the journalists or any writers who write on the internet... When you have all of these laws around you, then you censor yourself and step by step, eventually you don't realize that you have censored yourself a lot and you have lost your critical views... [The KDP and PUK] don't need to kill journalists to scare us and they don't need to beat us. They just need to use like all of the modern authoritarians around the world... the judiciary and the legal procedures against critics and decent politicians... and they have been successful if you look at... the KRG officials, they say, "No, whatever we are doing is according to law." But most laws are not just.

Chomani himself was charged and arrested under Article 2 of Law 6/2008 for allegedly incorrectly attributing the ownership of *Kurdistan 24*, a television station based in Erbil, to Masrour Barzani in several articles and social media posts. *Kurdistan 24* is an example of "semi-party media," or media outlet that is a mouthpiece for a particular political party, but ownership by the party cannot be definitively proven (Taha 2020, 73). Chomani acknowledged that although *Kurdistan 24* is legally owned by Noureddin Waysi, the station is bankrolled by the KDP and is widely known to be linked to the current prime minister. Thus, Chomani would have been held liable for defamation for disseminating information that was technically untrue.

Although he attempted to have the charges reduced to a violation of Law 35/2007, Chomani claimed that the Journalists Syndicate was unwilling to advocate for him because he was not a member of the organization: "I told the Syndicate, 'I don't need you to do anything for me except tell the judges and tell the complainant that 'he is a journalist' and I should be tried per the Journalism Law. But again, they try to do something like if you are not a member of the syndicate, how can you prove that you are a journalist?"

The KRG dropped the charges against Chomani after he left for Germany to pursue his master's degree but, several weeks later, commenced retaliatory litigation under Article 2 of Law 6/2008 against two other journalists who paid Chomani's bail (Chomani 2020).[10]

Even where the law is applied to the purpose for which it was intended, in case of phone or internet harassment or blackmail, the politicization of the courts and the history of selective enforcement has reduced public confidence in the integrity of the judiciary and has also concerned feminists and victims of harassment. MP Shady Nawzad pressed charges in 2019 under Law 6/2008 against Shaswar Abdulwahid, the president of one of the KRI's largest and most important opposition news outlets, *NRT*, for blackmailing her with a nude video taken without her consent (*Kurdistan 24* 2019). Abdulwahid is also the secretary of the opposition political party, New Generation, which Nawzad represented in the Kurdistan Region Parliament.[11] Nawzad has since been criticized by members of her former party for allegedly aligning with the dominant political parties to persecute Abdulwahid, the head of a media organization that has frequently been made the target of violent crackdowns. Nawzad (2020) holds that she filed charges because she "could not accept harassment" and she

---

[10] As documented by Human Rights Watch (2020a), the families and acquaintances of journalists and dissidents are often targeted by *asayish* for coercion.
[11] Nawzad currently sits as an independent in the Kurdistan Region Parliament

resents the politicization of her case by the KDP and PUK:

> It has become clear to me that this case is becoming a political case and the case has been neglected in terms of women's rights and the fact that [Abdulwahid] used social media to threaten a woman . . . that hasn't been recognized. In the Kurdistan Region, we still have two [partisan administrative] zones, and the way that cases are dealt with, they are used by one zone against another when it's convenient for them . . . and within one zone, certain politicians use it against one another. And it's a tragedy that my case is being used against New Generation in Sulaimaniyah . . . every political party wants to use your voice for their own purposes.

Although Nawzad insists that she will prevail in her struggles in court, with the political controversies surrounding her case, she regrets that she has been revictimized for seeking justice. "I have lost so much," she said, "I cannot be happy like I was before, I cannot engage in politics like I did before, I cannot come and go freely."

Controlling the Narrative

In recent years, the KRG and its political parties have established a robust online presence. While many ministries and local governments do not have functioning webpages, nearly all have Facebook pages through which they circulate news, information about new regulations and decisions, and even interact with constituents directly (Mohammad 2019, 106). As Jiyad, Küçükkeleş, and Schillings (2020, 39) note, the single-district electoral system does not incentivize engagement with constituents, so social media fills this gap by opening channels for direct feedback, complaints, and other interactions with political officials. The parties and their individual branches also have pages through which they promote their party platform and keep the public abreast of their activities. In addition, the parties support "fan pages" (Mohammad 2019, 115) for powerful leaders like Masoud Barzani and Lahur Sheikh Jangi Talabani through which "fans" can express their adoration for the leaders.

But the KRG and its parties also attempt to control the conversation by flooding platforms with misinformation or information favorable to the government into the social media discourse and dominating the online narrative. Social media accounts created by government or party operatives are now frequently used to discredit and demoralize the opposition. "Huner" (2020), who has left work as a journalist and now works for a political party, described how the parties use social media pages and messaging to dissuade users from participating in protests: "Sometimes they said, 'The protests are bad, the protests will be detrimental to people. If the protests happen then the shops will close and the market will close.' And they tried in this way to suppress them. Sometimes . . . by disseminating threats, but there were fewer threats . . . it was mostly the protests will be detrimental, they will cause economic problems for people, the shops will not reopen, the teachers strike will be detrimental for students, people are creating problems for governmental institutions; this way."

Sirwan (2020) reported that the political parties use social media to discredit and defame protest organizers, noting that party operatives, like dissidents, benefit from the anonymity of social media:

> Now, the two parties have several platforms: on websites, on radio TV. But because this attracts less attention, they are trying to transfer their activities to social media. They are attempting to convey their message, platforms, political activities to the people through social media . . . Now this has created a problem, which has become dangerous because those pages and accounts that they use, and nobody knows who moderates them, they use them to defame people. For example, activist teachers, religious scholars, civil rights activists; they produce videos of them, and most of it is false, and they accuse them of being immoral, to assassinate their character, so that they will no longer have popular influence and people won't listen to them . . . So anybody who writes against the elites becomes a target of those pages.

While the source of many of these accounts remains unknown, the KDP and PUK security forces have used both their verified accounts and troll accounts to intimidate and harass members of other political parties as well as journalists. A recent study identified four hundred accounts managed by the PUK's Zanyari intelligence agency, which is headed by PUK Co-president Lahur Sheikh Jangi, that appeared to be designed for the purpose of disseminating anti-KDP propaganda (Nimmo et al. 2020).

In another example, the official page of the Kurdistan Counter Terror Forces, a branch of the Kurdistan Region Security Council linked with Masrour Barzani, published a post that accused journalist Rebwar Karim Wali, who is regarded as being close to Masrour's cousin and rival, Nechirvan Barzani, of "reveling" in the assassination of a Turkish diplomat in Erbil when he questioned the KRG response to the incident, implying that he was behind the killing and seeking to undermine the authority of the Kurdistan Region Security Council: "Rebwar is happy to tell lies to propaganda tabloids like *Lvin* and *Millet* [two PUK publications], and not reveal his identity as an *agha*. Arrogance cannot protect the damned *aghas*" (*Spee Media* 2019).

The KDP and PUK also use social media to publicize their rapport with foreign leaders and thus enhance their credibility as statesmen. Party leaders frequently post photographs of themselves participating in "fruitful" meetings with international delegations on Twitter in English rather than Kurdish for an audience of foreign observers. On their Facebook pages, which tend to target Kurdish audiences, these posts are often accompanied with videos containing no dialogue but with triumphal music played over scenes of these statesmen and party leaders engaged in apparently animated conversation. The message is that the party leader engages in diplomatic relations with foreign states and, thus, exercises sovereignty. The use of this type of social media post is also, to some extent, an instrument of competition between the parties. For example, photographs of Masoud Barzani meeting with diplomats that are posted to the official Baregaye Barzani (Barzani Headquarters) social media pages have caused controversy because the captions continue to describe him as "President" notwithstanding his resignation in 2017.

Conclusion: Overcoming Networked Authoritarianism

In August 2020, the Kurdistan Region Parliament considered an internet governance bill that would have placed severe restrictions on "any electronic content." As with journalists, it required app and website developers and editors to register with the Journalists Syndicate and introduced character fitness, age, and other restrictions for licensing. Most seriously, it prescribed punishment under counterterrorism legislation for electronic posts and publications that violate its terms and holds editors liable for the publication of "terrorist propaganda" on their webpages (2020). Lawmakers from all the major parties, including Gorran, backed the proposed legislation. Yet ironically, lawmakers pulled support from the bill after an intense social media campaign, with many denouncing the bill as "diminishing freedom of expression" (*Xendan* 2020).

Civil rights and labor activists organizing online have also won other victories. Several high-profile journalists charged under Law 6/2008, including Draw Media's Niyaz Abdullah, were acquitted with courts citing a lack of evidence (*NRT* 2020a). An outcry on Twitter and Facebook was also credited with pressuring prosecutors to drop an IPC criminal charge against Surkew Mohammad (Hawrami 2019). Most significantly, Baddel Barwari, a teacher arrested in Duhok for calling for protests of non-payment of teachers' salaries, was acquitted in October 2020 after a social media campaign publicized his and his son's arrest. In its ruling, the criminal court applied Article 38 of the Iraqi Constitution, which pertains to press freedom, and the international human rights treaties to which Iraq is a party in construing the meaning of Law 6/2008, holding that the content of Barwari's internet posts fell within the permissible bounds of lawful speech (H. Ahmad, personal communication, October 9, 2020; *NRT* 2020c).

Yet, the Kurdistan Region's online dissidents, journalists, and organizers continue to face mounting crackdowns, particularly as fresh wage cuts drive more people into the streets and onto online platforms to organize. Dozens of journalists and ordinary citizens throughout the Kurdistan Region, and particularly in the KDP-held governorates of Duhok and Erbil, were arrested in protests throughout the summer of 2020, and many of them were charged under Article 2 of Law 6/2008 or federal statute. Some of these detainees have been held without charge or access to their families and attorneys.

In October, the KDP bloc in parliament initiated another bill to punish "disrespect and insults" against undefined "patriotic and national symbols"[12] under Article 226 of the IPC, a section which prohibits insults to government officials and punishes violations by up to seven years in prison.[13] According to KDP member of parliament, Bahman Kaka'Abdullah the bill addresses "a legal vacuum with regards to protecting national sanctity" and is consistent with democratic norms: "Every free country in the world has [sacred symbols], and they are protected by law . . . Those who think of it as a restriction on freedom . . . feel it is more important to fight and insult on Facebook than to protect sacred things in this country" (*VOA Kurdish* 2020). Thus, while social media remains an important platform for criticism and organization, the latest legislative proposals amid a wave of arrests demonstrate that the Kurdish political parties are more serious than ever about securitizing online space and enshrining their rhetorical linkages between terrorism, sabotage, and dissent on

---

[12] "National symbol" is defined in the bill as including "the flag, national anthem, peshmerga, historical leadership, and liberators of the people of Kurdistan" ("Legislative Proposal on Patriotic and National Symbols, Kurdistan Region of Iraq" 2020)

[13] Article 226 reads: "Any person who publicly insults the National Assembly or the government or the courts or the armed forces or any other constitutional body or the public authorities or official or one semiofficial agencies or departments is punishable by a term of imprisonment not exceeding seven years or detention or a fine."

social media in law.

Postscript: On February 16, 2021, five of the more than 70 journalists and activists arrested the previous summer in Duhok and Erbil, were brought to trial on new charges – under Law 21/2003 which punishes any person who commits or attempts to commit an act "with the intent to undermine the security, stability, and sovereignty of the institutions of the Kurdistan Region-Iraq." Using evidence derived primarily from Facebook posts and messenger chats, the defendants were sentenced to six years in prison in proceedings regarded by human rights organizations to be "deeply flawed" (Human Rights Watch 2021) and "a new low for press freedom in Iraqi Kurdistan" (CPJ 2021). Notwithstanding his acquittal on charges arising under Law 6/2008, Baddel Barwari has since been charged under Law 21/2003. He remains in prison awaiting trial (Peregraf 2021).

References

Abdullah, Farhad Hassan, and Hawre Hasan Hama. 2020. "Minority Representation and Reserved Legislative Seats in Iraqi Kurdistan." *Contemporary Review of the Middle East* 7 (4): 381–402.

Akgül, Mustafa, and Melih Kırlıdoğ. 2015. "Internet Censorship in Turkey." *Internet Policy Review* 4 (2): 1–22.

Ali Saleem, Zmkan, and Mac Skelton. 2020. "Assessing Iraqi Kurdistan's Stability: How Patronage Shapes Conflict." LSE Middle East Centre.

Blakkisrud, Helge, and Pål Kolstø. 2011. "From Secessionist Conflict Toward a Functioning State: Processes of State- and Nation-building in Transnistria." *Post-Soviet Affairs* 27 (2): 178–210.

Brancati, Dawn. 2014. "Democratic Authoritarianism: Origins and Effects." *Annual Review of Political Science* 17: 313–26.

Broers, Laurence. 2014. "Mirrors to the World: The Claims to Legitimacy and International Recognition of De Facto States in the South Caucasus." *Brown Journal of World Affairs* 20 (2): 145–59.

Carpentier, Nico, Peter Dahlgren, and Francesca Pasquali. 2013. "Waves of Media democratization: A brief history of contemporary participatory practices in the media sphere." *Convergence* 19 (3): 287–94.

Chomani, Kamal. 2019. "Judiciary in Kurdistan Region in Peril." Tahrir Institute for Middle East Policy, January 11. https://timep.org/commentary/analysis/judiciary-in-kurdistan-region-in-peril/

Chomani, Kamal. 2020, September 25. Personal interview.

Connelly, Megan. 2018. "Why Kurdistan's college grads can't just roll their sleeves up and get to work." Medium blog post, August 4. https://medium.com/@meganconnelly/why-kurdistans-youth-can-t-just-roll-their-sleeves-up-and-get-to-work-18670c88f4f0

Cottle, Simon. 2011. "Media and the Arab uprisings of 2011." *Journalism* 12 (5): 647–59.

CPJ (Committee to Protect Journalists). 2021. "'Spaghetti against the wall': How Flimsy Evidence Sent 2 Iraqi Kurdish Journalists to Jail for 6 Years." March 12. https://cpj.org/2021/03/spaghetti-against-the-wall-flimsy-evidence-iraqi-kurdish-journalists-jail/

Deibert, Ronald, John Palfrey, Rafal Rohozinski, and Jonathan Zittrain. 2010. *Access Controlled: The Shaping of Power, Rights, and Rule in Cyberspace*. The MIT Press.

Draw Media. 2019. "پەرلەمانتارێک به ١٣ ملیۆن دینار سزا دەدرێت" [MP is fined 13 million dinar]. September 22. https://drawmedia.net/page_detail.php?smart-id=4514

Draw Media. 2020. "دهۆک به سلێمانی کردنی" [On the Slemani-ization of Duhok]. May 19. https://drawmedia.net/page_detail?smart-id=5942

European Asylum Support Office (EASO). 2019. *Country of Origin Report Iraq: Targeting of Individuals*. https://www.easo.europa.eu/sites/default/files/publications/EASO-COI-

Report-Iraq-Targeting-Individuals.pdf

Euro-Mediterranean Human Rights Monitor. 2020. "Iraqi Kurdistan: Exacerbating Crises and Stolen Rights." https://euromedmonitor.org/en/article/3979/New-Report:-200-detainees-in-two-months-of-demonstrations-in-Iraqi-Kurdistan

Gallup. 2014. *Media Use in Iraq and Iraqi Kurdistan.*

Gandhi, Jennifer, and Adam Przeworski. 2006. "Cooperation, Cooptation, and Rebellion Under Dictatorships." *Economics & Politics* 18 (1): 1 –26.

Gibson, Edward L. 2005. "Boundary Control: Subnational Authoritarianism in Democratic Countries." *World Politics* 58: 101–32.

Ginsburg, Tom, and Tamir Moustafa. 2008. *Rule by Law: The Politics of Courts in Authoritarian Regimes.* New York: Cambridge University Press.

Hama, Hawre Hasan. 2020. "The Rise and Fall of Movement for Change in the Kurdistan Region of Iraq (2009–2018)." *Asian Journal of Comparative Politics.*

Hanna, Reine, and Matthew Barber. 2017. "Erasing Assyrians: How the KRG Abuses Human Rights, Undermines Democracy, and Conquers Minority Homelands." *The Assyrian Confederation of Europe.*

Hardi, Choman. 2013. "Women's activism in Iraqi Kurdistan: Achievements, shortcomings and obstacles." *Kurdish Studies* 1 (1): 44–64.

Hassan, Awat. 2017. "Teacher, Amanj Hassan, brother of Awat Hassan, has some messages for his friends." Facebook, https://www.facebook.com/watch/live/?v=1158275807619773&ref=watch_permalink

Hassan, Kawa. 2015. *Kurdistan's Politicized Society Confronts a Sultanistic System.* Washington, DC: Carnegie Endowment for International Peace. https://carnegieendowment.org/files/CMEC_54_Hassan_11.pdf

Hawrami, Fazel. 2019. Twitter, January 19. https://twitter.com/FazelHawramy/status/1218856106736353281

Herrmann, Julián Durazo. 2010. "Neo-Patrimonialism and Subnational Authoritarianism in Mexico. The Case of Oaxaca." *Journal of Politics in Latin America* 2 (2): 85–112.

Human Rights Watch. 2007. *Caught in the Whirlwind: Torture and Denial of Due Process by the Kurdistan Security Forces.* https://www.hrw.org/reports/2007/kurdistan0707/

Human Rights Watch. 2018. "Kurdistan Region of Iraq: Protestors Beaten, Journalists Detained." April 15. https://www.hrw.org/news/2018/04/15/kurdistan-region-iraq-protesters-beaten-journalists-detained

Human Rights Watch. 2020a. *We Might Call You in at Any Time.* https://www.hrw.org/report/2020/06/15/we-might-call-you-any-time/free-speech-under-threat-iraq

Human Rights Watch. 2020b. "Kurdish authorities clamp down ahead of protests." May 19. https://www.hrw.org/news/2020/05/19/kurdish-authorities-clamp-down-ahead-protests

Human Rights Watch. 2021. "Kurdistan Region of Iraq: Flawed Trial of Journalists, Activists." April 22. https://www.hrw.org/news/2021/04/22/kurdistan-region-iraq-flawed-trial-journalists-activists

Huner. 2020, September 25. Personal interview.

Invest in Group. 2013. "Plugging In: Telecom and Internet." https://investingroup.org/review/242/plugging-in-telecom-and-internet-kurdistan/

IOM (International Organization for Migration). 2018. *Demographic Survey: Kurdistan Region of Iraq.* https://iraq.iom.int/files/KRSO_IOM_UNFPA_Demographic_Survey_Kurdistan_Region_of_Iraq.pdf

Jiyad, Sajad, Müjge Küçükkeleş, and Tobias Schillings. 2020. *Economic Drivers of Youth Political Discontent in Iraq: The Voice of Young People in Kurdistan, Baghdad, Basra and Thi-Qar.* https://www.gpgovernance.net/publication/economic-drivers-of-youth-political-discontent-in-iraq-the-voice-of-young-people-in-kurdistan-baghdad-basra-and-thi-qar/

Jüde, Johannes. 2017. "Contesting Borders? The Formation of Iraqi Kurdistan's de facto state." *International Affairs* 93 (4): 847–63.

Kirkuk Now. 2020a. "دوو سکاڵای لەسەرە: پۆلیس سەرنوسەری پەرمگراف دەستبەسەردمکات"

[Two charges: police arrest editor of Peregraf]. January 19. https://kirkuknow.com/ku/news/61217

Kirkuk Now. 2020b. "Impunity: A motivator for continuous assassinations and violence against Journalists in the Kurdistan Region." May 14. https://www.kirkuknow.com/en/news/62228

Kolstø, Pål, and Helge Blakkisrud. 2012. "De facto states and democracy: The case of Nagorno-Karabakh." *Communist and Post-Communist Studies* 45 (1-2): 141–51

Kurdistan 24. 2019. "Court issues warrant against New Generation's Shaswar Abdulwahid." May 16. https://www.kurdistan24.net/en/news/39e890fc-2f3b-4df5-907c-eb5bd8fc703a

Levitsky, Steven, and Lucan Way. 2002. "Elections Without Democracy: The Rise of Competitive Authoritarianism." *Journal of Democracy*, *13*(2), 51-65.

Mansour, Renad, and Christine van den Toorn. 2018. *The 2018 Iraqi Federal Elections: A Population in Transition?* LSE Middle East Centre Report, July 2018. http://eprints.lse.ac.uk/89698/7/MEC_Iraqi-elections_Report_2018.pdf

Mohammad, Munir. 2019. *Social Media and Democratization in Iraqi Kurdistan*. Rowman & Littlefield.

Mufti, Adnan Rashad 2008. "The Report of the Human Rights Committee." *Parliament of the Kurdistan Region – Iraq: Session Minutes Volume No. 47*. https://www.parliament.krd/media/4692/

Natali, Denise. 2010. *The Kurdish Quasi-State: Development and Dependency in Post-Gulf War Iraq*. Syracuse, NY: Syracuse University Press.

Nawzad, Shady. 2020, September 7. Personal interview.

Nimmo, Ben, C. Shawn Eib, Lea Ronzaud, and Thomas Lederer. 2020. *Facebook's Kurdistan Takedown: Platform Takes Down Inauthentic Network in Iraqi Region*. Graphika. https://public-assets.graphika.com/reports/graphika_report_kurdistan_takedown.pdf

Niqash. 2018. "After Protests Turn Violent, Iraqi Kurdish Stop Worshipping Their Military." January 4. https://www.niqash.org/en/articles/politics/5803/After-Protests-Turn-Violent-Iraqi-Kurdish-Stop-Worshipping-Their-Military.htm

Nouri, Dana. 2020, September 3. Personal interview.

NRT. 2018. "Woman participated in Erbil protests says her name removed from payroll list." July 1. https://www.nrttv.com/EN/News.aspx?id=2227&MapID=1

NRT. 2020a. "Journalist Niyaz Abdulla Acquitted by Erbil court over lack of evidence." March 1. https://www.nrttv.com/En/News.aspx?id=19839&MapID=1

NRT. 2020b. "Journalist arrested in defamation lawsuit filed by President Barham Salih: Metro Center." September 22. https://www.nrttv.com/En/News.aspx?id=24042&MapID=1&fbclid=IwAR0YXwEQxpJldpHiJ4By_DbYrPNxDpE4xiVhRJtCe4NsjoTG-kidKLDEfp4

NRT. 2020c. "دادگا دنیکردازا یرایرب تنیرکان دازائ مڵبه هو دا یروبه لدهب" [Court decides to free Baddel Barwari but he has not been released]. October 9. https://www.nrttv.com/News.aspx?id=35376&MapID=1

O'Donnell, Guillermo A. 1994. "Delegative democracy." *Journal of Democracy* 5 (1): 55–69

O'Driscoll, Dylan, and Bahar Baser. 2019. "Referendums as a Political Party Gamble: A Critical Analysis of the Kurdish Referendum for Independence." *International Political Science Review* 41 (5): 652–66.

O'Loughlin, John, Vladimir Kolossov, Gerard Toal, and Gearóid Tuathail. 2011. "Inside Abkhazia: Survey of Attitudes in a De Facto State." *Post-Soviet Affairs* 27 (1): 1–36.

Pearce, Katy E., and Sarah Kendzior. 2012. "Networked Authoritarianism and Social Media in Azerbaijan." *Journal of Communication* 62 (2): 283–98.

Peregraf. 2020a. "60 days behind bars: Story of a Kurdish teacher calling for public rights." October 19. http://peregraf.com/en/political/57

Peregraf. 2020b. "یناکاڵاچ اتشێه تیرکدم یناززراب رورسم هل دنووت یهنخهر هل هوادغهب هل ناڕگۆ ؛ناندنیز هل نانیداب" [Badinan activists remain in prison; Gorran harshly criticizes Masrur Barzani from Baghdad]. October 25. http://peregraf.com/news/1246

Peregraf. 2021. "دادگا یهناوهڕ هرابوود یروربه لدهب یهیسۆد ارک" [Baddel Barwari's case goes back to court]. April 28. http://peregraf.com/ku/news/3121/

Rashid, Bilal Najmaddin, Azhi A. Faraj, and Twana H. Shareef. 2016. "Investigating and

Evaluating Internet Usage in Kurdistan Region of Iraq." *International Journal of Multidisciplinary and Current Research* 4 (May/June): 474–79.

Rauf, Mohammad. 2014. *February 17: A Comparative Documentary Analysis.* Sulaimaniyah: Livin.

Reuter, Ora John, and Graeme B. Robertson. 2015. "Legislatures, Cooptation, and Social Protest in Contemporary Authoritarian Regimes." *The Journal of Politics* 77 (1): 235–48.

Reuter, Ora John, and David Szakonyi. 2015. "Online Social Media and Political Awareness in Authoritarian Regimes." *British Journal of Political Science* 45 (1): 29–51.

Richards, Rebecca, and Robert Smith. 2015. "Playing in the Sandbox: State Building in the Space of Non-recognition." *Third World Quarterly* 36 (9): 1717–35.

Rudaw. 2017. "Migration of young people still a major challenge in Kurdistan," February 23. https://www.rudaw.net/english/kurdistan/23022017

Salih, Cale, and Maria Fantappie. 2019. *Kurdish Nationalism at an Impasse: Why Iraqi Kurdistan is Losing Its Place at the Center of Kurdayeti.* https://tcf.org/content/report/iraqi-kurdistan-losing-place-center-kurdayeti/

Shan Press. 2020. "Because of a complaint by Aram Sheik Mohammad, journalist arrested," January 19. http://www.shanpress.com/details.aspx?jimare=23205

Sheikh Mohammad, Barzan. 2020, September 18. Personal interview

Shirky, Clay. 2011. "The Political Power of Social Media: Technology, the Public Sphere, and Political Change." *Foreign Affairs*, 28–41.

Sika, Nadine. 2019. "Repression, cooptation, and movement fragmentation in authoritarian regimes: Evidence from the youth movement in Egypt." *Political Studies* 67 (3): 676 –92.

Sirwan. 2020, September 26. Personal interview.

Spee Media. 2019. "Counterterror forces: Rebwar Karim and his aghas are afraid of a strong government." July 23. http://speemedia.com/dreja.aspx?=hewal&jmare=78314&Jor=1

Svolik, Milan. 2008. "Authoritarian Reversals and Democratic Consolidation." *American Political Science Review* 102 (2): 153–68.

Svolik, Milan. 2012. *The Politics of Authoritarian Rule.* New York: Cambridge University Press.

Taha, Mohammedali Yaseen. 2020. *Media and Politics in Kurdistan: How Politics and Media are Locked in an Embrace.* London: Lexington.

Talabani, Jalal. 2012. *Kurdistani Nwe: How Do You Want It?* Chapkhana Shivan.

Tucker, Joshua A., Yannis Theocharis, Margaret E. Roberts, and Pablo Barberá. 2017. "From Liberation to Turmoil: Social Media and Democracy." *Journal of Democracy* 28 (4): 46–59.

U.S. Department of State. 2015. *Report on Human Rights Practices: Iraq.* https://2009-2017.state.gov/j/drl/rls/hrrpt/humanrightsreport//index.htm

Varol, Ozan O. 2014. "Stealth Authoritarianism." *Iowa Law* Review 100 (4): 1673–1742.

Warf, Barney. 2011. "Geographies of global Internet censorship." *GeoJournal* 76 (1): 1–23.

Xendan. 2020. "گۆڕان: پەرلەمانتارانمان واژۆکەیان لەسەر پڕۆژەیاسای ڕێکخستنی میدیای ئەلیکترۆنی دەکشێننەوە" [Gorran: Our MPs have withdrawn their signatures from the bill to regulate electronic media]. August 16. https://www.xendan.org/detailnews.aspx?jimare=109710

VOA Kurdish. 2013. "نیاز عەبدوڵا: ئێستا هەرێمی کوردستان نیوەندێکی مەترسیدارە بۆ ڕۆژنامەوانان" [Niyaz Abdullah: The Kurdistan Region is a Danger Zone for Journalists]. December 23. https://www.dengiamerika.com/a/1816399.html

VOA Kurdish. 2020. "بەهەمن کاکەعەبدوڵا: لەمێژووی بزوتنەوەی ڕزگاری خوازی کوردا غاندی و چیڤارا هەیە و زوریش لەوان خەبات و قوربانی دانیان زیاترە" [Bahman Kaka'Abdullah: Throughout the history of the Kurdish liberation movement, it has had its Ghandis and Guevaras and they have struggled and sacrificed more]. October 20. https://www.dengiamerika.com/a/kurdistan/5628248.html

Zebari, Dindar. 2020. "The Kurdistan Press Law is Active, and it is Legally Implemented." Facebook. May 19. https://www.facebook.com/dindar.zebari.5/posts/3170220066362136

Laws and Bills

Iraqi Penal Code, No. 111 of 1969

Law Enacting Amended Article 156 of the Iraqi Penal Code (No. 111 of 1969), No. 21 of 2003

Journalism Law of the Kurdistan Region of Iraq, No. 35 of 2007
Law to Combat Terrorism in the Kurdistan Region of Iraq No. 3 of 2006
Law of Non-Governmental Organizations in the Kurdistan Region of Iraq No. 1 of 2011
Law of the Journalists Syndicate of the Kurdistan Region of Iraq No. 4 of 1998
Law Regulating the Misuse of Electronic Communication Devices, Kurdistan Region of Iraq No. 6 of 2008
Legislative Proposal on Patriotic and National Symbols, Kurdistan Region of Iraq 2020
Legislative Proposal on Regulating Electronic Media in the Kurdistan Region-Iraq 2020
Third Amendment to Law No. 1 of 1992, for the Election of the Kurdistan National Assembly No. 47 of 2004

CHAPTER 3

CONSTRUCTING THEIR OWN LIBERATION: YOUTH'S REIMAGINING OF GENDER AND QUEER SEXUALITY IN IRAQI KURDISTAN

Hawzhin Azeez

Youth across the Kurdistan Region of Iraq (KRI) are consistently an influential generational cohort that contributes to progressive and evolving visions of Kurdishness. Not only are they impacting the nature of Kurdish identity through their activism and shrewd use of social media, but they are also moving toward a more critical views of patriarchal nationalism (*Kurdayeti*) and challenging gender norms. In the past half century, the KRI has become the locus of Kurdish nationalism, which has acted as a means of entrenching patriarchal, clientelistic, and patrimonial attitudes in the name of the national and Kurdish struggle against the Iraqi state. More recently, this patriarchal nationalism has become increasingly fragmentary, promoting a sense of disconnect and apathy within society, since the political elite has reduced *Kurdayeti* to a tool used to loosely legitimize their diminishing claims to power. This approach by the political elites has failed to create a united and consistent shared sense of belonging in society for a largely adolescent and youth cohort. Kurdish leaders continue to use past glories, struggles, successes, and achievements to maintain power, even as their current policies no longer feasibly represent or entice the evolving interests of a substantially youthful population.

Consequently, Kurdish youth are caught between competing and alternative visions of Kurdishness that fail to capture their imagination, desires, and interests. Since the tactics of the Kurdish leadership in the region, especially following the 2017 referendum, have resulted in a strong sense of alienation and increasing detachment from politics, youth are seeking out alternative spaces in which they can speak out. If nations can be defined as an "invented tradition" (Hobsbawm and Ranger 1983, 1) or, in the words of Benedict Anderson (1991, 6), as "imagined communities" then it is possible to conceive of Kurdish youth and queer communities, with unprecedented access to information and technology, as being capable of impacting and influencing the Kurdish national identity and gender norms. Bereft of a space in formal political structures, youth are forging new traditions and producing new narratives around identity, solidarity, democracy, civic responsibility, gender, and Kurdishness by effectively utilizing social media and Information and communications technology. Queer communities play an important role in this process despite significant institutional and cultural barriers. Collectively, as youth seek out political spaces, they also face multiple challenges including Islamists groups' vying for their attention and being just as savvy in their use of social media and technology as well as patriarchal norms that continue to marginalize queer individuals and hinder women's participation in the public sphere. In response, youth are increasingly utilizing civil society and NGOs, challenging gender and sexual norms, establishing startups, and turning to activism and solidarity in their efforts to reimagine an alternative sense of civic identity and belonging.

This chapter first aims to highlight the exclusion of youth from political participation and representation in formal politics in the KRI, a situation that has ultimately created the need for alternative spaces and platforms for representation and expression. Using the LGBTQIA+ community's efforts to achieve visibility and demand access to political spaces, the chapter highlights the socio-political, ethno-religious, and economic issues that youth continue to face as they challenge the established patriarchal notions of *Kurdayeti*. The chapter argues that, despite a tendency to exclude them from formal politics, youth use social media and communication technology to sustain an influential level of political activism, particularly in the reimagining of gender and sexual norms. Many barriers remain, yet the increasing visibility of progress around gender norms is also undeniable, persistent, and present.

Youth in Kurdistan

Youth in the KRI live amid the complex and multifaceted legacy of decades of nationalist liberation efforts by Kurdish leaders and political elites against the Ba'athist regime. From their inception, the Kurdish nationalist efforts in Southern Kurdistan (the KRI) were defined by tribal and patriarchal attitudes, as a result of which young men led the national resistance. Women were confined to the traditional role of providing domestic labor, food, care, or services away from the frontlines. The response of the Ba'athist regime employed gender-based violence as an explicit tool to undermine the resistance movement. The threat of this gender-based violence, including the notorious sexual violence inflicted by Ba'athists, had the desired effect of limiting women's participation. The old tropes of women being the honor of the nation and feminization of Kurdistan being synonymous with motherhood were predominant during this time. Politics and national liberation in the KRI were a masculinist, securitized, and patriarchal domain and remain largely so today. The simultaneous development of Kurdish movements, such as the People's Democratic Party (*Halkların Demokratik Partisi*, HDP) or the YPG and YPJ forces in Northern Kurdistan (southeastern Turkey), and an increasingly visible and active women's force, especially in the recent fight against ISIS in Western Kurdistan (northern Syria), has failed to produce real and meaningful change in the KRI (Gunes and Lowe 2015). It merely produced imitations that failed to effect long-term change for women (Marouf 2018). Nevertheless, gender liberation has steadily increased ever since the achievement of semi-autonomous status developed through the imposition of the No-Fly Zone resulted in Kurdish self-rule. The rates of female genital mutilation (FGM), for example, have diminished significantly in the past three decades (Johnston 2020). More women are in the workforce, the right to divorce is becoming normalized, education is becoming more accessible, and women are generally marrying later in life and having fewer children (Vilardo and Bitter 2018; Kaya 2017). But many challenges remain today, including ongoing patriarchal values that are reinforced through the influence of many Islamic groups and organizations as well as youth's increased access to social media and information technology, which has produced a surge in violence and honor-based crimes.

Before delving further, it is important to mention the results of the region's most recent demographic survey and consider its implications for youth. According to the International Organization for Migration's "Demographic Survey: Kurdistan Region of Iraq" (IOM 2018), over 35 percent of the population is younger than fifteen, while 61 percent of the population is of working age (fifteen to sixty-five). Youth constitute the majority of the population, while children aged fifteen and younger represent the second largest segment in society. The report indicated that 90 percent of households are headed by men, and the average age of marriage is 20.7 for women and 24.5 for men. The average number of children was found to be three, but more educated women tended to have fewer children. The report also revealed important conclusions about literacy, with over 45 percent of the population above the age of six not having a primary education degree, though 80 percent of this group could read and write. Seventeen percent of young people between the ages of eighteen and twenty-four had not completed primary school. In relation to employment, only 40 percent of the population aged fifteen to sixty-four were employed. However, there is a staggering gender gap, with 15 percent of women being employed compared to 70 percent of men. Women's level of economic participation correlates to their level of education, including finishing secondary and graduate degrees. The public sector employs 75 percent of the women in the workforce, cementing the notion that only certain types of positions—respectable desk jobs affiliated with government branches and institutions—are appropriate career pathways (IOM 2018).

Likewise, over 1,628,074 IDPs and refugees live in the region, according to the Ministry of Interior's Joint Crisis Coordination Centre (2020), impacting certain aspects of life for youth such as their access to education, freedom, and employment. Overall, these statistics highlight a number of issues that youth face, including persistent gender inequality in the labor force, the continuing male economic and cultural dominance in households, and low rates of formal education. Some of these challenges are fairly significant and undoubtedly have a detrimental impact on youth's desire for gender liberation and additional freedoms, especially due to the extremely limited and conditional nature of political spaces. In the KRI, for instance, politicians are elected based on a system called *Muhasasa*, which prioritizes affiliation with particular parties or politicians rather than their policies, ideas, merit, or competence. This is largely due to the legacy of the civil war between the two political parties as well as the pretext of power-sharing imposed after 2003. This process yielded a formalization of *Muhasasa* rather than a full merger. Consequently, elections, which lack fairness or transparency, do not produce real and meaningful change.

Political structures in the region remain top-down configurations in which a small number of elite political leaders make decisions in order to perpetuate party and individual interests rather than those of the region. As a result, the last three decades of self-government have resulted in "a broken political and economic region" (Saeed 2019), serving as a barrier to progressive gender norms. The outcome has been that youth have been "stripped of Kurdish patriotism" (Saeed 2019) and deprived of alternative spaces in which they can formally participate in politics or access platforms to raise their voices or implement change. This, in turn, has underscored the imperative for youth to formulate or search for alternative spaces or platforms to find freedom and representation.

Across the Middle East, including in Iraq and the KRI, the exclusion of youth from formal politics has become strongly evident norm. This oppression often intersects with other forms of marginalization, including in the contexts of race, gender, religion, disability, culture, community, and sexuality. But youth are not passive bystanders. Research indicates that, since the Arab Spring, youth have remained politically involved with, but increasingly outside of, political parties (UN 2013). They often become and remain active through political movements, universities, organizations, and civil society groups. They exhibit high levels of distrust in, and disillusionment with, formal political parties. Consequently, youth tend to find themselves involved in unconventional forms of politics and political participation, through social media, activism, apathy (boycotting elections and conventional forms of politics), and protest movements. Research also indicates that formal participation in political institutions and processes such as parliament, elections, political parties, and policymaking is more prevalent among older generations compared with youth. Yet the UN (2013) emphasized that participation in informal political processes must be seen as a powerful tool for politicization, involvement, and democratization: "Meaningful youth participation and leadership require that young people and young people-led organizations have opportunities, capacities, and benefit from an enabling environment and relevant evidence-based programmes and policies at all levels. Realizing young people's rights to participate and be included in democratic processes and practices is also vital to ensure the achievement of internationally agreed development goals."

In the KRI, the extensive history of state oppression, marginalization, and genocide has culminated with the establishment of a system that embodies an age-based patriarchal authority. Accordingly, there is a general societal inclination to prevent youth politicization and participation unless it falls within the accepted boundaries of an established Kurdish political party, such as the Kurdistan Democratic Party (KDP) or the Patriotic Union of Kurdistan (PUK). A review of current MPs in the KRI shows that out of twenty-one parliamentary members, only two are under the age of forty (Ibrahim 2020). Formal political processes and institutions clearly reserve limited space for youth participation and involvement, resulting in a dearth of legal frameworks, policies, and plans. A recent change in Iraqi election laws, however, has reduced the minimum age for serving in the parliament from twenty-eight to twenty-five (Ibrahim 2020) and may open new spaces for participation. But the obstacles preventing youth from participating in formal politics are not only legal in nature. Much of it has to do with youth's increasing rejection of two-party politics. The KDP and PUK have both fielded numerous young MPs into the KRI parliament, but the parliament has been reduced to rubber stamping the whims of the leaders and parties.

An additional factor that contributes to the negative perceptions youth harbor regarding formal politics' ineffective representation of their interests is the ongoing ruling duopoly between the KDP and PUK. The patrimonial and clientelistic character of this monopoly has made them more apathetic toward political participation but has also effectively entrenched the two-party identity politics in the psyche of the youth. The recent example of presidential conflict in the parliament is a reflection of this issue, as is the lack of available space for new voices to enter politics. Nechervan Barzani became the KRG president in June 2019, two years after Masoud Barzani—Nechervan's uncle—had vacated the seat. Although the KRG constitution dictated that a president serves only a two-year term, Masoud Barzani had served for eight years and renewed his presidency for another two years in 2013. When, in 2015, he attempted to prolong his presidency by another two years, public discontent and protests by opposition parties failed to remove him from power. He went on to serve until November 2017, culminating with the disastrous September referendum, which called for the secession of the KRI from the rest of Iraq. The outcome was one of intense violence and the reimposition of the central Iraqi government over the region and all other territories the Kurdish Peshmerga forces had occupied since the start of the war with ISIS in 2014. Meanwhile, the September 2018 provincial council elections were marred with allegations of fraud and inconsistencies and prompted smaller parties, including the Goran Party (Change Party), to reject the results. The two-party system also tacitly endorses a cisgender and heteronormative vision and characterizes all alternative, non-normative identities as a threat to Kurdishness (Robinson 2019). Other new parties such as Goran and the New Generation Party have been unable to challenge the dominance of the two-party system, often because their membership comprises former members or they are splinter groups and have become entrenched in the same clientelistic, patrimonial, and corrupt practices.

Women are generally chosen to participate in the political process based on their affiliation with key politicians or parties and often tend to be "yes-women" rather than representing women's interests in the parliament (al-Shadeedi and Van Veen 2020, 8). The same could certainly be said of younger MPs from the dominant political parties, as they are unable to sidestep their parties' line of politics in their legislating and monitoring of the executive. The Iraqi parliament has a 25 percent quota on women parliamentarians, while the KRG parliament legally reserves 30 percent of its seats for women. While this number has been surpassed in the current parliament, women tend to be placed in the service sector and given "low-level" positions, while men tend to be awarded higher profile cabinet positions (Dri 2019). Women's rights advocates are working to push the 30 percent threshold to 40 percent, but the above evidence and current trends evoke the question of whether increased women's participation could have any long-term or meaningful impact. Nevertheless, the current speaker and deputy speaker of the parliament are both women, and while women only previously occupied one cabinet position, the ministries of agriculture and social and labor affairs are now held by women, as is the cabinet position overseeing parliamentary affairs. This suggests a positive trend in spaces becoming increasingly open to women in formal politics. Unsurprisingly, some women have called the role of women in parliament and the political parties as "decorative" or tokenistic efforts that do not bring about real or lasting change (Dri 2019). Likewise, accusations that women continue to be excluded from decision-making councils or politburos appear to have some credibility. Generally, women from younger generations are strongly discouraged from participating in formal political platforms and parties, not only for the reasons mentioned above but also because of the ongoing sexual harassment of women in public (Menmy 2020) and because of general societal perceptions in which women in politics and public spaces are viewed in a derogatory manner (Johansen 2019; Dexter 2016).

A number of other obstacles that youth face in the KRI produce an alternative vision that better aligns with their experiences living in the post-Saddam era. The historical period of Kurdish resistance against the authoritarian and genocidal policies of the Ba'athist regime under Saddam Hussain continues to play an important role in the lack of youth participation and their exclusion from politics. It was largely youth who resisted against the regime and paid the highest price in lives, blood, and commitment. But those who rebelled against the Ba'athist regime are now the parents of today's youth and actively deter their own children from participating in politics due to the disillusionment and fatigue of Kurdish liberation since the establishment of the KRI. Likewise, the political parties, conscious of the potential of youth to challenge their patron-clientelistic and entrenched corruption, have used a number of violent tactics to dissuade them from engaging with politics. The high-profile murders and arrests of journalists, academics, anti-government protesters, and activists have spawned an atmosphere of fear and deterrence (HRW 2018; CPJ 2020). The International Federation of Journalists has noted that murders of journalists in KRG "remain scandalously high" (Rwanduzy 2019). Additionally, each political party has its own affiliated security forces, military, and intelligence agencies as a legacy of the civil war between the KDP and PUK, making them formidable opponents of dissenting voices and movements.

Overall, Kurdish politics is driven by an age-based, "patriarchic, personality-centric" (al-Shadeedi and Veen 2020) configuration, which engenders ongoing issues for youth relating to democracy development, governance, and representation. The repercussions of the September 2017 referendum demonstrated that change and progress come at a cost, serving only to consolidate the authority of the old, patriarchal order. It is becoming increasingly evident that unless youth also follow the same conventional two-party identity line, political spaces are unavailable to them. The ongoing tribal, nepotistic, and patrimonial nature of the political system and culture as well as the establishment of institutions and party practices continue to reinforce the status quo. Another problem within this context is the increasingly localized character of identities and loyalties, which create an added layer of divisive identity politics between the KDP-controlled Erbil and the PUK-controlled Sulaimani governorates. A factor that promotes localized loyalties is the establishment of a large number of local, public, and private universities, which encourages youth to remain in their hometowns, reducing cross-regional experiences and interaction between governorates (Salih and Fantappie 2019).

However, there are also some positive trends. One way in which youth reclaim public spaces, promote representations of their interests, and nourish the development of civil society within the region is through startups. Youth launch new startups, businesses, associations, and independent, online media outlets, and they utilize social media to advance their values and interests. From eco-friendly clothing brands to vegan foods, language-learning interactive cafes to art classes, disability service providers to babysitting, and coworking spaces to food delivery services, youth are taking a critical stance and rejecting the client patronage system of salary in return for loyalty and acquiescence (Cooper 2020). Young women are also at the forefront of this important movement. According to Alice Bosley, the cofounder and executive director of Five One Labs, "Older industries like cement and oil are still much more male dominated, but when you look at new, innovative business, women are making a huge impact . . . These are the ones that are going to modernize Iraq's economy" (Cuthbert 2020). The number of women-led businesses and startups has increased significantly in recent years, and their success is becoming increasingly commonplace and accepted. According to one female entrepreneur, this is largely due to social media opportunities and exposure, which allow society to be grow more familiar with successful women working in their chosen careers

(Cuthbert 2020). Young women are leading many of the emerging socially focused startups and businesses in the region. Yet Iraq and the KRI have developed a political and economic environment that is "unaccustomed to and skeptical of independent advocates," meaning that many independent voices and youth-run businesses encounter problems and fail (National Democratic Institute 2011).

Local and international NGOs and civil society groups have filled much of the gap in the representation and promotion of youth interests. These organizations continue to work on a range of urgent and necessary issues, including peacebuilding, democracy development, combating violence against women, and promoting multiculturalism. However, civil society and local NGOs have faced a number of challenges in pursuing their goals such as struggling with a "credibility gap" and societal acceptance, being deprived of access to decisionmakers and political figures, and lacking clear strategies and the capacity to determine the overall impact of what strategies they do have (National Democratic Institute 2011, 1). As a result, social media tools such as Facebook or Twitter have become important platforms of political engagement, resistance, liberation, and self-expression for youth. Conroy, Feezell, and Guerrero (2012) noted that information-sharing on social media outlets such as Facebook encourages "civil participation, trust, political and life contentment among youth." Similarly, Abdu, Mohamad, and Muda (2017, 2) concluded that social media enables youth to be more politically active relative to other previous generations, because they feel that their voices resonate on these platforms. Furthermore, social media allows more intimate and immediate access to political parties and figures and, in turn, permits them to communicate their views and preferences and impact policy and decision-making (Skoric and Poor 2013).

In response, a unique Kurdish youth political culture is emerging, through the use of social media platforms, activism, and leadership of local organizations, that seeks to implement change and subsequently contribute to the organic establishment of a civil society and the active promotion of peacebuilding. Such activism breaks down primordial loyalties and traditions across ethno-religious lines while deradicalizing and preventing alienation among marginalized youth. It also promotes the creation of a transformative, civic, and secular citizenship. Nevertheless, the recent 2018 demographic survey indicated that death rates for youth in the region tend to be higher and involve cultural factors such as political issues, honor or revenge killings, and casualties due to conflict and war. In contrast, the primary causes of death for other generational cohorts are illness and sudden death (IOM 2018). This suggests that youth bear the brunt of cultural and political conflicts and violence, especially if they attempt to implement changes that mainstream society views as "foreign" or "alien."

Another major challenge that competes for attention among youth is that of Islamist or radical groups wishing to exert their own influence over the region. With the increasing levels of corruption, lack of institutional reforms, a rentier economy, intra- and inter-party conflicts, leadership contests, and gaping economic inequality, Kurdish nationalism—though not necessarily its associated patriarchal norms—has been on a steady decline. The matter crystallized with the ill-organized 2017 referendum, which dashed any remaining hopes of independence despite a 93 percent vote in favor of the initiative (Yoshika 2018). While the high turnout and considerable support for independence demonstrate the persistence of Kurdish patriotism, the ensuing violence and invasion by Iraqi military forces into the Kurdish-controlled, disputed territories illustrated the persistent division and tensions simmering within the Kurdish identity and the liberation cause. The failure of the Kurdish forces to oppose to the Iraqi army, their disintegration, and the incoherent, chaotic, and poorly organized response to Baghdad's incursion all contributed to a decline in trust within society and between the main Kurdish political parties. The death of a number of Peshmerga forces who broke rank and stood their ground evoked an emotional and traumatic response in society regarding the futility of Kurdish nationalism in light of the enduring apathy, failure, and corrupt self-interested policies of the leadership. Experts and observers noted that since the referendum, the KRI's "role as the hub for the evolution of Kurdish nationalism is declining," largely because the political leadership "fails to meet the expectations of a changing society" (Salih and Fantappie 2019). Consequently, the results of the referendum "convinced many Kurds that the leadership's statehood-focused vision of *Kurdayeti* is obsolete, and cannot provide for the civil rights they have come to expect. Only a true political transition that makes way for new leaders proposing a new social contract can solve Iraqi Kurdistan's impasse" (Salih and Fantappie 2019). Youth became even more vulnerable in the circumstances they faced after 2017.

As the chasm between the political leadership and the public widens, society has been left increasingly defenseless against internal conflicts, regional interference, and alternative ideologies such as radical Islam. This trend has significant impacted youth's attempt to locate alternative means of identity, belonging, and connection that transcend the conventional definitions imposed by Kurdish nationalism. This is the gap that Islamist groups have sought to fill. According to Meleagrou-Hitchens and Alaaldin (2018), terrorist organizations have been incredibly successful at using social media and the internet to locate and recruit possible members "among sections of the region's vulnerable and impressionable youth." The KRG region experienced a similar trend in which youth, alienated and disconnected from mainstream parties and lacking alternative avenues leading to change, were captivated by the allure of participation and the impact for which fundamentalist groups have advocated. The ongoing disillusionment with politics has played a crucial role in this regard. It is no wonder that regions such as Halabja—the site of Saddam's infamous chemical bombings, which killed five thousand men, women, and children overnight in March 1988—has been most influenced by Islamists (Hauslohner 2014). The ongoing neglect by the political parties and their failure to support development projects, job growth, and progress in the region have created a community that is vulnerable and easily swayed by alternative arguments, including that of Islamists. One of the most vulnerable groups that continues to be ostracized and erased is the queer community in the KRI.

Queer Youth

Queer youth are another important minority within the younger generations in the region. They are a critical and increasingly visible and active component of society who challenge traditional and patriarchal gender norms around Kurdish identity in multiple ways. With their increasing visibility and self-representation on social media for emerging pro-queer organizations, queer communities are an integral part of civil society groups and promote democratization and the promotion of diversity.

As a legacy of the neo-liberal policies of the US invasion in 2003, Iraq has one of the more progressive queer laws in the region. Typical remnants of the most recent colonial practices of the Western world—a far cry from the actual values of the people in these countries—same-sex sexual relations are legal under the Iraqi Penal Code, which is enforceable in the KRI (Robinson 2019). In reality, homosexuality and displays of queerness remain taboo and deeply frowned upon or, worse, precipitate acts of violence toward individuals suspected of being queer (Robinson 2019). Many exist in a state of constant fear and struggle to live freely and authentically. The situation is exacerbated when cases of honor killings and murder of family members for suspected homosexuality are not legally punishable and occur frequently. Violence and oppression inflicted upon queer youth originate from a range of different groups and actors within society, including the government, militias, employers, family, and friends. In the widespread anti-government protests in 2019 in Baghdad, members of the queer community were present and involved in demanding democratic rights, better services, action to address unemployment, and an end government corruption. While queer youth played a key role in the protests, they have had to exercise higher levels of caution to ensure that they are not identifiable as queer people, lest they be targeted by government forces or religious militias. Prominent religious leaders, such as Grand Ayatollah Ali al-Sistani, the leading religious authority in the Shi'ite sect of Iraq, explicitly call homosexuality "forbidden" and actively promote anti-queer violence and oppression (McCarthy 2013). In an unprecedented move, Muqtada al-Sadr, another prominent religious leader whose militia the Mehdi Army was responsible for a spate of anti-queer violence in Iraq in 2009, called for an end to anti-LGBTQIA+ violence in 2016 (Human Rights Watch 2016). However, the influence of such a call on curbing violence is questionable, and, for all appearances and purposes, the anti-queer violence has endured. With the majority of the population in the KRG being of the Sunni religious sect, many religious and political leaders in the region actively promote homophobia as an integral aspect of a Sunni Muslim-Kurdish identity (Hawramy 2017). Even if the desire for change does exist, the KRG's "democratic institutions lack the strength to contain the influence of long-standing power brokers" (Freedom House 2020).

Societal change, from increasing levels of tolerance to acceptance of plurality in recent years, has contributed to a new generation of youth that is increasingly conscious and actively supportive of queer rights. According to the local journalist Rebaz Majeed (2020), however, it is essential to view Kurdish youth not as a homogenized entity but, rather, as a diverse group of people who are driven by myriad interests and desires. Rebaz argues that while elements of youth are moving toward conservative, patriarchal, and traditional notions of Kurdishness, others are shifting toward a leftist framework inspired by the Rojava Revolution. The civil war in Syria provided a space for the Kurds in Western Kurdistan to practice self-governance for the first time. Unlike the ruling KDP and PUK, the YPG/YPJ have adopted a bottom-up, progressive, and egalitarian political system heavily reliant on women and youth to participate in the nascent governing and self-administrative system. Meanwhile, in the KRI, others "are just people hoping for a better day, either becoming refugees in the West or becoming some sort of nihilists who reject everything and do not find any hope in regards to change" (Majeed 2020) These competing visions are, perhaps, a natural outcome in a region and a country that has suffered decades of civil war, conflict, invasion, bombings, and foreign interference combined with the ongoing corruption and exclusion of dissenting voices in domestic politics. And the increasingly neo-liberal, consumerist economic policies as well as the visions of Western freedom, sex, and wealth flooding from satellite televisions, online streaming sites, and social media continue to drive home the hollow foundation of the limited freedoms and social changes youth are able to experience. Online communities across social media constitute the intermediate space for these two realities. While this trend is applicable in the region, youth bear an additional and intersecting layer of oppressions and barriers, which could explain why they are so adamant—and have been somewhat successful—in their push for gender and sexual freedom.

According to activists, queer communities in the Middle East face a two-pronged struggle. "They are battling oppressive forces within" their communities while also "resisting the global narrative that tries to use our 'oppression' for broader military or political goals" (Haddad 2017). A recent example aptly illustrates this issue. On May 17, 2020, the EU mission in Iraq raised the pride flag in Baghdad to celebrate International Day Against Homophobia. This was a tone-deaf and dangerously ignorant attempt at inclusivity, reminiscent of the ill-conceived 2003 Iraq invasion and subsequent state-building efforts. For experts, queer bodies in the Middle East have become a battleground in a much larger war. After all, one activist said, it is no secret that both liberals and conservatives in "North America and Europe have, since 9/11, waved the flag of women's rights, and to a lesser degree LGBT rights, as a way to gain Western public support to wage wars in the Middle East. Images and stories of oppressed Afghan women drove the call to war in 2001, and the more recent footage of ISIS throwing gay men off towers and enslaving Yazidi women stoked the fires of intervention in Syria" (Haddad 2017). Another wave of outrage ensued when a similar incident occurred in July 2017 and the American consulate raised the rainbow flag in Erbil. Some argued that such a practice was "alien" to Kurdish culture, while the media office for Erbil province stated, "This is an attempt to distort the social norms in Kurdistan and defame Kurdish culture . . . the governor has not given permission to any person, group or organization to behave like that" (Hawramy 2017). Nevertheless, although social media is a platform for criticism, it is also the avenue for others to express open support of queer communities, which indicates burgeoning tolerance.

Predictably, a wave of anti-queer violence erupted across the central and southern parts of the country immediately after the EU mission raised the pride flag in May 2020, including angry politicians and clerics calling for the expulsion of the visiting ambassadors. The queer community, activists, and allies in the Kurdish region responded with a wave of support through savvy use of social media platforms, engaging in critical discussion and dialogue online. Social media, parallel to the crucial role it played in the rise of anti-government youth protests in Baghdad in 2019, was similarly pivotal in this case. Activists, supporters and allies, feminists, and pro-democracy voices across the KRI and the country condemned the waves of violence. Studies have demonstrated that youth engagement with social media increases their capacity to access and understand political information, which in turn has resulted in greater participation (Abdulrauf, Abdul Hamid, and Ishak 2015). Moreover, the cost of accessing information is reduced significantly with social media, while youth are able to better comprehend the nature of the political system within their societies. Likewise, experts indicate that, while demographics and psychological factors were the dominant influence on political engagement in the past, social media and technology have more recently played an equally significant role (Abdulrauf, Abdul Hamid, and Ishak 2015). The role of local and international NGOs in the promotion of peace and democracy and their relationship with and support of queer youth groups have likewise been important yet limited by the persistence of the age-based political system and the prevalence of nepotistic, clientelistic, and clan-based political parties and organizations. In relation to youth's lack of access to safe and formal political representation and avenues, social media can play a defining role in promoting tolerance and democratization as well as alternative visions of gender and sexuality within society. The above example indicates the growing importance of social media as a safer alternative for self-expression and dissent. This potential, however, may be limited by increasing efforts to crack down on online activists (Abdulrauf, Abdul Hamid, and Ishak 2015).

Consequently, brave local organizations such as IraQueer and Rasan in the KRI are actively working to fight against the persistent oppression and exclusion of queer youth in the country. Rasan works to promote coexistence and social cohesion using art, music, focus groups, seminars, workshops, and training as well as to engage with community leaders in order to advance LGBTQIA+ and gender rights (Laveres 2017). The organization also provides essential services such as "psychosocial support, legal aid, and consultation" to queer people (Rasan 2020). The organization was initially established as a feminist association in 2004, but, as the members became aware of the plight of the LGBTQIA+ communities in the region, it became necessary to promote and involve queer voices. Rasan has run a number of successful campaigns, including painting pro-diversity, pro-queer, pro-women, and multicultural murals across cities. Rasan believes that the greatest barriers to further activism are "governmental institutions, which are, unfortunately, often run by biased and conservative people" (Rasan 2020). This was exemplified with the Ministry of Education's decision to ban the organization from holding workshops or seminars at schools because of the rainbow colors in the organization's official logo. With examples including the refusal to accept the official registration of pro-LGBTQIA+ organizations, defamation campaigns on social media, direct threats of violence by the Directorate of Non-Governmental Organizations, and the refusal to refer to Rasan as an active and successful organization in the community, pressure on such associations immensely limit their capacity to effectively achieve their goals (Rasan 2020).

Yet ongoing crackdowns against LGBTQIA+ organizations and people across Iraq continue to foster the same oppressive and exclusionary message targeting vulnerable queer communities. For example, there were numerous instances of the kidnapping, torture, and killing of queer men in 2009, while the Iraqi army launched a series of attacks against people who appeared to be gay or transgender in 2012 (Human Rights Watch 2012). Violence has continued over the years, despite the fact that a committee designed to address and prevent abuses toward queer people was established in an effort to reduce ongoing marginalization. Activists have argued that little or no action has been taken by the central government to curb violence against queer people in the country. Across the Middle East, the same repetitive cycle of erasure, humiliation, and denial of rights for queer people is constantly reinforced, with examples such as the 2001 Queen boat incident in Egypt in which thirty-six men were arrested, the 2012 arrest of another group of thirty-six queer men at a cinema in Bourj Hammoud in Beirut, and the ongoing attacks against pride parades in Turkey, (Haddad 2017; Kirchick 2007). The public execution of gay men by ISIS seemed to be merely an extension of the existing hatred and homophobia in the region, as such violence against queer people was commonplace even before ISIS emerged (William and Maher, 2009).

According to Rasan, however, the situation for queer communities is relatively better and safer in the KRI compared to the rest of Iraq, though many queer people refuse to contact the police due to a history of oppression and violence at the hands of security forces. In Iraq, according to the organization, many people are attacked or murdered simply "for looking gay" (Rasan 2020): "Many of the LGBT+ people feel unsafe when it comes to police and Asaiysh because of the mistreatment they face when they have to deal with them, we had a transgender case who was detained and her hair was cut against her will and the police verbally assaulted her. In Iraqi law, there is nothing against homosexuality, but Penal Code 393 of Iraqi law has been falsely translated into Kurdish, and is used to detain LGBT+ people."

Rasan believes that social media is an essential tool for their work to spread awareness and inclusion and to promote the rights of queer youth. There is a growing body of research on the importance of social media in the encouragement and advancement of activism, engagement, and politicization among youth over the past decade. An important trend, the literature suggests, is youth's acquisition of political information and content from the network of their friends on social media, thereby increasing their levels of political interest. Consequently, politically interested social media users influence their network of friends to be more politically informed or engaged (Boulianne 2009). At the same time, social media can help "convert or mobilize" individuals who may not have been involved in offline political activities, with research showing that social media platforms such as Facebook are more powerful than traditional media (Gromping 2014). When asked what essential tools are available to them to promote their work, Rasan gave the following response:

> We live in a time where everyone has access to social media and the internet, so digital advocacy is really important in the activism field. We have a great media strategy, and we are always engaging the community we have built so far. At the beginning, LGBT+ people seemed very hopeless, they would accept insults hurled at them by homophobes in our comment sections and they would tell us that our activism would never be successful, but now we are seeing them getting more confident, defending themselves and work with us to build their future. Some of the people that were frustrated even became great activists that work with us (2020).

Conversely, many queer youth feel increasingly disconnected from the traditional version of Kurdishness and gender norms. Lack of formal support and rights and ongoing oppression have cultivated a sense of alienation from

Kurdayeti, even while queer communities are accused of becoming Westernized and emulating Western culture because of their identities. Many queer youth are deemed sex workers or are strongly associated with "nothing but sex" (Majeed 2020). In other words, queerness is associated with immorality or hypersexuality and is viewed as dangerous and threatening for conservative cultural and religious visions of Kurdishness. A queer Kurdish youth is judged as "a sinner, an outsider, immoral, disgusting and a subject to make fun of" (Majeed 2020) and made to feel a distinct lack of belonging in society. These negative views may account for the selective and deliberately misinterpreted representations of Iraqi Penal Codes 393, 394, 400, and 401, which are translated from Arabic to Kurdish and, according to Rasan (2020), are applied selectively to prevent and curb queer people's rights in the KRI. For example, Code 400 entails the punishment of immodest, nonconsensual acts. However, consenting queer people are still detained and punished under this code, indicating a propensity to view queerness as immoral rather than focusing on the "nonconsensual" aspect of the law.

Homophobia is often used as a critical lens to accuse queer youth in the region of betraying their culture and identity and adopting fashionable Western personas. There is a persistent failure to view the increasing visibility and the rise of queer voices as legitimate, organic and locally produced; rather, this visibility is perceived as the negative influence of Western modernity through communication technologies and social media opening avenues of representation that were previously denied to them. The recent public coming out of Darin, a famous Kurdish singer living in Denmark, provoked important questions and prompted discourse across social media regarding inclusivity, gender, democracy, freedom, and choice. It also contributed to the critical discussions among Kurdish diaspora communities and their increasingly Westernized and liberal approaches as opposed to those of Kurds living at home who continue to grapple with a lack of safe and available avenues of self-expression and representation (*Ziv Magazine* 2015).

Despite these positive trends, decades of conservative education, media, and religious and cultural values promoting an intensely homophobic and exclusionary view of Middle Eastern societies have become deeply rooted in the region. According to Renwar Najm (2020), a journalist from Sulaimani, LGBTQIA+ communities are some of the most vulnerable groups in society and are under pressure from "all sides; family, friends, and society as a whole ." Renwar noted that "discrimination, insults (sometimes violence), and lack of acceptance" are three major challenges facing queer communities. Rebaz Majeed, mentioned previously, identified the main challenge facing queer communities as a "lack of awareness about the community" (2020) among mainstream society. Another issue that promotes feelings of alienation arises from the psychological toll of being a member of the queer community in a deeply conservative society that denies queerness or accuses LGBTQIA+ people of simply emulating Western trends. It is unsurprising that many queer youth wish to leave the region. According to Rasan, an estimated fifteen thousand youth have emigrated from the region to first world countries in the past few years. While there are no data regarding the number of queer people among them, it is believed that many LGBTQIA+ youth wish to immigrate to countries with increased freedoms. Despite these challenges, including lack of personal safety, queer communities across the KRI continue to become increasingly emboldened and visible and utilize spaces to amplify their voices and promote an alternative vision of Kurdishness that is the antithesis of the old, patriarchal, traditional, and tribal view of *Kurdayeti*.

Conclusion

Youth throughout the KRI are attempting to reformulate and reimagine gender norms and values. The old, traditional, patriarchal Kurdish identity is increasingly seen to belong to a past that is no longer relevant and is nonexistent in the living memory of youth today. It is considered an ideology that has served to institutionalize existing age-based hierarchies, corruption, and estrangement from politics, actions to which youth do not feel a sense of belonging. *Kurdayeti* has become a tool used and abused by the old order that only provides benefits based on patrimonial, clientelistic, and nepotistic behaviors and promotes a cisnormative and heterosexual identity. Nevertheless, this patriarchal system remains entrenched and continues to act as a barrier silencing, shaming, and erasing dissenting voices calling for progressive gender and sexual norms.

The activism and work of youth and queer communities in the KRI, especially through their online work, reveals a transition toward more progressive visions of gender and sexuality. Kurdishness has never been a static concept, nor have its representations, and it is now being expanded to increasingly involve queer communities and progressive gender norms. Kurdishness has always evolved and, in fact, requires this evolution to counter the persistent challenges and conflicts that it has faced. Being deprived of their own state and being divided across the borders of four countries—each run by authoritarian and fascist regimes—have resulted in a multitude of intersecting forms of oppression and violence that have been inflicted on the Kurds since the Sykes-Picot Agreement. Kurdish youth communities, including LGBTQIA+ groups, are caught in between the tribal, patriarchal, and corrupt politics of Southern Kurdistan, that of the radical leftist ideologies of the Kurdish vision in Northern and Western Kurdistan, and Islamists filling the gap between disenfranchised and alienated youth throughout the region. Adding to this complex web is the persistent lure of the alternative, Western lifestyle, promoted and normalized by social media to represent a fickle and sexually promiscuous existence filled with an extravagant amount of free time and inexplicable wealth.

Overall, the traditional patriarchal model of Kurdishness is deemed a barrier for Kurdish youth who are now moving toward a more progressive, cosmopolitan view of identity and rights. The region, despite experiencing unprecedented economic growth after 2003, has remained largely mired in internal power struggles, oppression, political killings, silencing of dissident voices, and the suppression of protests and activists. Queer communities are often caught at the crossroads of this process. The new generation of youth who did experienced the oppression under the Ba'ath regime do not identify with the unifying external forces that upheld patriarchal *Kurdayeti* structure and are instead searching for alternative platforms to represent and express their evolving identities. Social media and information technologies will be indispensable for the promotion of progress, solidarity, tolerance, and gender liberation, even as it remains a tool for alienation and censorship.

References

Abdu, Shamsu Dauda, Bahtiar Mohamad, and Suhaini Muda. 2017. "Youth Online Political Participation: The Role of Facebook Use, Interactivity, Quality Information and Political Interest." In *SHS Web of Conferences*, Vol. 33: 00080. EDP Sciences. doi: 10.1051/shsconf/20173300080.

Abdulrauf, Aishat Adebisi, Norsiah Binti Abdul Hamid, and Mohd Sobhi bin Ishak. 2015. "Social Media and Youth Online Political Participation: Perspectives on Cognitive Engagement." *New Media and Mass Communication* 44.

al-Shadeedi, al-Hamzeh and Erwin Van Veen. 2020. "Iraq's Adolescent Democracy: Where to Go from Here." Clingendael Institute. https://www.clingendael.org/sites/default/files/2020-06/iraqs-adolescent-democracy.pdf

Anderson, Benedict. 2006. *Imagined Communities: Reflections on the Origin and Spread of Nationalism*. New York: Verso Books. Revised version with added material, 1983.

Boulianne, Shelley. 2009. "Does Internet Use Affect Engagement? A Meta-analysis of Research." *Political Communication* 26 (2): 193–211.

CPJ (Committee to Protect Journalists). 2020. "Iraqi Kurdish Police Arrest Journalist Sherwan Amin Sherwani." https://cpj.org/2020/10/iraqi-kurdish-police-arrest-journalist-sherwan-amin-sherwani/

Conroy, Meredith, Jessica T. Feezell, and Mario Guerrero. 2012. "Facebook and Political

Engagement: A Study of Online Political Group Membership and Offline Political Engagement." *Computers in Human Behavior* 28 (5): 1535–46.

Cooper, Havovi. 2020. "This Incubator is Helping Entrepreneurs in War-Torn Iraq Launch Startups like Vegan Meal Services and Art Classes." *Business Insider*, March 26 https://www.businessinsider.my/iraq-business-entrepreneurs-five-one-labs-2020-3

Cuthbert, Olivia. 2020. "Startup Networks Bring a Whole New Autonomy in Kurdistan." *Wired Middle East*, March 1. https://wired.me/business/startups/startup-networks-bring-a-whole-new-autonomy-in-kurdistan/

Dri, Karwan Faidhi. 2019. "Women seek 30 percent share in new Kurdistan Regional Government." *Rudaw*. https://www.rudaw.net/english/kurdistan/120620193

Hobsbawm, Eric, and Terence Ranger, eds. 1983. *The Invention of Tradition*. Cambridge University Press.

Fazel Hawramy. 2017. "LGBT Community Struggles for Recognition, rights in Iraqi Kurdistan." *Al-Monitor*, June 16. https://www.al-monitor.com/pulse/originals/2017/06/lgbt-iraq-kurdistan-human-right-gender-quality.html.

Freedom House. 2020. "Iraq Overview." https://freedomhouse.org/country/iraq/freedom-world/2020

Garam, Dexter. 2016. "Kurdistan Regional Government: Toward inclusion of women in the economy." *World Bank Blogs*, January 5. https://blogs.worldbank.org/psd/kurdistan-regional-government-toward-inclusion-women-economy

Gromping, Max. 2014. "Echo Chambers' Partisan Facebook Groups during the 2014 Thai Election." *Asia Pacific Media Educator* 24 (1): 39–59.

Haddad, Saleem. 2016. "The Myth of the Queer Arab Life." *Daily Beast*, April 2. https://www.thedailybeast.com/the-myth-of-the-queer-arab-life.

Human Rights Watch. 2012. "Iraq: Investigate 'Emo' Attacks." https://www.hrw.org/news/2012/03/16/iraq-investigate-emo-attacks.

Human Rights Watch. 2016. "Clerics Call Against Anti-LGBT Violence." https://www.hrw.org/news/2016/08/18/iraq-clerics-call-against-anti-lgbt-violence

Human Rights Watch. 2018. "Kurdistan Region of Iraq: Protesters Beaten, Journalists Detained." https://www.hrw.org/news/2018/04/15/kurdistan-region-iraq-protesters-beaten-journalists-detained

Ibrahim, Ara. 2020. "Iraqi Youth in the Middle of the Way: A Fight for Participation in the Political Arena." *Kirkuk Now*, March 11. https://kirkuknow.com/en/news/61691

IOM (International Organization for Migration). 2018. "Demographic Survey: Kurdistan Region of Iraq." https://iraq.iom.int/files/KRSO_IOM_UNFPA_Demographic_Survey_Kurdistan_Region_of_Iraq.pdf

Johansen, Henriette. 2019. "Breaking the Cycle of Shame in Iraq." Middle East Research Institute. http://www.meri-k.org/publication/breaking-the-cycle-of-shame-in-iraq/

Johnston, Holly. 2020. "Long road to eradicating FGM in Kurdistan." *Rudaw*, February 6. https://www.rudaw.net/english/kurdistan/06022020

Joint Crisis Coordination Centre. 2020. "KRG hosts 40% of all IDPs and 97% Syrian refugees in Iraq." http://jcc.gov.krd/en/article/read/56

Kirchick, James. 2007. "Queer Theory." *The New Republic*, October 7. https://newrepublic.com/article/62069/queer-theory

Lavers, Michael K. 2017. "Kurdish Group Launches Pro-LGBT Human Rights Campaign." *Washington Blade*, January 3. https://www.washingtonblade.com/2017/01/03/kurdish-group-launches-pro-lgbt-human-rights-campaign/

Majeed, Rebaz. "Queer Identity and Nationalism in Youth Demographics." Interview by Hawzhin Azeez. Sulaimani, Iraq. October 17, 2020. In interview with the author.

Marouf, Hanar. 2018. "Peshmerga Female Fighters: From Frontline to Sideline." The Washington Institute, October 10. https://www.washingtoninstitute.org/fikraforum/view/peshmerga-female-fighters-from-frontline-to-sideline

McCarthy, Andrew, C. 2013. "Obama's Gay-Rights Hypocrisy." *National Review*, August 14. https://www.nationalreview.com/2013/08/obamas-gay-rights-hypocrisy-andrew-c-

mccarthy/
Meleagrou-Hitchens and Alaaldin Ranj. 2018. "The Kurds of ISIS: Why Some Join the Terrorist Group." *Foreign Affairs*, August 16. https://www.foreignaffairs.com/articles/syria/2016-08-08/kurds-isis
Menmy, Dana Taib. 2020. "Haunted by Online Sexual Harassment: Iraqi-Kurdish women fight back." *Middle East Eye*, May 16. https://www.middleeasteye.net/news/haunted-online-sexual-harassment-iraqi-kurdish-women-fight-back
Najm, Renwar. October 15, 2020. In interview with the author.
National Democratic Institute. 2011. "The Voice of Civil Society in Iraq: An Assessment." https://www.ndi.org/sites/default/files/Civil_Society_Assessment_Iraq.pdfp0
Rasan Organization. "The Role of Queer Organisation and Rights in KRI." Interview by Hawzhin Azeez. Sulaimani, Iraq. October 2020. In interview with the author.
Robinson, A.C. 2019. "LGBT Community Fear Living Openly in Kurdistan." *Rudaw*, January 29. https://www.rudaw.net/english/kurdistan/29012019
Rwanduzy, Mohammed. 2019. "International Federation of Journalists Urges KRG President to Protect Journalists." *Rudaw*, December 20. https://www.rudaw.net/english/kurdistan/20122019
Saeed, Yerevan. 2019. "Without Diversifying its Rentier Economy, Pessimism Among Kurdish Youth Will Increase." The Washington Institute, September 25. https://www.washingtoninstitute.org/fikraforum/view/without-diversifying-its-rentier-economy-pessimism-among-kurdish-youth-will
Salih, Cale and Maria Fantappie. 2019. "Kurdish Nationalism at an Impasse: Why Iraqi Kurdistan Is Losing Its Place at the Center of Kurdayeti." The Centenary Foundation. https://tcf.org/content/report/iraqi-kurdistan-losing-place-center-kurdayeti/
Skoric, Marko M. and Nathaniel Poor. 2013. "Youth Engagement in Singapore: The Interplay of Social and Traditional Media." *Journal of Broadcasting & Electronic Media* 57 (2): 187–204.
UN (United Nations). 2013. "Youth, Political Participation and Decision-Making." https://www.un.org/esa/socdev/documents/youth/fact-sheets/youth-political-participation.pdf.
Vilardo, Valeria and Sara Bitter. 2018. "Gender Profile Iraq: A situation analysis on gender equality and women's empowerment in Iraq." Oxfam International. https://oxfamilibrary.openrepository.com/bitstream/handle/10546/620602/rr-gender-profile-iraq-131218-en.pdf
Williams, Timothy and Tareq Maher. 2009. "Iraq's Newly Open Gays Face Scorn and Murder." *New York Times*, April 7. https://www.nytimes.com/2009/04/08/world/middleeast/08gay.html
Yoshioka, Akiko. 2018. "What Caused the KRG Miscalculation on the Independence Referendum?" Washington Institute. https://www.washingtoninstitute.org/fikraforum/view/what-caused-the-krgs-miscalculation-on-the-independence-referendum-of-the-k
Zeynep Kaya. 2017. "Outperforming Baghdad? Explaining Women's Rights in the Kurdistan Region of Iraq." London School of Economics (blog), February 8. https://blogs.lse.ac.uk/wps/2017/02/08/outperforming-baghdad-explaining-womens-rights-in-the-kurdistan-region-of-iraq/
Ziv Magazine. 2015. "When Will Kurdish Politicians Talk Officially About Gay Rights in Kurdistan?" July 14. https://zivmagazine.com/2015/07/14/when-will-kurdish-politicians-talk-officially-about-gay-rights-in-kurdistan/

CHAPTER 4

KURDISH YOUTH AND CIVIC CULTURE: SUPPORT FOR DEMOCRACY AMONG KURDISH AND NON-KURDISH YOUTH IN IRAQ

Dastan Jasim

The foundations of the Kurdistan Region of Iraq (KRI) were laid in 1991 and what started as a form of de facto autonomy became official in 2005, being enshrined in the new Iraqi constitution. This brought major changes to how Kurdish people were socialized in the newly established Kurdish region. A new generation was born in this decisive period during the 1990s that has now grown up to be citizens of the Kurdistan Region and Iraq, with the cohort of people under the age of thirty constituting most of the country. The systematic changes of governance in Kurdistan and Iraq in 1991 and 2003 have led to a situation in which the members of this cohort were politically socialized much differently than their parents.

For members of this generation born after 1990, the situation further changed depending on whether they were born in the Kurdistan Region or in Iraq. Starting in 2003, the Kurdish political parties—namely the Kurdistan Democratic Party (KDP) and the Patriotic Union of Kurdistan (PUK)—became close allies of the United States, and the KRI subsequently became a safe haven for Kurds. The rest of Iraq, on the other hand, had to endure much greater instability and repeatedly descended into episodes of insurgency.

Many in this cohort barely experienced the authoritarian rule under Saddam and mostly experienced the post-2003 political order. Based on this assessment, this chapter assumes that lived political experiences have differed significantly for Kurdish and non-Kurdish[1] youth from 1991 onward, evoking questions about what has shaped this new generation.

This study will demonstrate how a generational split, gender, and Kurdish

---

[1] Though the greatest portion of the non-Kurdish population in Iraq is Arab, the author is explicitly not subsuming all non-Kurds as Arab, as political realities of other minorities also differ substantially from the groups under observation. However, the datasets used in this chapter did not cover enough Yazidis, Assyrians, Chaldeans, Shabaks, and other minorities to be able to provide a representative analysis of these groups as well.

citizenship in the KRI make a difference in the civic culture of Iraq's citizenry. The question this research seeks to answer, therefore, is whether there are generational, gender-based, and ethnic differences in the civic culture of the population of Iraq. The chapter highlights a host of socio-economic and political dimensions of this question that warrant consideration when discussing these differences in the political reality in Iraq and that justify the choice of covariates. The theory of civic culture and its modern expansions are introduced to illustrate the assumed causal relationship. The deduced hypotheses are tested based on a merged dataset of 6,110 Iraqis who were interviewed between 2010 and 2019. This analysis will show how age, gender, and citizenship in the Kurdistan Region greatly shape patterns of civic culture in Iraq.

Youth in Iraq and Kurdistan Region: Demographics, Economy and Gender

Like many other Middle Eastern countries, Iraq has a large youth population, where people aged thirty and younger account for 60 percent of the population (see IOM 2018; Al-Ali 2014). The share of the population that youth constitute will continue to increase due to high fertility rates, and it is paramount to ask what shapes this generation and what can be expected as this new generation enters the political sphere. Figure 1 shows that there were two major increases in population growth: One around 1990–1998 and another around 2009. While those born around 2009 are just now becoming teenagers, the wave of Iraqis born in the 1990s has been of legal age for years, representing a range of ages from twenty-two to thirty. With an increasing number of adolescents pursuing higher education, the share of those in this age cohort who have earned at least a bachelor's degree is growing, and gender as well as divides between urban and rural residents and internally displaced persons (IDP) and non-IDPs are highly impactful in this growth (see IOM 2018). Still, unlike their forebears, this generation is more connected with the world via the internet and social media, embodying a group that, to a much greater extent, can contextualize politically what happens in their own country and is fully aware of the potential to effect change that exists with social media (Aljubooria, Fashakhb, and Bayat 2020, 134f).

The generational shift is also closely connected to the economic situation, as we see that birth rates often rise during times of economic crisis, such as during Iraq's invasion of Kuwait in 1991 or amid the regime change in 2003. This brings some major difficulties, since the state is the biggest employer in Iraq, and recent economic developments have highlighted the flaws in this system.

The older generation in public service cannot be laid off and must receive wages until retirement and a pension for afterwards, while an ever-growing young generation searching for employment can hardly be included in this inefficient public employment system that is struggling to pay its existing employees, let alone hire new ones. A deregulated and insecure private sector has developed parallel to the public sector since the mid-2000s and is giving young people some employment opportunities but cannot provide any assurance for long-term planning and development (Abboud 2008). Additionally, the job market is neither expanding nor capable of supporting Iraqi professionals in particular. While private corporations from the Middle East and other international partners receive substantial deals in construction, engineering, energy engineering, and the health sector, these enterprises bring their own professional workforce to the country, giving only low-level jobs to local workers (e.g., Skelton 2019a; World Bank 2019).

Figure 1. Annual GDP and population growth in Iraq (%)[2]

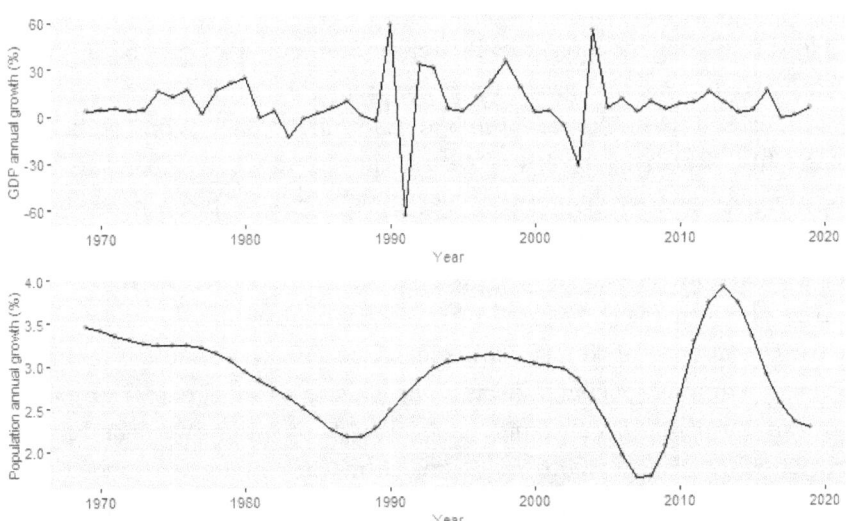

With the combination of these factors, we see, on the one hand, that the generational cohort born after 1990 struggles to find employment despite often being highly skilled and qualified. On the other hand, we also have the birth wave in 2009, a cohort that now comprises teenagers and the potential workforce. With insecurity of guaranteed oil revenues and of the distribution of

---

[2] Data obtained from Wordbank.org via https://data.worldbank.org/indicator/NY.GDP.MKTP.KD.ZG and https://data.worldbank.org/indicator/SP.POP.GROW?locations=IQ

public jobs these revenues create, we expect that the future of Iraq's youth will be precarious, something the youth fully understand as the October 2019 and December 2020 protests showed (O'Driscoll et al. 2020, 10–13).

For the KRI, the last twenty years have arguably not been easier but, rather, more manageable when it comes to this insecurity. The KRI was able to thrive economically starting in 2005 as many international businesses became willing to invest more into the KRI, which was considered more stable relative to the rest of Iraq (Rafaat 2018, 167f). Moreover, KRI fertility rates were sinking, especially in the cities, parallel to the economic growth of the 2000s (see IOM 2018, 18). Similar to Iraq, however, the largest employer in the KRI was the public sector, in which the two ruling parties—the KDP and PUK—offered jobs in exchange for political loyalty and voter agitation (Bali 2018, 100f). The Daesh onslaught in 2014, slumping oil prices, revenue sharing disputes with Baghdad, and an influx of IDPs into the KRI reversed this fortune. Young Kurdish graduates found themselves immersed in struggle and uncertain about how to make a living as their parents had done (Snow 2018).

However strong the refugee or ISIS crises in recent years have been, studies have shown in detail that patronage and corruption are driving factors behind the unequal distribution of means in both Iraq and the KRI (World Bank 2015; Al-Ali 2014; Rubin 2018; Saleh, Azhar, and Azeez 2020; Abdullah 2019). International auditors and experts are often hired to provide proof that economic turmoil is caused by refugee crises, incomplete accounting, or organizational inefficiency in the public sector. But clearly, the roots of the problem also lie in the party-based structure that controls the allocation of jobs, the large amounts of foreign investment, and a poor and unsustainable distribution of multi-million projects in the housing or industrial sector to non-Iraqi and non-Kurdish companies, as Bache (2018) has shown. The Kurdish and non-Kurdish generations of youth in Iraq are aware that, under these circumstances, motivation, diligence, and excellent degrees are never enough to secure economic prosperity in the KRI or Iraq. On the economic level, the situation of non-KRI youth used to be much more precarious than that of the young population of the KRI, but the structures of the dysfunctional public sector as well as the generational divide between the older and the younger populations are very similar. With the protest movements of youth in KRI intensifying in December 2020, we can assume that the once privileged economic situation of KRI citizens is diminishing.

Another important covariate to consider is gender. Substantial research has been conducted on the roles of Iraqi and Kurdish women in the recent decades of political turbulence, with Al-Ali and Pratt (2010) and Hardi (2011) having published some of the most extensive work. Much of this research, however, mostly focuses on the period stretching from the 1980s to the 2000s. New gender dynamics and an emergent generation in which men and women have fundamentally different experiences and in which there is an increasingly visible queer scene have not been studied in detail. There is reason to assume, though, that gender plays a considerable role in the political views of both adolescents and population as a whole.

IOM (2018) reported that the role of women in the Kurdistan region is ambiguous with many women in urban areas having tertiary degrees and many of those being employed. Women from rural areas as well as IDP women experience a much different situation and face enormous economic and social hardships. Many IDP women are widows and, therefore, the heads of their households. Female-headed households on average are less educated and have more limited financial resources than male-headed households (IOM 2018, 20). In the age group between fifty-five and sixty-four throughout the KRI, more than one in four women is a widow, a consequence of both past wars and the lower life expectancy for men (IOM 2018, 24). The war has had an immense impact on the older generation of Iraqi women, especially on the social level, and a respondent in a study published by Al-Ali and Pratt (2010, 37) adequately illustrates this point: "The Iran-Iraq War had a big effect on society. It showed the efficiency of women in a very clear way. Most of the men were fighting at the front. There was a great dependence on women. And women proved their strength and their resourcefulness. You could even see women at gas stations or women truck drivers. They not only took responsibility for work but also for the home and the children. Our women all became super-women."

Though the image of the nurturing mother defending the homeland is used in various war-related narratives with romanticized descriptions, the influence of the widespread socio-cultural changes that war imposes on societies and gender roles should not be underestimated. War can further emphasize patriarchal gender roles while giving women a practical position of power that is unprecedented and can, in effect, transform into a shifting social position of power (see Goldstein 2003, 114f).

The KRI is generally perceived as a haven, especially for progressive women, a characteristic that is considerably influenced by the presence of international organizations (Al-Ali and Pratt 2010, 50) and local women's organizations

(Hardi 2011, 143) starting in 1990 as well as the pro-Western image that the KRI government vehemently tries to foster (see Glastonbury 2018). Yet female genital mutilation (FGM) as well as domestic violence and femicide are persistent issues in the KRI as well as throughout the rest of Iraq (Abdulah, Sedo, and Dawson 2019; Al-Atrushi et al. 2013; Al-Ali and Pratt 2011). Relative freedom in the KRI and Iraq is, therefore, highly dependent on education, economic status, and whether one lives in the urban centers of the country. In all cases, however, political perception is extremely gendered, and women are more often occupying leading positions in political grassroots movements, and the causalities between gender and democratization can also be assumed to be significant in the case of Iraq. Overall, the review shows that there are many reasons to assume that the generational shift, the difference in economic prospects for the younger generation as well as an increasingly visible gender divide influence political and democratic thought among the population.

Language and Education

As already indicated, another major difference between Iraq's Kurdish and non-Kurdish adolescents is that they often do not speak the same language, an element of separation that substantially impacted the political self-perception of Kurdish youth in Iraq (Dodge 2005, 38f). For the generation born after 1990, this is not surprising, as the curriculum of the nascent KRI was mostly in Kurdish. Their parents' generation, however, could barely use the Kurdish language in professional settings. After several attempts to grant the Kurds cultural autonomy in the 1970s, the Ba'ath Party finally ordered Arabic to be mandatory starting in the fourth grade and closed down bilingual and Kurdish schools as well as the bilingual University of Sulaimaniya in 1981 (Vanly 1986, 167f). Since the Iraqi regime supported a targeted approach of disinvestment in the Kurdish region, those whom Saddam did not forcibly resettle had to move to bigger cities such as Mosul or Baghdad to pursue higher education, which was only available in Arabic (Rafaat 2018, 114f). The Kurdish intelligentsia emerging from these circumstances is characterized by strong traditions of interaction with different Arab populations in Iraq, and based on this interaction, groups like the Iraqi Communist Party were able to materialize from both a strong Kurdish and Arab background, diversifying the Iraqi opposition (see Ismael 2007, 268f).

University campuses now are much more divided than they were in the 1970s or 1980s. Kurdish youth who completed their secondary education in Kurdish often do not have a strong command of Arabic and are less likely to study in Iraqi universities outside of KRI and vice versa for Arabic-speaking students from Iraq. What is developing, rather, is a generation of youth that is fragmented along ethnic lines, class divides, and urban-rural areas.

Furthermore, we now see a growing group of young people pursuing bachelor's degrees in the KRI's urban centers as well as in Iraq, with a consistently increasing share of women among them, while the rural areas in the KRI and elsewhere in Iraq still suffer from unwaveringly low rates of primary school completion for adolescents, especially women (IOM 2018). Therefore, when studies like Costantini (2020, 16) suggest that "there is a new generation of activists emerging from civil society committed to advance both a materialist and postmaterialist agenda," it is important to keep in mind that this is often a very urbanized and privileged segment of society. The situation looks much more precarious for IDP youth, who have sometimes missed years of education while being scattered over different IDP camps in central and northern Iraq. The IOM (2018, 34f) even determined that at least 30 percent of the IDPs in the KRI—of whom many are Yazidi or Arab—have never attended school. These observations indicate that when it comes to the political culture of these adolescents, education may not play the great predictive role that it has in developed countries. Education does not necessarily correspond to social exchange and certainly not economic progress for most young Iraqis.

Youth throughout Iraq have organized protests in this context. Many share the same ideas and protest because of the same grievances but are divided in their lived realities. Costantini (2020, 15) offered an assessment of the recent protests in southern Iraq: "It hardly managed to attract the majority of the Sunni population, who, mostly out of fear, have been reluctant to engage with the protests and did not extend to the KRI, showing as a minimum, the limits that a developing across-identity movement face." However, the December 2020 protests that were widespread in KRI showed that the increasing economic crisis is slowly ending this threefold division. Accordingly, with towering class and language barriers, there is a case for a growing generation of youth that generally maintains similar political beliefs but is not connected socially and, therefore, is unable to perform or communicate a common democratic discourse.

War, Violence, and Mental Health

For a society that has rarely seen a year without major political impasse, economic crisis, or civil war, it is essential to ask how youth are socialized in an environment of generational trauma while studying how they perceive their own political system. According to the UN Office of the High Commissioner for Human Rights (OHCHR), 298 people committed suicide between January and August 2020 in Iraq—the highest number since 2003 (Al-Hussein 2020). Among them is an increasing number of youth as young as sixteen who took their own lives in the face of a general lack of perspective, economic problems, and great political and social insecurity, with traumatized Yazidi women also constituting a large part of this group (Kizilhan et al. 2020; Saadoun 2020). It is therefore important to consider the political framework of insecurity and violence in which these adolescents were socialized when researching their civic culture in Iraq.

The traumatologist Ilhan Kizilhan estimates that the rate of people suffering depression and post-traumatic stress disorder in Iraq is more than double the average in Western countries (Percy 2019). Some studies (e.g., Freh 2016) report that the situation is no better for adolescents. There is no reason to believe that the factors that fuel violence and trauma in Iraq are declining. The ACLED data from Raleigh et al. (2010) suggest that sources of violence may be changing but are not decreasing.

As Figure 2 shows, there are clear patterns when it comes to sources of violence and conflict-related fatalities in Iraq. Though there are fatalities in the KRI, as the graph illustrates, they are largely linked to battles and remote violence originating from the Turkey-PKK conflict fought mainly in the border regions between Iraq and Turkey (Crisis Group 2020). This form of violent conflict in the KRI, although regularly killing civilians in these regions, is often rather isolated from the everyday lives of many people. This is the case especially for youth, who more often make their way to safer city centers for economic reasons. The picture is different elsewhere in Iraq, where deaths due to violently suppressed protests and riots have surged since 2018, even in governorates that were free of greater regional conflict in the last four years. For example, the recent wave of protests starting October 2019 has resulted in the deaths of at least six hundred people, most of them minors or teenagers (Amnesty International 2020). Although there repeatedly are human rights abuses by KRI groups and the recent protests in December 2020 were violently oppressed, killing at least eight adolescents (Euro-Med Monitor 2021), the probability of targeted or arbitrary killings as well as kidnappings is much higher outside of KRI.

Figure 2. Fatalities in Iraqi governorates over conflict type 2016–2020 (Raleigh et al. 2010)

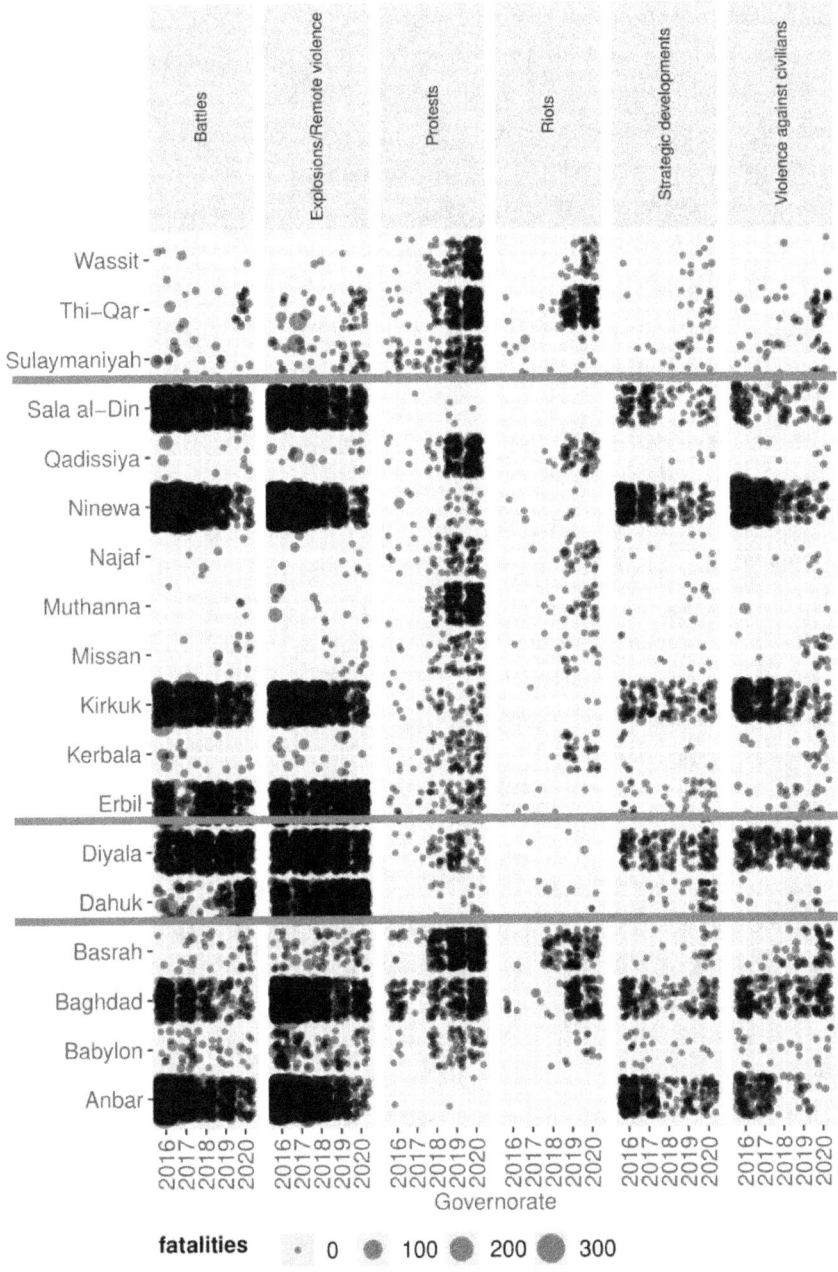

Violence and potential life-endangering situations are more decentralized outside the Kurdistan Region, where a vast number of militias and paramilitary groups conduct acts of violence against not only rival groups but also unarmed civilians, especially amid the waves of protest in Baghdad and several southern provinces since October 2019. For residents of the so-called disputed territories as well as territories previously under ISIS occupation, the greatest source of violence is the ongoing hit-and-run operations of ISIS remnants and various militias dispersed throughout the region (Skelton 2019b). Personal security risks vary based on where an individual resides in Iraq, a situation that has always been a reality of life in Iraq, particularly since 2003. With the great death toll among young protesters since the beginning of the 2019 protests, however, Iraqi youth and especially those who choose to be politically active and protest have come to expect a much more individualized type of violence (Amnesty International 2020). We must assume that this influences how citizens of a country perceive their position in a democratic system along with their avenues of participation and non-participation.

Insecurity and the omnipresence of violence have shaped the generation born after 1990 to a considerable extent, and the desire for stability and security has led many into the arms of radical organizations (McCue et al. 2017). On many levels, one can also assume that this longing for stability trumps the desire for a functioning democracy. With the Iraqi state and its democratic institutions in disarray, it is difficult to imagine how this new constituency can be stabilized in its democratic beliefs when anti-democratic alternatives seem to be presenting themselves everywhere in Iraq.

In studies of Kurdish and non-Kurdish youth, trauma plays an important role that could not yet be quantified on a national level. This theoretically important covariate can therefore not be accounted for empirically but must be considered while analyzing data on political culture as well as experience of security and insecurity among adolescents. War and insecurity have had discrete impacts on the everyday life of the Iraqi population and highlight the differences between being raised in the KRI versus elsewhere in Iraq. Being an IDP also engenders its own tremendous psychological and sociological differences.

Political Systems

The goal of state-building after the end of Saddam Hussein's reign was to put Iraq on a path toward democracy, at least institutionally. However, this goal has not been fulfilled in many regards. For the Kurdish population, the approach to a parliamentary system first started with the elections of 1992, which ended in a bloody civil war between the two competing parties, the KDP and PUK. An analysis of political culture among adolescents in the KRI and the rest of Iraq must consider the nature of the political in which the generation born after 1990 was socialized as well as the image of democracy that these systems have conveyed. When talking about civic culture as "attitudes toward the political system and its various parts, and attitudes toward the role of the self in the system" (Almond and Verba 1963, 9), it is crucial that we understand how the political system and various forms of participation have fundamentally changed after 1990.

For the Kurdistan Region, the political system before 1991 was not only authoritarian but deeply genocidal. Furthermore, Kurdish life was deeply influenced by the practice of permanent observation—typical for Ba'ath regimes all over the region—and, therefore, the Kurdish parties challenging this order had a profound reason d'être (Chaliand 1984, 320f; Rafaat 2018, 122). Being an entity of uprising and anti-genocidal defense, Kurdish parties and institutions never had to justify themselves. After the Kurdish uprising of 1991, a generation of political cadres established themselves in both the KDP and PUK as political members or Peshmerga fighters and have assumed a natural legitimization to become prominent figures in the newly established Kurdistan Region. This has resulted in grave repercussions. Criticizing the partisan structure of today's Kurdistan Region and the lacking civil-military relationship between the Peshmerga, Asayish, and civil population is treated as an offense to the very idea of an independent Kurdistan forced to establish itself in decades of war against Ba'ath rule (see Hama 2019). Youth in Kurdistan are raised in a political system strongly impacted by patronage.

Whether one can be admitted to a university, employed, buy land or a house, or publicly participate in politics is highly dependent on the backing of one of the major parties. While the Gorran movement used to be an oppositional movement that fought against party patronage starting in 2009 and wielded influence over the protests of 2011, experts agree that now there are few differences between its own party structure and that of the clientelism of the PUK and KDP (Hama 2020; Azeez 2018; Chomani 2018). Kurdish youth are also disenfranchised from the Gorran movement, as they were involved in the 2011 protests that were met with violence and even resulted in the deaths of several young protesters and journalists (Tawfeeq 2011). To see a movement in which young people invest so much time and energy transform into the same top-down party apparatus that has previously been rejected alienated many people.

Not having seen the horrors of Saddam Hussein yet being socialized in the de facto and, later, de jure autonomy of the KRI, this generation of adolescents targets its criticism specifically toward the Kurdish party-establishment rather than the Iraqi one.

All criticism aside, though, a profound loyalty toward the idea of Kurdistan can be seen among many. The Kurdistan referendum of 2017 was a major example of that. Although many have shown in several polls that they are critical of the referendum, a great majority voted in favor of the referendum (Connelly and Jasim 2017). Despite the presence of oppositional convictions, this basic loyalty to the idea of Kurdish independence and regarding the Kurdish parties as lesser evils compared to a centralist Iraqi power is still strong.

In this environment, protest and youth protest is exceedingly issue-based. Whether it is about corruption, a stagnating job market, or a lack of electricity or infrastructure, protest in the Kurdistan Region often has a specific conception of what it wants yet is not characterized by greater ideological notions regarding the direction in which the ideal political system should progress (Chomani 2011). All issues aside, there is a general awareness among Kurds in the Kurdistan Region that, compared to other areas in the region, one is relatively better off, an idea that could explain the issue-based nature of these protests. However, this notion is greatly challenged in the last years of repeated anti-system protest.

A much more anti-systemic approach was apparent in the most recent Iraqi protest wave, which began in October 2019 and was a significant step for Iraqi youth. The average Iraqi adolescent was born into harsh economic sanctions and widespread poverty, which turned into chaos and militia rule following the regime change in 2003 (see Ali and Shah 2000; Garfield 2001; Alnasrawi 2001). With a political system strictly divided along ethno-sectarian divides, Iraq's institutions—supposedly democratic—were built on the American premise that the basic Iraqi citizen is Kurdish, Sunni, or Shi'a before embodying political beliefs that could be conveyed into a democratic system (Al-Ali 2014, 65f). Therefore, before any civic culture could emerge in modern Iraq, the notions and premises of identity-based politics were, ironically, institutionalized through

Muhasasa,³ a system of ethno-sectarian, quota-based governance in Iraq.

This has heavy repercussions for the Iraqi youth who were socialized in this system. Costantini (2020) noted the existence of an educated urban milieu pursuing a post-modernist agenda. Reports from the 2019 protests in Iraq such as Ibrahim (2019) illustrate that *Muhasasa* represents a blatant obstacle to democracy. Although a precarious political and economic environment of upbringing is influencing this generation and has radicalized some, there is considerable support for such non-sectarian civilian protest movements as well as a sophisticated structure of political beliefs. What these structures look like and what social covariates influence them is not clear and has not been the focus of much research. Previous research has neglected to analyze Iraqi and Kurdish youth as political agents.

The Theory of Civic Culture

As the previous overview has shown, there is reason to believe that political socialization in Iraq differs historically and contemporarily based on age, gender, and place of residence in Iraq. Many factors are key to understanding how people perceive democratic institutions and what compels them to support democracy as a system contrary to authoritarianism. The theory of civic culture by Almond and Verba (1963) is one of the most famous and most widely used approaches to do so.

Almond and Verba define civic culture as the "attitudes toward the political system and its various parts, and attitudes toward the role of the self in the system" (Almond and Verba 1963, 9). It seeks to address how citizens' relation to their democratic system stabilizes the democratic order. The theory of civic culture looks at how constituents create and influence their participatory structures and how those structures influence them. In theory, that means that if people have the role of being a part of a democratic public, if they learn and repeat practices such as participation, deliberation, and democracy-compatible dissent, distinct sociological and even psychological features emerge. The study of civic culture therefore always tries to connect the macro- and micro-analyses of causalities in democratic transition and development (Almond and Verba 1963, 31).

---

[3] Al-Amin (2016) described the term *muhasasa* as "either of the interpretations of the inclusivity of the executive branch of the Iraqi State... The word *muhasasa* is derived from the Arabic word for apportionment. The *muhasasa* ethno-sectarian quota system has been used by successive Iraqi governments to distribute cabinet positions for so-called 'National Unity' and 'National Partnership' governments."

Political cultures can have a parochial, subjective, and participant character. Table 1 presents a matrix on the existence of orientations toward the political objects: given (1) or not given (0).

Table 1. Typology of political cultures following Almond and Verba (1963, 16)

	System	Input objects	Output objects	Self as participant
Parochial	0	0	0	0
Subject	1	0	1	0
Participant	1	1	1	1

In parochial political cultures, no parts of the policy process, including the overarching system, are objects of any evaluation, affect, or cognitive information for an individual. Such a system is comparable with the traditional authority described by Weber (2013, 122f) in contrast to the rational or charismatic authority. Tribal or feudal as well as monarchic systems are such types, and, therefore, Ottoman rule would constitute an example for the Iraqi case.

Subject civic cultures have a population that adopts ideas and attitudes regarding the general system and political outputs but do not have an influence on the input or self. Examples for such a political culture are publics in authoritarian states where general system function and political outputs such as economic performance are objects of public evaluation, even if unsuccessfully. An example of this could be Saddam's rule, during which people could demand policy inputs but, indeed, maintained a certain stance on the system and the political outputs.

A participant civic culture where citizens can expect their impact to have some importance is one in which citizens consequently adopt orientations toward a variety of political objects, including both inputs and themselves as participants. However, individuals can be free of orientations in a democratic system, too. Citizens can be participants but have mainly negative orientations toward specific or all political objects. Almond and Verba are therefore interested in the roots of civic culture as a stabilizing means of democracy. The important issue, therefore, is about the *congruence* of political structure and culture (Almond and Verba 1963, 20). Here, Almond and Verba (1963, 21) differentiate between the congruence or incongruence of political culture and structure and outline three typologies: allegiance, apathy, and alienation. As Table 2 shows, citizens' orientations toward political objects can be positive (+), indifferent (0), or negative (-). The cognitive side of orientations is a baseline of this typology, so Almond and Verba assume that the actual difference in congruence starts with the affective and evaluative level of orientation.

Table 2. Typology of system/culture congruence following Almond and Verba (1963, 21)

Orientation	Allegiance	Apathy	Alienation
Cognitive	+	+	+
Affective	+	0	-
Evaluative	+	0	-

An allegiant political culture emerges when a political culture is characterized by a public that trusts its political objects and evaluates them positively. However, if that culture mostly comprises individuals who are indifferent to the system in their affect or evaluation, no congruence is present but the apathy of the constituency toward the system. An alienated civic culture goes further and consists mostly of individuals who have negative orientations toward the system. Here lies the key theoretical argument of Almond and Verba (1963, 33): Stable democracies have a "relationship of affective and evaluative allegiance between culture and structure."

Modern works based on this theory illustrate greater variation in country-level data and see a diffusion of emancipatory values even in non-democratic countries (Dalton and Shin 2014, 94f). This suggests a worldwide trend toward a new conceptualization of emancipatory values and their correlation with support for democratic systems. Also, as this study has elaborated for the Iraqi case, there is reason to assume, contrary to the causal relationship established by Almond and Verba (1963), that the Iraqi citizenry is more critical of—and, perhaps, completely dissatisfied with—their institutions as they grow more supportive of a democratic order.

Whom Klingemann (2014) describes as dissatisfied democrats and Norris (2010) describes as critical citizens should also be considered in the case of the Iraqi citizenry. Civic culture must address a citizenry in a country where institutions are created to be democratic but fail to provide both basic services and democratic responsiveness. We must assume that someone who is dissatisfied with the Iraqi status is not necessarily opposed to democracy but, rather, how democracy was established. If Iraqi institutions were not built on the premise that Iraqis can be rational and equal citizens but instead views them as a sectarian mass whose political beliefs are predicated on ethno-sectarian grounds, as Baker III and Hamilton (2006) famously stated, then there is no reason for a correlation between trust and support for these institutions and this democratic system to emerge for Iraqis, as this simply not embodied by any part of the ruling *Muhasasa* system. Based on these conclusions, the following hypotheses were tested:

H 1. There is a significantly negative correlation between trust in institutions and support for democracy.

H 2. There is a difference between the civic attitudes of KRI respondents and non-KRI respondents in the tested models.

H 3. There is a difference between the civic attitudes of KRI and non-KRI respondents older than thirty and younger or thirty in the tested models.

H 4. There is a significant difference in civic attitudes between men and women.

Methodology

The inferential analysis will calculate a multivariate linear regression on a dataset comprising different waves from the Arab Barometer as well as the World Values Survey, which were merged by the author. The overall sample contains 6,110 Iraqi respondents. The dataset consists of 1,234 respondents from Arab Barometer wave 2010–2011, 1,215 from Arab Barometer wave 2013–2014, 2,461 respondents from Arab Barometer wave 2018–2019, and 1,200 from the World Values Survey of 2013. The goal of this pooled analysis is not to incorporate data from the years of Iraqi institutional building in the 2000s but only to include respondents from 2010 and later—when Iraqi state-building can be seen as consolidated. The sample includes respondents from all Iraqi governorates with a representative share of adolescents, as Table 4 shows.

The linear regression model assumes that the independent variables of civic culture as well as age, gender, and education can account for most of the variance in the dependent variable of the democracy index that was created. The model can be described as

$$y_i = \beta_i + \beta x_i + \varepsilon_i \quad (1)$$

where y_i represents the dependent variable of measured support for democracy versus autocracy, βx_i represents the covariates, and ε_i represents the error term for all observations (James et al. 2013, 63). Putting this in terms of the produced operationalization, the tested model is

$$DemocracyIndex = PoliticalInterest + AffectiveSupport + Gender + Age + Education + Error(\varepsilon) \quad (2)$$

where we assume that a set of predictors influences the outcome of the index created to measure the support for democracy but that the effects inside the countries are stable.

The dependent variable is an index created out of the variables measuring (1) support for democracy, (2) support for an army rule, (3) support for experts ruling, and (4) support for a strong leader ruling. Support for democracy affects the overall value positively while support for the other three factors that are forms of authoritarian rule is subtracted from the index, similar to the index calculated by Dalton and Shin (2014). The analysis, therefore, assumes a rather strict measure for support of a democratic system, where support for democracy is not measured by the respondents indicating their support but by measuring whether they, in return, reject authoritarian forms of politics. The calculation of the index can be described as

$$Index = |ProDemocracy - ProArmyRule - ProExpertRule - ProStrongLeader| \quad (3)$$

where the final index is > 0 and measures the overall support of democracy subtracted by the support of autocratic forms of rule from least democratic (0) to most democratic (12). One key assumption of the multivariate analysis is the normal distribution of the measured variables, which is a given as Figure 3 shows.

Table 4. Age distribution by governorate

	Total			Row %		
	18–30	31–45	>46	18–30	31–45	>46
Anbar	41	48	40	32	37	31
Babylon	163	79	90	49	24	27
Baghdad	619	395	374	45	28	27
Basra	305	242	183	42	33	25
Dhi Qar	130	171	104	32	42	26
Diyala	150	109	79	44	32	23
Erbil	168	99	78	49	29	23
Karbala	105	65	41	50	31	19
Kirkuk	132	60	58	53	24	23
Maysan	40	24	19	48	29	23
Najaf	56	58	70	30	32	38
Nineveh	216	140	85	49	32	19
Niniveh	133	144	71	38	41	20
Qadisiyyah	102	46	20	61	27	12
Salahaddin	142	56	62	55	22	24
Sulaymaniyah	190	101	109	47	25	27
Wasit	49	34	15	50	35	15

The variable measuring rating of the political system could not be included in the overall model, as it has too many missing values. The overall model can only be calculated if enough data rows can be provided with all measured values present, which would not have been the case if that variable was included. For that reason, this variable is included in the descriptive analysis only.

The descriptive analysis will, therefore, give an account of simple distributions and correlations that can be seen between the variables of interest before in the inferential analysis the model tests the overall explanatory power of the chosen variables as well as the significance of the variables in explaining support for democracy. All of this is done first for the general sample and then for the KRI and non-KRI. I sample specifically to check for differences.

Analysis

The following analysis will give an overview of the tested correlations between age and support for democracy as well as age and the rating of the overall political system, which is repeated first for the overall sample and then the KRI and non-KRI sample.

Figure 3. Distribution of dependent variable: Index of support for democracy

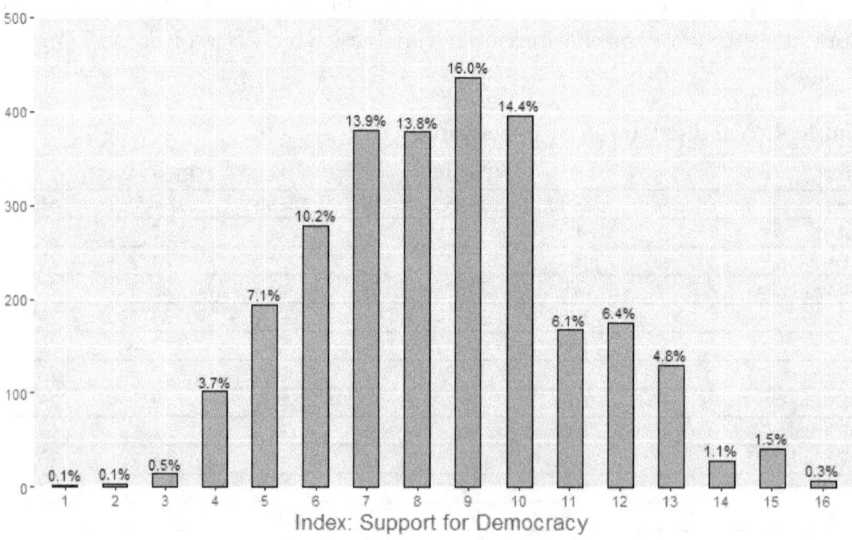

Figure 4 shows that the correlation between age and support for democracy, as measured by the additive index, is negative and significant with a p-value of < 0.5, indicating a 95 percent significance level. Therefore, we can see that younger respondents were more supportive of democracy compared to authoritarian types of rule, regardless of whether they resided in the KRI or elsewhere in Iraq.

Figure 4. Comparison of correlation between age, support for democracy, and rating of political system

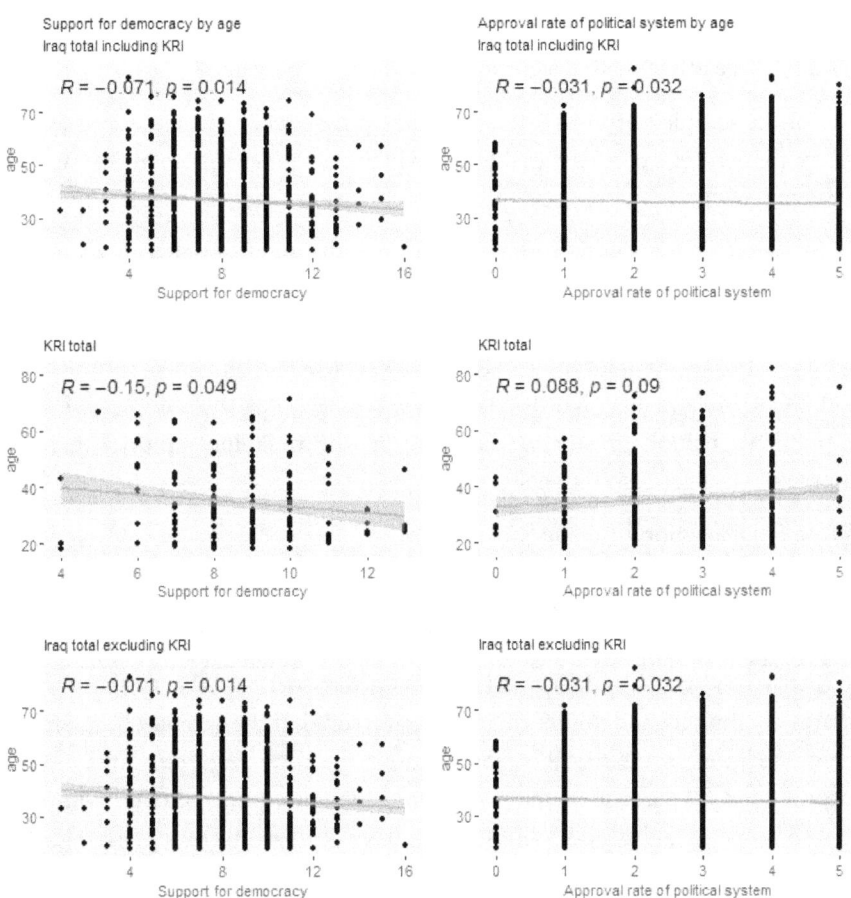

The correlation between age and the rating of the political system is different for the Kurdish and non-Kurdish Iraqi sample. While age and rating of the political system in the non-Kurdish sample are negatively correlated, with a 95 percent significance level, this is not the case in the Kurdish sample, in which the variables are positively correlated. This tells us that the younger respondents were more favorable of the performance of the political system, while this situation is reversed for the Kurdish sample.

Figure 4 shows the multilinear models divided up to the total sample and the sample of respondents aged thirty and younger. Figure 4 shows clear differences between the two age groups. In the sample of the older generation, we see that the strongest and most significant effects are the positive effect of gender on support for democracy versus autocracy, followed by a negative effect of political interest. Within the cohort, age has a significant, negative effect with a likelihood of error under 5 percent. On the scale of affective support, confidence in the government has a negative effect while confidence in parties has a positive effect, with a significance level of 90 percent.

For the sample born in 1990 or later, the picture changes. Here we see that, except for gender, no other variable has explanatory power in predicting support for democracy.

In Figure 4 we see a further division of the sample between older and younger respondents as well as between Kurdish and non-Kurdish samples. A substantial problem that appears in the young Kurdish sample is the limited number of cases to analyze, which takes away the strength of the model. For both Kurdish and non-Kurdish samples, we see that the samples of older respondents exhibit greater predictability in the multilinear model than the sample of younger respondents.

Table 5. Distribution of respondents

	Iraq (non-KRI)	KRI	Quota
Pre-1990	6110	473	4567
1990+	1502	79	171

Table 6 shows the specifics of the calculated models and the extent to which figures are missing and youth are underrepresented in the sample. If, as already mentioned, we assume that the general Iraqi population aged thirty and younger accounts for 60 percent of the population, then youth in the data from both Arab Barometer and World Values Survey have been greatly unrepresented. The data also show that many of these political variables have not been answered by the respondents and that the relation of urban versus rural populations does not represent the real distribution of the studied population. As Table 5 shows, if we assume that at least 60 percent of Iraqis are under the age of thirty and at least 15 percent of Iraq's population is Kurdish, the actual quota with 7,612 Iraqi respondents should be 4,567.2 respondents under the age of thirty, a Kurdish subsample of 1,141.8, and a Kurdish youth subsample of 171.27.

The overall pattern of the model shows—provided that enough respondents were included in the sample—that age, gender, confidence in parties and government, and political interest have the strongest influence on support for democracy. Political interest has a strong negative effect, which presents an interesting conundrum. Assuming that a respondent's support for democracy as a political system decreases as their claimed interest in politics increases, this may indicate the importance of media representation depicting responsibility and governance. Accordingly, confidence in parties has a positive correlation with the heavily party-based political system in Iraq. Both observations indicate that most Iraqis do not think of an abstract concept of a participatory rule when talking about democracy but think of precisely the system that was given to them by the United States after 2003 and has failed them on many levels.

Table 6. Statistical models

	Sample < 1990		Sample 1990+	
	Kurd	Rest Iraq	Kurd	Rest Iraq
(Intercept)	7.75***	9.45***	2.03	3.61
	(0.89)	(0.44)	(13.34)	(4.77)
pol interest	−0.14	−0.38***	2.31	0.09
	(0.17)	(0.07)	(1.46)	(0.25)
conf gov	−0.08	−0.20*	3.28	0.16
	(0.18)	(0.08)	(2.08)	(0.24)
conf armed	−0.18	−0.07	0.89	−0.25
	(0.17)	(0.10)	(1.13)	(0.36)
conf part	0.37*	0.24*	−1.90	0.35
	(0.17)	(0.10)	(2.03)	(0.31)
conf parl	−0.11	0.01	−1.65	−0.16
	(0.13)	(0.08)	(1.09)	(0.25)
conf police	0.28	−0.08	−0.78	−0.19
	(0.17)	(0.10)	(0.70)	(0.31)
gender	0.43	0.51***	−0.31	0.99*
	(0.26)	(0.13)	(1.44)	(0.43)
age	−0.01	−0.01**	−0.06	0.19
	(0.01)	(0.01)	(0.68)	(0.25)
edu	0.24*	0.05	0.43	0.03
	(0.09)	(0.04)	(0.50)	(0.19)
R2	0.19	0.05	0.46	0.08
Adj. R²	0.14	0.05	−0.14	0.01
Num. obs.	160	1052	18	126

***$p < 0.001$; **$p < 0.01$; *$p < 0.05$

Most interestingly, gender has strong predictive power for all Iraqi samples, suggesting that women are more likely than men to support democracy. Education is a significant factor in the Kurdish sector aged thirty and older, supporting the assumption that the older generation of Kurdistan's intelligentsia, which lived through resistance against Saddam, is more likely to still support democracy as a political system.

Figure 5. Multivariate regression

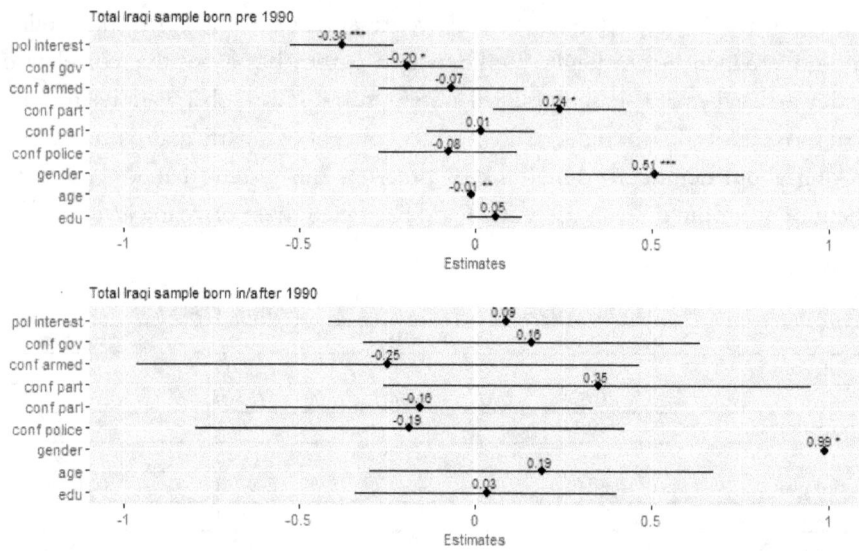

Figure 6. Multivariate regression.

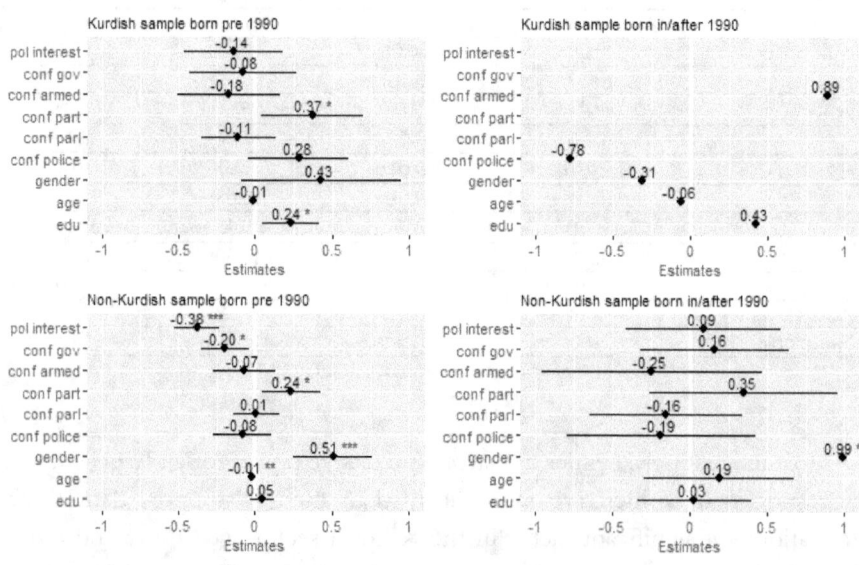

Overall, there is no clear support for Hypothesis 1. On the one hand, confidence in the government is negatively correlated with support for democracy, which underpins the hypothesis of dissatisfied democrats while, on the other hand, confidence in political parties is positively correlated in the sample of respondents born before 1990. Results for the other indicators, however, were too small and insignificant to be interpreted accurately.

Hypothesis 2 stated that there is a difference between the civic attitudes of KRI respondents and non-KRI respondents vis-à-vis support for democracy in the tested models, which can be supported for the sample of respondents aged thirty and older. The significantly negative correlation between political interest and support for democracy does not hold in the sample of Kurdish respondents aged thirty and older, supporting the assumption that the perception of democracy as a system was more positive for residents of the Kurdistan Region after 2003.

Gender fails to have a significant role in the Kurdish sample, while it—along with age—is highly significant in the Iraqi sample. For both samples, however, confidence in parties is positively correlated with support for democracy, indicating that democracy as a model is seen as equal to the Iraqi political system, which is, in practice, influenced primarily by political parties. Therefore, we reject the null hypothesis to Hypothesis 2, meaning we cannot definitively dismiss the possibility of a difference between the samples.

Hypothesis 3 stated that there is a difference between the younger and older respondents for both the KRI and non-KRI samples, where we fail to reject the null hypothesis. The sample of Kurdish youth especially is too small to be able to account for the hypothesis test. However, we can still see differences in patterns of direction when it comes to the used covariates. For the Iraqi sample, however, we can see differences in which the overall model does not have the same explanatory power for the sample of younger recipients and indicators like political interest and confidence in institutions have no effect.

For the Iraqi sample, the null hypothesis of Hypothesis 4 can be rejected, since we see that gender has a significantly positive impact on support for democracy for both older and younger respondents. This is not the case in the Kurdish subsample, in which we see a negative effect for the sample of younger respondents.

Conclusion

The goal of this study was to illustrate the influence of age, education, gender, and ethnicity on the civic culture of Iraqi citizens in the Kurdistan Region and Iraq.

This study was able to provide several observations. Firstly, the question is the extent to which Iraqi citizens connect the general term "democracy" to the system that governs them in Iraq. Although Iraq would not be considered a democracy in many scientific indexes, democracy was the overarching pretext of the US invasion of Iraq and the subsequent years of rule by the Coalition Provisional Authority. The outcome of this study strongly suggests that there is an overall negative perception of democracy due to this correlation. It also shows that the political system is mostly perceived in the context of political parties. A positive estimation of the parties is their correlation with positive notions of democracy. Within the Iraqi sample of respondents aged thirty and older, we further see a significant effect of age, indicating that support for democracy decreases with age.

In determining the importance of being born after 1990 and of being a Kurdish citizen of Iraq in the civic culture of the Iraqi population, we identified overarching differences for the analyzed difference in age cohorts as well as being Kurdish or not Kurdish in Iraq. These differences can be observed in the predictive strength of the used covariates, with gender interestingly having a strong effect on the non-Kurdish sample. The data suggest that the distinct political socialization of Iraq's public in terms of age and ethnicity have affected this population in recent years.

However, the overall models show that survey data collected on Iraq and the KRI specifically lacks many covariates and that survey questions are not asked in a context-specific manner, resulting in the absence of some values. We can therefore assess a difference based on age groups, ethnic groups, and gender.

A more sophisticated dataset is needed to calculate more detailed models. As for now, neither the World Values Survey nor the Arab Barometer have proven to include a sufficient share of respondents from rural areas let alone from Kurdish areas, a shortcoming that undermines the quality of their data. Nor is the share of respondents under the age of thirty sufficient, hindering research on this important population.

The causalities thought to be engendered within gender, age, ethnicity, and support for democracy must also be reconsidered in further research. Much of this can only be possible in a reproducible manner if reliable and representative data are gathered. Conducting the long-overdue census in Iraq and the KRI will be of great importance for this objective. Providing not only economic but sociological and political micro-level data while maintaining ethical standards and ensuring representativity is key for future research. Research approaches only looking at sectarianism are insufficient to explain the intricate web of youth-oriented and gendered political thought, and solving this puzzle is paramount for delivering science-driven policy advice.

References

Abboud, Samer. 2008. "Failures (And Successes?) Of Neoliberal Economic Policy In Iraq." International Journal of Contemporary Iraqi Studies 2 (3): 425– 42.

Abdulah, Deldar Morad, Bewar Abdulaziz Sedo, and Angela Dawson. 2019. "Female Genital Mutilation In Rural Regions of Iraqi Kurdistan: A Cross-Sectional Study." Public Health Reports,134 (5): 514– 21.

Abdullah, Samer. 2019. Corruption Protection: Fractionalization and The Corruption of Anticorruption Efforts in Iraq After 2003. British Journal of Middle Eastern Studies 46 (3): 358– 74.

Al-Ali, Nadje and Nicola Pratt. 2010. What Kind of Liberation? Women and the Occupation of Iraq. Berkeley, CA: University of California Press.

———. 2011. "Conspiracy of Near Silence: Violence Against Iraqi Women." Middle East Report 258 : 34–48.

Al-Ali, Zaid. 2014. The Struggle for Iraq's Future: How Corruption, Incompetence and Sectarianism Have Undermined Democracy. New Haven, CT: Yale University Press.

Al-Amin, Safwan. 2016. "What 'Inclusivity' Means in Iraq." The Atlantic Council, March 28.

Al-Atrushi, Hazha, Namir G. Al-Tawil, Nazar P. Shabila, and Tariq S. Al-Hadithi. 2013. "Intimate Partner Violence Against Women in The Erbil City of The Kurdistan Region, Iraq." BMC Women's Health 13 (1): 37.

Al-Hussein, I. 2020. "298 Suicides in Iraq Within 8 Months." Emirates News Agency.

Ali, Mohamed M. and Iqbal H. Shah. 2000. "Sanctions and Childhood Mortality in Iraq." The Lancet 355 (9218): 1851– 57.

Aljubooria, Abbas Fadhil, Abdulnaser M. Fashakhb, Oguz Bayat. 2020. "The impacts of social media on University students in Iraq." Egyptian Informatics Journal 21 (3): 139–144.

Almond, Gabriel Abraham and Sidney Verba. 1963. The Civic Culture: Political Attitudes and Democracy in Five Nations. Princeton, NJ: Princeton University Press.

Alnasrawi, Abbas. 2001. "Iraq: Economic Sanctions and Consequences, 1990–2000." Third World Quarterly 22 (2): 205– 18.

Alsaafin, Linah. 2020. "'Doesn't Affect Us': Iraq's Tahrir Square on Sadr Pulling Support." Al Jazeera, January 27. https://www.aljazeera.com/news/2020/1/27/doesnt-affect-us-iraqs-tahrir-square-on-sadr-pulling-support.

Al-Shadeedi, Hamzeh, Mac Skelton, and Zmkan Ali Saleem. 2020. "Why Iraq's Protesters Won't Go Home: 10 Voices from The Movement." Institute of Regional & International Studies.

Amnesty International. 2020. "Iraq: Protest Death Toll Surges as Security Forces Resume Brutal Repression." January 23. https://www.amnesty.org/en/latest/news/2020/01/iraq-protest-death-toll-surges-as-security-forces-resume-brutal-repression/

Arab Barometer. 2011. Arab Barometer Wave II. https://www.arabbarometer.org.

———. 2014. Arab Barometer Wave III. https://www.arabbarometer.org.

———. 2019. Arab Barometer Wave V. https://www.arabbarometer.org.

Azeez, Hawkar Abdullah. 2018. "Gorran: A Party of Words, Not Deeds." The Washington Institute for Near East Policy.

Bache, Christina. 2018. "Mutual Economic Interdependence or Economic Imbalance: Turkish Private Sector Presence in the Kurdistan Region of Iraq." Middle East Critique 27 (1): 61–75.

Baker III, James, and Lee H. Hamilton. 2006. The Iraq Study Group Report. New York: Vintage.

Bali, Ahmed Omar. 2018. "The Roots of Clientelism in Iraqi Kurdistan and the Efforts to Fight It." Open Political Science 1 (1): 98–104.

Chaliand, Gérard. 1984. Kurdistan Und Die Kurden. Band 1. Pogrom Reihe Bedrohte Völker.
Chomani, Kamal and Jake Hess. 2011. Pro-Democracy Demonstrations in Northern Iraq/South Kurdistan. Open Democracy.
Chomani, Kamal. 2018. "The Leadership Crisis of The Kurdistan Region Opposition Parties." The Tahrir Institute for Middle East Policy.
Connelly, Megan and Dastan Jasim. 2017. "Not All Iraqi Kurds Are on Board with Referendum." Middle East Institute, https://www.mei.edu/publications/not-all-iraqi-kurds-are-board-referendum
Costantini, Irene. "The Iraqi protest movement: social mobilization amidst violence and instability." British Journal of Middle Eastern Studies 0 (0): 1–18.
Crisis Group 2020. Turkey's PKK Conflict: A Visual Explainer. International Crisis Group.
Dalton, Russel J. and Doh Chull Shin. 2014. "Reassessing the Civic Culture Model." In The Civic Culture Transformed: From Allegiant to Assertive Citizens, edited by Russel J. Dalton and Christian Welzel. Cambridge University Press, 91–115. Cambridge: Cambridge University Press.
Dodge, Toby. 2020. "Beyond structure and agency: Rethinking political identities in Iraq after 2003." Nations and Nationalism 26 (1): 108–122.
———. 2005. "Adelphi Paper 372: Iraq's Future: The Aftermath of Regime Change."
Euro-Med Monitor (Euro-Mediterranean Human Rights Monitor). 2021. "Protesters unlawfully detained and tortured in Iraqi Kurdistan," February 8. https://euromedmonitor.org/en/article/4168/Protesters-unlawfully-detained-and-tortured-in-Iraqi-Kurdistan
Fantappie, M. 2019a. "A New Generation of Activists Circumvents Iraq's Political Paralysis." International Crisis Group.
———. 2019b. "Widespread Protests Point to Iraq's Cycle of Social Crisis." International Crisis Group.
Freh, Fuaad Mohammed. 2016. "PTSD, depression, and anxiety among young people in Iraq one decade after the American invasion." Traumatology 22 (1): 56.
Garfield, Richard. 2001. "Health and well-being in Iraq: sanctions and the impact of the Oil-for-Food Program." Transnational Law and Contemporary Problems 11 (2): 277.
Glastonbury, Nicholas S. 2018. "Building Brand Kurdistan: Helly Luv, the Gender of Nationhood, and the War on Terror." Kurdish Studies 6 (1): 111–132.
Goldstein, Joshua S. 2003. War and Gender: How Gender Shapes the War System and Vice Versa. Cambridge: Cambridge University Press.
Gunter, Michael M. 1996. "The KDP-PUK Conflict in Northern Iraq." The Middle East Journal 50 (2): 224– 41.
Hama, Hawre Hasan. 2019. "The Consequences of the Fragmented Military in Iraqi Kurdistan." British Journal of Middle Eastern Studies, 1–16.
———. 2020. "The Rise and Fall of Movement for Change in the Kurdistan Region of Iraq (2009–2018)." Asian Journal of Comparative Politics doi:10.1177/2057891120905902.
Hardi, Choman. 2012. Gendered Experiences of Genocide: Anfal Survivors in Kurdistan-Iraq. London: Routledge.
Ibrahim, Arwa. 2019. "Muhasasa, The Political System Reviled by Iraqi Protesters." Al Jazeera, December 4. https://www.aljazeera.com/news/2019/12/4/muhasasa-the-political-system-reviled-by-iraqi-protesters
IOM (International Organization for Migration). 2018. "Demographic Survey. Kurdistan Region of Iraq."
Ismael, Tareq Y. 2007. The Rise and Fall of the Communist Party of Iraq. Cambridge: Cambridge University Press.
Ismael, Tareq Y., and Jacqueline S. Ismael. 2015. Iraq in the Twenty-First Century: Regime Change and the Making of a Failed State. London: Routledge.
James, Gareth, Daniela Witten, Trevor Hastie, and Robert Tibshirani. 2012. An Introduction to Statistical Learning with Applications in R. New York: Springer.
Kizilhan, Jan Ilhan, Nadine Friedl, Johanna Neumann, and Leonie Traub. 2020. "Potential Trauma Events and the Psychological Consequences for Yazidi Women After ISIS

Captivity." BMC Psychiatry 20 (1): 256–63.
Klingemann, Hans-Dieter. 2014. "Dissatisfied Democrats: Democratic Maturation in Old and New Democracies." In The Civic Culture Transformed: From Allegiant to Assertive Citizens, edited by Christian Welzel and Russell J. Dalton, 116–57. Cambridge: Cambridge University Press.
McCue, Colleen, Joseph T. Massengill, Dorothy Milbrandt, John Gaughan, and Meghan Cumpston. 2017. "The Islamic State Long Game: A Tripartite Analysis of Youth Radicalization and Indoctrination." CTC Sentinel 10 (8): 21–26.
McDowall, David. 2004. A Modern History of the Kurds, 3rd Edition. London: I. B. Tauris.
Mohammad, Munir. 2019. Social Media and Democratization in Iraqi Kurdistan. Lanham: Rowman & Littlefield.
Norris, Pippa. 2010. "Critical Citizens Revisited: The Impact of Policy Performance, Process Performance and Cultural Modernization on Democratic Orientations." In APSA 2010 Annual Meeting Paper.
O'Driscoll, Dylan, Amal Bourhrous, Meray Maddah and Shivan Fazil. October 2020. "Protest and state-society relations in the Middle East and North Africa." SIPRI Policy Paper 56.
Percy, Jennifer. 2019. "How Does the Human Soul Survive Atrocity?" New York Times, October 31.
Rafaat, Aram. 2018. Kurdistan In Iraq. The Evolution of a Quasi-State. Routledge, London.
Raleigh, Clionadh, Andrew Linke, Håvard Hegre, and Joakim Karlsen. 2010. "Introducing ACLED: An Armed Conflict Location and Event Dataset: Special Data Feature." Journal of Peace Research 47 (1): 651– 60.
Rubin, Michael. 2018. "The Continuing Problem of KRG Corruption." In Routledge Handbook on The Kurds, edited by Michael M. Gunter, 329–40. New York: Routledge.
Saadoun, Mustafa. 2020. "Suicide ate among youth on the rise in Iraq." Al-Monitor, October 6.
Saleh, Subhi Mohamed, Zubir Azhar, and Bayan Sedeeq Azeez. 2020. "Corruption and Fraud Detection Through Foresic Accounting Practices in Kurdistan Region of Iraq." Qalaai Zanist Journal 5 (1): 148– 71.
Skelton, Mac and Zmkan Ali Saleem. 2019a. "Basra's Protests Movement and Unemployment: Contesting Party Dominance of The Oil Sector." Institute of Regional & International Studies.
Skelton, Mac and Zmkan Ali Saleem. 2019b. "Iraq's Disputed Internal Boundaries After ISIS. Heterogenous Actors Vying for Influence." LSE Middle East Centre Report.
Snow, Andrew. 2018. "Kurdistan Region's Debt Crisis Threatens Iraq's Economy." United States Institute of Peace.
Tawfeeq, Mohammed. 2011. "1 Killed, 57 Injured in Iraqi Kurdish Protests." CNN, February 17.
Vanly, Ismet Cherif. 1986. Kurdistan Und Die Kurden. Band 2. Pogrom Reihe Bedrohte Völker.
Weber, Max. (1922) 2013. Wirtschaft Und Gesellschaft: Grundriss Der Verstehenden Soziologie. Mohr Siebeck, 5. Auflage Edition.
World Bank. 2015. "The Kurdistan region of Iraq: assessing the economic and social impact of the Syrian conflict and ISIS ."
———. 2019. "Iraq Economic Monitor, Fall 2019: Turning the Corner-Sustaining Growth and Creating Opportunities for Iraq's Youth."
World Values Survey. 2015. "1981–2014 Official Aggregate Dataset V.20150418." Aggregate File Producer: Jdsystems, Madrid. World Values Survey Association.

CHAPTER 5

YOUTH AND NATIONALISM IN THE KURDISTAN REGION OF IRAQ

Sofia Barbarani

No matter where in the world you find yourself, the idea of youth and youth movements will always be a highly romanticized one. From the young men intent on bringing down France's absolute monarchy in the late eighteenth century and Mazzini's Young Italy movement in the nineteenth century, to the Edelweiss Pirates in 1930s Nazi Germany and the student-led anti-gun group founded three years ago in the United States following a deadly shooting at the Marjory Stoneman Douglas High School. For the nostalgic soul, youth movements are vestiges of days gone by—a time with few complications, other than fighting for one's ideals. Although eruptive and episodic, these movements were far from unstudied; they were, instead, organized and conscious. They were attempts by young men and women to bring about or resist societal change and took on a variety of forms, including "student rebellions, cultural innovations (literary, artistic, music) scientific revolutions, religious reforms, ethnic revolts, nationalist and political generations, and environmental, peace and anti-war movements" (Braungart and Braungart 2001, 16668). Having focused on young diaspora Kurds during my master's degree in London, I was introduced to Kurdish youth movements both from afar and within an academic setting. It wasn't until I relocated to the Kurdistan Region of Iraq (KRI) in 2013 that I began to truly appreciate the intricacies of today's youth and the challenges they face. In this chapter, I highlight such challenges while focusing on nationalism and the ways in which it is being championed by the youth of today.[1] To better understand the current brand of youth nationalism, I will explore what the movement meant to Kurdistan's forebears, why it changed so dramatically after the mid-twentieth century, and how it became multifaceted and unfixed.

For the young men and women of the second half of the twentieth century, Kurdish nationalism revolved around an ethnic revolution intent on acquiring

---

[1] For the purpose of this chapter, the term youth will be used to identify any person aged between eighteen and thirty.

basic rights and battling non-Kurdish oppressive forces. And while the dissatisfaction that galvanized the now renowned Peshmerga fighters into taking up arms against their enemies is not dissimilar to the disenchantment of modern-day youth, today's young men and women are reacting to internal threats, including their own ruling class. With more than a quarter of its population aged between eighteen and thirty-four (Demographic Survey 2018), the KRI boasts a young society. Despite being filled with brilliant, young minds, the region's system has for decades catered primarily to the old and established elite, creating many hurdles for the young men and women who lack significant connections or a privileged status. Government corruption, high unemployment, and a general sense of stagnation has fractured trust and shifted the youth's sense of national pride—where the Kurds of Iraq once looked to their leaders for national inspiration, today's youth are reshaping nationalism. While some are turning to ancient religions to underscore their Kurdishness, others find it in myths and history books rather than real life, or describe it as a feeling that changes depending on the state of the country. Unlike their forebears, today's youth have better access to information and to the world outside the KRI, and, as a result, *Kurdayeti* has become less homogenous and more subjective. A key difference between Kurdistan's youth and the older generations is that today's young were born after or not long before the 1991 implementation of the "No Fly Zone" by the international community in northern and southern Iraq. With Saddam Hussein's Ba'ath regime no longer an imminent threat, the KRI was ushered into a period of relative calm. But even with the Ba'athist menace gone, the newly established safe haven turned into a warzone when the region's ruling parties—the Kurdistan Democratic Party (KDP) and the Patriotic Union of Kurdistan (PUK)—turned on each other, sparking a bloody civil war that lasted from 1994 to 1997. This was arguably the marked beginning of how Kurdistan's leadership would go on to undermine its own nationalist dream and lose its appeal among younger generations. But first, let's go back to a pre-civil war Kurdistan, when morally dubious politicians were still courageous guerrilla leaders fighting in the mountains and the Kurdistan Regional Government (KRG) had yet to be established—when the meaning of nationalism was inextricably linked to survival.

The Youth of Yesterday: Survival

The Kurdish youth rise bravely,

With their blood they colored the crown of life

The Kurdish youth are ready and prepared,

To give their life as the supreme sacrifice.

- Yunis Reuf, better known by his pen name Dildar

Renowned Kurdish poet Dildar was just twenty years old in 1938 when he was imprisoned by the Iranian government for his involvement in the Kurdish separatist movement led by Qazi Muhammad. During his time behind bars, the young poet from Koya unwittingly penned what would later become the national anthem of the KRI, "Ey Reqib"—or Oh Enemy. Dildar became a symbol of defiant Kurdish nationalism, and his poem a battle-cry for an increasingly restless people. Amid references to Kurdish bravery, historical kingdoms, and wars gone by, he also addressed his fellow youth, thus turning "Ey Reqib" into not just a love poem to Kurdistan but also a thank you note to the young men and women who, like himself, were putting their lives on the line for their borderless homeland. At just thirty years old, Dildar died young, but not before he had carved out a space for himself in Kurdish literature, adding to the dominant themes of nationalism and resistance.

From the tale of young Feraydun and his battle against the tyrannical king Zahhak to the young Peshmerga fighters who, in 2014, took up arms against ISIS, youth, as courageous central figures in the battle against enemies both real and mythical, have been part of Kurdish identity from time immemorial. Before the KRI became, for all intents and purposes, a country, a mythical shared past replete with ancient symbols and stories was key in maintaining a collective identity. Myths, says Macdowall, "are valuable tools in nation building, however dubious historically, because they offer a common mystical identity, exclusive to the Kurdish people" (Macdowell 2004, 4). But it wasn't until the collapse of the Ottoman Empire in the early twentieth century and the dawn of nation - states in the Middle East that the Kurdish struggle acquired nationalist undertones. This is not to say that a Kurdish people had not existed as an identifiable group for more than two thousand years, but it wasn't until the late nineteenth century that a sense of national community began to emerge.

According to Saleh and Fantappie (2019, 6), "Sheikh Ubaydallah, a prominent religious and tribal leader from what is today southeast Turkey, was among the first to assert the Kurds as a 'people apart.' He aimed to unite Kurdish sheiks across localities in the form of an independent state, leading a rebellion against the Ottomans in pursuit of this goal in 1879."

In 1918, as the aged Ottoman Empire took its dying breath and the Turks and Arabs began to embrace their own ethnic sense of identity, the British joined the vilayets of Basra, Baghdad, and Mosul under a single flag. "The dismemberment of the Ottoman Empire had left chaos and a political vacuum in the Kurdish inhabited regions . . . the Kurdish nationalists, like other nationalists within the Empire, tried to take advantage of this situation and establish a Kurdish state" (Ali 1997, 521). But in 1923, the Kurds suffered what would be the first in a long string of American and European betrayals when the allied powers at the Treaty of Lausanne guaranteed the division of Kurdish-inhabited areas among Turkey, Iraq, and Syria and, thus, the absence of a self-governed Kurdish state. Even in 1932 after the British were gone and Iraq became independent, the Kurds failed to separate themselves from the young Arab country. The region had been redrawn, and Iraq's Kurds penciled into the confines of a nation state that would soon show signs of strong pan-Arab nationalism as well as an aversion to a Kurdish minority and its growing hunger for self-determination.

Pursley (2015, para. 20) argued "that independent Iraq was often imagined—both by Iraqi nationalists and by the British—as an 'Arab state' was very significant for Iraq's non-Arab populations . . . Arabism shaped the formation of an Iraqi national identity and thus the formation of Iraq as a nation-state."

So Iraq's Kurds mobilized, intent on fueling a nascent national consciousness and staying relevant amid a rapidly changing region. To do so, they pushed for what Michael Hechter called peripheral nationalism: when minority nationals refuse to assimilate and instead call for autonomy (Spinner-Halev and Theiss-Morse 2003). But what did nationalism mean for a people without a nation-state? It would be limiting to attribute a single definition to Iraqi Kurdish nationalism; it is a multi-faceted movement, influenced by historical, social, and economic contexts and is in continuous development. It cannot be defined in the clear cut-manner with which the *Encyclopedia Britannica* would like to define it: "an ideology based on the premise that the individual's loyalty and devotion to the nation-state surpass other individual or group interests." Instead, Louis L. Snyder's less succinct but more encompassing definition of nationalism allows for a realistic analysis of *Kurdayeti*. Snyder argues that nationalism should be viewed as a force for many purposes: a "force for unity . . . a force of disruption . . . a force of independence . . . a force of colonial expansion . . . a force of aggregation to obtain greater territory, capital, power and entourage . . . [and] a force for anti-colonialism" (Aghapouri 2018). Depending on whom you ask, one or all of these examples can be used to define Kurdish nationalism.

Similarly, youth movements are not defined by a single characteristic but, instead, are changing and "rooted in specific sociohistorical conditions" (Braungart and Braungart 2001, 16668). In 1930s Baghdad, for example, the founding of a young Kurdish men's club where members could meet and discuss politics became a watershed moment for Kurdish nationalism. "It marked the awakening of national consciousness among the first generation of secular educated and urban Kurds" (McDowall 2007, 288). Gradually, over the first half of the twentieth century, Kurdish nationalism in Iraq continued to intensify and solidify into a collective and coherent force set to spark Baghdad's ire in decades to come. Many of the men and women who rose to prominence for their involvement in the nationalist struggle were still in their twenties—fueled by pride and a pinch of youthful recklessness. While the Kurdish intelligentsia in the Iraqi capital discussed the country's state of affairs in smoky tea houses, a different type of revolt brewed in the north. In 1931, a twenty-eight-year-old Mustafa Barzani readied himself to embark on one of his first insurrections against Baghdad and its autocratic prime minister, Nuri al-Said. Thirty years later, prominent poet Sherko Bekas was just twenty-five years old when he followed in Mala Mustafa's footsteps and became deeply involved in the Kurdish fight against Iraq's pan-Arabist president, Abdul Salam Arif. In the late 1970s, Hero Talabani was in her twenties when she joined the Peshmerga in the mountains, while in Baghdad Saddam Hussein consolidated his power. In 1985, the legendary Peshmerga fighter Najmadin Shukr Rauf—also known as Mama Risha—was ambushed and killed at just twenty-eight years old. For the youth of yesterday, Kurdish nationalism was inextricably linked to survival—and more concretely, to the survival of their ethnic group. Maintaining the idea of a Kurdish community meant enduring and fighting back against the Ba'ath regime's attempts to quash the Kurdish people along with their culture, language, and history. The suffering of the Kurds under Hussein resulted in a collective feeling of resistance as well as victimhood, both of which became ingrained in Kurdish identity. What started with the Arabization policy[2] in the

---

[2] This policy entailed the mass displacement of ethnic Kurds from northern Iraq and the repopulation of these areas with Arabs to deny Kurdish majority in certain areas. The legacy of Arabization has yet to be resolved in a number of provinces, including Kirkuk. The policy also affected Assyrians and Turkomans.

1970s and the execution of eight thousand Barzani men and boys in 1983 came to a head when Hussein launched a full-blown genocidal campaign against his own Kurdish civilians. The Al Anfal campaign and its methodical killing of an estimated 182,000 Kurds between 1986 and 1989 is arguably the starkest example of how nationalism and survival became intertwined. As Hussein's regime attempted to stamp out Kurdish ambitions for basic human rights and autonomy through the destruction of towns, villages, and farmland, the Kurds became increasingly resolute. Just two years after the official end of Al Anfal, the 1991 Kurdish uprisings began, prompting Baghdad's violent response and the consequent displacement of more than one million Kurds. This in turn resulted in the implementation of the aforementioned "No Fly Zone," a new chapter that would culminate in 2003 with the US-led invasion of Iraq, the end of Hussein's regime, and the beginning of a more prosperous Kurdistan Region. All of this marked an important shift in how the youth related to nationalism. The nationalist dream that their parents and grandparents had risked their lives for was beginning to pay off, and the following generations were set to reap the benefits—or so they thought.

The Youth of Today: Let Kurdistan Be for the House of Barzani

"Loyalty to country always. Loyalty to government, when it deserves it."

– Mark Twain

By 2013, Iraq's Kurdish region was riding a wave of social and economic recovery, seemingly leaving behind decades of crippling problems. Unlike the rest of Iraq, Kurdistan offered an enclave of stability amid volatile neighbors. The KRG was quick to begin developing its own oil and gas resources while also expanding into non-oil sectors as well as attracting foreign investment and Western-educated young diaspora Kurds and non-Kurds. In Erbil and, to a lesser extent, Sulaymaniyah and Duhok, upscale hotels, malls, and new residential compounds were being built at extraordinary speed. The foundations had been laid for a prosperous new Kurdistan, and pride in the homeland was bursting at the seams. But while some hopefuls referred to the KRI as the "next Dubai," the more cynical among Kurdistan's watchers were careful to use the term with a large pinch of salt. And as is often the case, the cynics turned out to be the realists. As quickly as they took off, the Kurds of Iraq came crashing down when in January 2014 Baghdad's central government froze the KRG's take of the federal budget. The economic downfall and consequential social unrest were then exacerbated by that year's plummeting oil prices and followed by one of the region's gravest security threats to date: the rise to power of the Islamic State. By 2015, the mass influx of internally displaced people and refugees had begun to weigh heavily on the region's economy while the ongoing war against ISIS eroded the once-pristine security résumé the KRG took pride in. And thus, the young men and women who had been promised a more prosperous future than that of their parents watched as their homeland's short-lived renaissance imploded, fizzled out, and settled into an impasse that continues to this day. With virtually no job opportunities in the private sector, civil servant salaries reduced or unpaid, and trust in the government in free-fall, resentment began to bubble among a generation of Kurds on the brink of adulthood and manifested itself in widespread protests and migration as well as complete apathy and disenchantment.

In 2015, Iraq's Ministry of Migration estimated that approximately twenty-five thousand people from Iraq's Kurdish region had left the country. Jiyad, Küçükkeleş, and Schillings (2020) argued that while there are no recent public data on the exact number of Iraqi Kurds who have travelled to Europe illegally, images of Kurds from Iraq who died while trying to cross the Mediterranean Sea, in addition to daily conversations with people, suggests more have been leaving the KRI in recent years. One such person was a young man from Zakho, whom we'll call Dana. In the summer of 2020, Shwan (also not his real name) stumbled upon Dana at an airport in southern Turkey. Both men were making their way to Istanbul. It soon transpired that Dana—who Shwan described as a weary man in his early thirties—was there not on holiday but to be smuggled to Europe. Dana explained that he had tired of the hardships of living in the Kurdish region, particularly following the uptick in violent protests that took place in August and September 2020 as a result of continued unpaid public salaries and pay cuts. Nearly half of the active workforce in the KRI is employed in the public sector, and his city—Zakho, on the border with Turkey—had been particularly affected by it. Dana saw no reason to stay in Kurdistan and hoped to cross from Turkey into Bulgaria before starting a new life elsewhere in Europe. His homeland, he lamented, had been monopolized by one ruling family: *"Bila ba Kurdistan bo mala Barzani beit,"* he said. "Let Kurdistan be for the house of Barzani."

Iconic figures such as ex-guerrilla fighters Masoud Barzani and late Jalal Talabani no longer spark the same level of national pride (nor enthusiasm) among younger generations. Even the late charismatic Nawshirwan Mustafa's

Goran Movement, which presented itself as a force for change amid the KDP-PUK duopoly, gave in to nepotism and was technically inherited by Mustafa's sons following the leader's death in 2017. Indeed, it's no surprise that many resent the ruling families' long-standing control, cronyism, and alleged corrupt dealings. Even in 2012 prior to the region's collapse, Denise Natali warned that despite Kurdistan's hard-won autonomy and newfound safety, the Iraqi Kurdish population was becoming increasingly critical of the KRG. Natali argued that the regional government would be wise to show its commitment to nationalism through increased accountability, transparency and equal distribution of oil revenues or risk undermining its own nationalist project (Natali, 2012). But accountability, transparency, and equal revenue distribution remain mere aspirations. According to anti-corruption center U4, one of the key obstacles in Kurdistan's fight against corruption are Barzani and Talabani's political parties—the KDP and PUK, respectively (Pring 2015, 2). As a result, the leaders who once served as the glue that strengthened nationalism have lost much of their relevance among a generation of youth that has admitted to feeling excluded from shaping its own country's future. "This generation gets disappointed every single day, if not every single hour when seeing and witnessing what other countries are enjoying," twenty-nine-year-old Hanar Marouf, an analyst based in Erbil, explained over the phone. "Unemployment is rising, and we don't have a proper private sector, so graduates are waiting on the government to employ them [but] the employment system is corrupted. You go to the [government] offices and you see the discrimination, the injustice." For Marouf, nationalism as her parents knew it is a thing of the past. "It has faded with this new generation [and] generation after generation it will fade even more," she explained, mirroring the frustration and disillusion that has become widespread among young Kurds over the past five years. Despite offering high job security, low upward mobility and income inequality has led the majority of young people to support the KRG's plan to reduce public employment. But with a private sector that is both unable to absorb the tens of thousands of students who graduate each year (Jiyad, Küçükkeleş, and Schillings 2020) and that remains monopolized by politically embedded cronies, free market competition is a mere mirage. Meanwhile, unemployed youth grow increasingly restless. The Kurdish region's state-society relationship, argued Sediq (2018), has been deeply damaged by its own leaders, politicians and decision-makers. As a result, nationalism is no longer linked solely to leadership and is instead being reshaped to fit the youth's reality, rather than that of their parents and grandparents.

But not everyone has lost faith, and some interviewees expressed a moderate degree of optimism when asked about the region's leadership. "In every [political] party there are people who are good and less good," said thirty-year-old content creator and policy advisor Polla Garmiany, who was born and raised in Sulaymaniyah before moving to Europe at the age of seven. "These symbols [of nationalism] are unfortunately sometimes misused," he added. Elections, noted Marouf, are the perfect example of how the ruling elite has misused and exploited nationalist sentiments through "slogans and fake promises." This is arguably what happened in the KRI in the lead-up to what should have been the culmination of the Kurdish nationalist dream—the independence referendum in September 2017. For weeks, then president Masoud Barzani traveled the region to encourage voters to say "Yes" to an independent Kurdistan. An uplifting surge in public displays of nationalism were seen and heard across the region, as jubilant images of young and old dressed in *jili Kurdi* (Kurdish clothes) and clutching the Kurdish tricolor made the rounds online—a reminder to the international community and to Baghdad that this was the will of the people, whether the world agreed with it or not. Just days before the vote Masoud Barzani and top PUK members even took to the stage together in a rare show of political unity. Predictably, the "Yes" ballot was victorious with more than 92 percent of voters saying they wanted independence from Baghdad. But neither the international community nor Baghdad accepted the outcome, and the referendum's success was soon overshadowed by the central government's retaliation, including the KRG's painful loss of Kirkuk to Baghdad. The somber episode dampened the widespread optimism, with many young Kurds expressing dismay. In September 2020 on the third anniversary of the referendum, Masoud Barzani took to Twitter to reach out to his younger followers, vowing, "We do not bow down." The succinct message sparked mixed reactions online, with some Twitter users referring to the leader as a "father of a nation" and "hero" while others questioned the outcome, asking, "Where is our country?" According to Bzhar Aziz Husain, a twenty-five-year-old medical student from Erbil, the referendum divided Kurds into two categories: those who "have completely given up and say we cannot be a nation and others who strongly believe there is still hope." Fellow medical student, twenty-two-year-old Ilaf Sabah Othman, belongs to the latter category. "It made us stronger and awakened the feeling of nationalism '*Kurdayeti*' among Kurds," she said. "And if we go back to the time, we will vote for an independent Kurdistan, again and again. It was a huge step in our history, and we are proud of it." Others, like twenty-year-old Ray Karim, argue that calling for a referendum at that moment in time was "the biggest mistake Kurdish leaderships have ever made." The young woman from the southern city of Kalar was quick to underscore why: "I love my Kurdistan more than anything in the world and I want the best for it and my people . . . [but] there are so many reasons why it was wrong," she explained, before adding, "We don't have a strong economy, we still don't have a united Peshmerga force, [and] we didn't have international support." The fundamental problem, as noted by Saleh and Fantappie, is that instead of focusing the narrative of Kurdish national identity on civil rights and nurturing the region's future generations, the ruling elites continue to emphasize the importance of an independent statehood and leverage "their historical roles (or those of their elder relatives) in fighting for Kurdish autonomy in order to compensate for their shortcomings in developing effective governance institutions" (Saleh and Fantappie 2019, par. 2). For the youth of yesterday, nationalism was a force of independence in which Kurds aspired to self-determination. But in a secure and largely self-governed region where nationalism no longer stems from battling outside oppressors, KRG leaders have not tailored their policies toward a new kind of Kurdish society.

As in other countries across the globe, today's youth is arguably more multifaceted than previous generations. Unlike their forebears, the Kurdish youth of today are scattered across cities, countries, and continents, and many have the world at their fingertips, access to airports, and freedom of movement. They have adopted a more "liberal and civic form of Kurdish nationalism" that is "closely linked with broader developments that are taking place in Kurdistan's transnational space" (Jiyad, Küçükkeleş, and Schillings 2020, 40). A large number of Iraqi Kurds, for example, were born and raised in the diaspora—while nearly 85 percent of the Kurdish diaspora in the West comes from Turkey, the Kurds from Iraq come second and form a large part of the communities in Great Britain, the Netherlands, the United States, and Sweden (Fondation Institute Kurde de Paris). Having lived briefly or not at all in Kurdistan, their brand of nationalism usually differs from that of their counterparts in the KRI, and like most diaspora communities, many romanticize their homeland. No matter where in the world they find themselves, Kurdish households abroad tend to maintain a sense of Kurdishness through language, culture and simple day-to-day habits. "We had the same celebrations, I wore Kurdish clothes to every celebration, we ate the same food," explained thirty-year-old Heliz Mazouri, who was born and raised in rural Michigan. For Mazouri, whose mother and father left Kurdistan in the seventies and eighties, respectively, nationalism is "a hundred percent linked to heritage and not political parties."

The advent of the internet and social media platforms also allowed for the nationalist discourse to grow stronger and bring diaspora Kurds closer to their homeland.

In 2018, Aghapouri (2018, 64) argued, "As a result of nationalist practices, migrants and diasporas have produced economic, cultural, and social networks. They are increasingly involved in and aware of their ethnic and national identities through 'rediscovering national histories,' disseminating their culture and politics, and 'pressing for recognition of their distinctness,' as well as bringing about and reconsidering new demands under the name of self-determination, independence, autonomy and sovereignty in an increasingly interconnected world."

Both diaspora and local Kurds, for example, have been looking into their past to redefine their identity. In 2017, local media reported that an estimated ten thousand Kurds had converted to Zoroastrianism, a pre-Abrahamic faith once widespread throughout the Kurdish territories. For some, turning to ancient practices became a way to assert their Kurdishness. But even then, argued Fatah (2015, par. 41), "subversion and manipulation of religion throughout the centuries for political gain have left the region struggling with its identity and stability." Reclaiming pieces of a cultural heritage often drowned out by the noise of an increasingly Westernized world is another form of nationalism on the rise among younger Kurds. Young entrepreneurs have set up businesses that are rooted in Kurdish culture and history. Huda Serhang is the founder and owner of Lala Candles, a thriving business that uses traditional tea cups as candle holders and Kurdish folk tales as names for her collections. Kurdish creative Raz Xaidan's poetry, illustrations, and photography focus on Kurdish identity and culture. Organizations such as the Erbil branch of Global Shapers create a sense of social cohesion and national pride through projects that focus on volunteering and giving back to the community. Cultural heritage as a form of nationalism can also be seen in the common refusal among young Kurds to learn the Arabic language or to refer to themselves as Iraqi as well as the immense displays of pride in their flag, music, and traditional clothing. For others, like Marouf, nationalism is "something from the past," an emotion fueled by history books rather than a tangible social movement. While some, like twenty-nine-year-old Decan Dana, define nationalism as "going out of your way to prioritize your country," Othman, a medical student, similarly defined it as "the loyalty that we, Kurds, give to the beautiful nature of Kurdistan and its people." The idea of sacrificing yourself for the homeland is a theme that continues to play heavily among young Kurds—the tricolored flag, for example, uses the color red to recall the men and women who sacrificed their lives for Kurdistan. However, noted Dana, nationalism can often dwindle as quickly as it spikes. "If you have invaders coming into the country, everyone is going to be the first one saying, 'We're going to defend our land.'" This was true of the Peshmerga volunteers who took to the frontlines with little more than a rusty Kalashnikov to defend Kurdistan from ISIS, even in 2015 when support for the leadership was visibly in decline and public employees were taking to the streets to demonstrate against unpaid wages and what they viewed as a corrupt government.

In August 2020, similar frustrations once again bubbled to the surface, sparking protests in Duhok as well as the southern Sulaymaniyah province. In the town of Ranya, twenty-seven-year-old Krdar Mohammad Hussein took an active role in organizing the demonstrations. The vast majority of the protesters, he explained, were young. "We are not able to do this alone," he said from his home in Ranya. "We have to make the older people join the demonstration to demand our basic rights." Like many of his peers, Hussein says he has lost hope in Kurdistan and is planning to travel to Europe. "In my region, most of the youth are leaving the country because we have no opportunities, most are jobless, they have no monthly income," said Hussein. In the first half of 2020, the KRG paid only two months of salaries while unemployment and poverty rates were on the rise, in part due to the Covid-19 crisis (Jiyad, Küçükkeleş, and Schillings 2020). By October 2020, Hussein said he had been unemployed for months after his mobile coffee shop was forced to shut down due to the pandemic. "Nationalism will fade away if you don't serve your own people," he said. "The rulers and leaders are ruining the definition of nationalism, that's the problem . . . nationalism is not a thing anymore for the youth."

As long as they feel that the government is monopolizing nationalism, it is unlikely that the young men and women of the KRI will turn to their leadership for national fervor. For many, "Even the factual parts of the Kurdish nationalist narrative—namely, the former generation's resistance against a repressive regime in Baghdad—are being tainted by their association with the establishment" (Saleh and Fantappie 2019, par. 25). As a result, they are more likely to become less engaged with the region's political elite while continuing to shape their own brand of nationalism. This in turn could see a further widening of the gap between today and yesterday's youth—the rulers and the ruled.

In addition, Jiyad, Küçükkeleş, and Schillings (2020) argue that "As well as frustration with the governing elites, new nationalism in the KRI also features liberal conceptions of social well-being and government-citizen relationship. While independence still animates collective emotions, growing numbers of educated middle class Kurds prioritize self-reliance, good governance and effective delivery of public services over large-scale political questions ."

And while critics may claim that younger generations are not involved enough in the nationalist dream that fueled the aspirations of their parents and grandparents, it is worth noting that many young men and women have been given very little space to nurture their political and professional dreams. And thus, where nationalism once meant the collective struggle for survival, today it has taken on a myriad of different meanings and a redefining of *Kurdayeti* that is based on the youth's own realities, which are far removed from those of the men and women who came before them.

References

Aghapouri, Hossein Jiyar. 2018. "Nationalism, Diaspora and Cyberspace: The case of the Kurdish diaspora on social media." PhD diss., University of Auckland. https://researchspace.auckland.ac.nz/bitstream/handle/2292/37012/whole.pdf

Ali, Othman. 1997. "The Kurds and the Lausanne Peace Negotiations, 1922 –23." *Middle Eastern Studies*, 33 (3): 521 –34.

Braungart, R.G., and M.M. Braungart. 2001. "Youth Movements." In *The International Encyclopedia of the Social & Behavioral Sciences*, edited by Neil J. Smelser and Paul B. Baltes, 16668–71.

Elsevier. Salih, Cale, and Maria Fantappie. 2019. "Kurdish Nationalism at an Impasse: Why Iraqi Kurdistan Is Losing Its Place at the Center of Kurdayeti." The Century Foundation, April 29. https://tcf.org/content/report/iraqi-kurdistan-losing-place-center-kurdayeti/

Fatah, Lara. 2015. "The Curious Rebirth of Zoroastrianism in Iraqi Kurdistan." Projects for the Study of the 21st Century, November 26. https://projects21.org/2015/11/26/the-curious-rebirth-of-zoroastrianism-in-iraqi-kurdistan/

Institut Kurde De Paris. "The Kurdish Diaspora." https://www.institutkurde.org/en/kurdorama/

International Organization for Migration Iraq Mission. 2018. "Demographic Survey Kurdistan Region of Iraq." https://iraq.iom.int/files/KRSO_IOM_UNFPA_Demographic_Survey_Kurdistan_Region_of_Iraq.pdf

Jiyad, Sajad, Müjge Küçükkeleş, and Tobias Schillings. 2020. "Economic Drivers of Youth Political Discontent in Iraq: The Voice of Young People in Kurdistan, Baghdad, Basra and Thi-Qar." Global Partners Governance.

Kohn, Hans. 2020. "Nationalism." In *Encyclopedia Britannica Online*, November 28. https://www.britannica.com/topic/nationalism

McDowall, David. 2004. *A Modern History of the Kurds*. 3rd ed. New York: IB Tauris.

Natali, Denise. 2012. "The Persistent Boundaries of Kurdish Nationalism." *World Politics Review*, May 9. https://www.worldpoliticsreview.com/articles/11926/the-persistent-boundaries-of-kurdish-nationalism

Pring, Coralie. 2015. "Kurdistan Region of Iraq: Overview of corruption and anti-corruption." U4 Anti-Corruption Resource Centre. https://www.u4.no/publications/kurdistan-region-of-iraq-overview-of-corruption-and-anti-corruption

Pursley, Sara. 2015. "Lines Drawn on an Empty Map: Iraq's borders and the Legend of the Artificial State." *Jadaliyya*, June 3. https://www.jadaliyya.com/Details/32153/%60Lines-Drawn-on-an-Empty-Map%60-Iraq%E2%80%99s-Borders-and-the-Legend-of-the-Artificial-State-Part-2

Sediq, Ayad. 2018. "Opportunities to rebuild trust in the KRI." *LSE Blogs*. https://blogs.lse.ac.uk/mec/2018/04/19/opportunities-to-rebuild-public-trust-in-the-kri/

Spinner-Halev, Jeff, and Elizabeth Theiss-Morse . 2003. "National Identity and Self-Esteem ." *Perspectives on Politics* 1 (3): 515 –32.

CHAPTER 6

AN ELITIST INTERPRETATION OF KRG GOVERNANCE: HOW SELF-SERVING KURDISH ELITES GOVERN UNDER THE GUISE OF DEMOCRACY AND THE SUBSEQUENT IMPLICATIONS FOR REPRESENTATION AND CHANGE

Bamo Nouri

One consequential political breakthrough on the road to Kurdish independence was the formal establishment of the Kurdistan Region of Iraq (KRI) in Iraq's 2005 Constitution, which granted autonomy to the KRI and allowed the Kurdistan Regional Government (KRG) to govern through parliamentary democracy. Proponents of Kurdish statehood viewed the official recognition of the Kurdistan Region as a crucial step toward furthering Kurdish autonomy in the neighboring states of Turkey, Iran, and Syria, with grander aspirations of an independent Kurdish nation-state. The possibility of Kurdish autonomy evolving further would be heavily dependent on the KRG's establishment of a constitutional, democratic, and prosperous governance model that could represent a blueprint for similar structures in neighboring countries. Many viewed this as a momentous opportunity for the Kurds to build on previous soft-power gains—as popular proponents of freedom and democracy—by building a prosperous and democratic KRI. However, after fifteen years of formal KRG rule, the KRI has failed to live up to these expectations. Instead, the region has become a haven for repression, political violence, corruption, and oppression. This chapter posits an elitist argument based on empirical and analytical coverage of the KRG's relations with the Government of Iraq (GOI), patronage politics, clientelism, partisan institutions, and constitutional violations by ruling elites in the KRI, analyzing how this has subverted democracy and prevented progressive change. The drawbacks are almost immeasurable and limitless, as symptomatic disseminations of a stagnated elitist system span far and wide. One key implication that this chapter will highlight is how a dysfunctional elitist political system has contributed to a disillusioned generation of youth who have lost faith in the KRI's political system. This is evidenced by significantly low—and decreasing—voter turnout in tandem with a diminished reliance on political participation as an avenue for political change in addition to a festering mental health crisis.

The KRG's Political System

Elite theory challenges the arguments of pluralism, which suggests that power is shared or divided among various interest groups and classes as opposed to purely single-class domination (Parry 1986). Pluralism in the context of the KRG is the conception that power, or the ability to make decisions, is diffused and that negotiation is the method for decision-making (Prewitt and Stone 1973). Prima facie, the existence of numerous parliamentarians from a diverse range of political parties would support the notion that the KRG is a representative body. Therefore, a negotiation or bargaining process is expected to exist in every societal domain, particularly health, security, labor, and education. This is important to acknowledge, as the KRG claims to be pluralistic and an advocate of democracy and, therefore, should not be elitist. The existence of a minority Kurdish elite, dominating the political system in the KRI, produces theoretical implications, including concerns about legitimacy and representation in the region.

The doctrine of elite theory provides a convincing explanation with an argument that there is inevitably a minority of the population in every society that dominates decision-making processes and that this dominant subgroup cannot be controlled by the majority regardless of existing democratic instruments (Pareto 1916; Mosca and Livingston 1896; Mills 1956). The members of the elite exploit their power to serve the interests of their own domination (Parry 1986). This enables decision-making elites in the KRI to implement policies and act in order to serve their own self-interests, which tend to reflect the domination of Iraq's resources by dividing authority over the Iraqi ministries that maintain the state's budgets. This is based on the conception that, once elites are in decision-making positions, groups of like-minded individuals—regardless of internal division—collaborate in order to dominate the decision-making process. It must be acknowledged that elites can also have disagreements, an inevitable human tendency that arises from differences in judgement and opinion. However, it is equally important to remember that intra-elite disagreements are tactical and concern the smaller aspects of the details regarding the implementation of their tactical dominance and, therefore, do not concern the more fundamental particularities and strategies such as sharing authority in controlling Iraq's resources.

Elitist Political System: Government Formation, Patronage Politics, and the Subversion of Democracy, 2005–2019

Government Formation Based on Ministerial Fiefdoms

In order to understand the dynamics of post-Saddam Kurdish politics, it is important to recognize the precedent of government formation in the GOI. Sanctified by Iraq's 2005 constitution, sectarian politics metamorphized into an ethnic, religious, and tribal-based patronage system that controls and clenches public-sector positions that maintain control over budgetary matters as a key source of this structure (Yahya 2017). At no point since 2003 has the winner of the parliamentary elections in the GOI become prime minister. In 2005, the victory of Ibrahim al-Jaafari, the leader of the United Iraqi Alliance coalition, was overruled by fellow Islamic Dawa party member Nouri al-Maliki, who was a compromise candidate following the breakdown of negotiations over government formation (Mansour 2018). In the 2010 elections, Ayad Allawi, the head of the al-Iraqiya list coalition, narrowly won the elections by a margin of two votes but failed to form a government, leading to Maliki's reappointment. As the head of the State of Law coalition, Maliki won the 2014 elections but, due to disagreements over government formation and strategy in the fight against the Islamic State of Iraq and al-Sham (ISIS), was replaced by Haider Al-Abadi. In the 2018 elections, Muqtada al-Sadr's Saairun coalition won a majority, but ultimately, Adil Abdul-Mahdi, a compromise candidate between the two emerging post-election coalitions—Al Bina and Al Islah—was chosen as prime minister.

The lengthy government formation process is entirely reliant on the division of key state institutions based on tribal identities. This is achieved through political parties forming blocs with and against each other to achieve their goals. Ministerial fiefdoms, where political parties are given ministries in exchange for support, have created a dysfunctional government due to the lack of clear—and, more importantly, united—governmental strategy, a deficit that consequently impedes development. A key drawback of the patronage system is the implications it creates where there is a lack of qualified decision-makers in positions of development, with intellectuals or individuals who can add real value being prevented from contributing (Paasche 2016).

The Kurdistan Region of Iraq (KRI) is no different in that government formation is entirely dependent on the division of the region's ministries.

Parliamentary elections and the subsequent formation of governments between 2005 and 2019 have been dominated by the battle for ministries, with coalitions formed based on ministerial fiefdoms. The 2005 KRI parliamentary elections aimed to bring an end to party rule when a coalition called Democratic Patriotic Alliance of Kurdistan (DPAK) was formed between the Kurdistan Democratic Party (KDP) and the Patriotic Union of Kurdistan (PUK). In winning 104 of the 111 seats in the Kurdistan Parliament, the KDP and PUK were the most represented parties in the coalition, with forty and thirty-eight seats, respectively. However, divisions between Kurdish elites reduced the number of seats DPAK won in the 2009 KRI parliamentary elections, as Gorran (meaning "change" in the Sorani dialect of Kurdish), a new political party comprising former pro-reform PUK members, emerged to win twenty-five seats. Gorran included itself on its own list entitled "movement for change list" and exposed the deeper flaws from within the KDP and PUK, with former members of both parties campaigning against the practices of nepotism and corruption. During the 2009 KRI parliamentary elections, the former DPAK lost fifty-nine seats and was renamed the "Kurdistani list," and the KDP and PUK won thirty and twenty-nine seats, respectively. With Gorran's twenty-five seats posing a threat to KDP-PUK dominance (Hiltermann 2010), an agreement over the exchange of ministries was reached, and a cabinet was formed on October 28, 2009, just over three months later. Turbulence and controversy surrounding the legitimacy of the ruling parties became more prevalent, driven and inspired largely by Gorran and new opposition allies, the Kurdistan Islamic Union and Kurdistan Islamic Group.

Fueled by the revelation of the corruption in the internal processes and institutions led by the ruling elites, tens of thousands of Kurds in the KRI staged their own version of the Arab Spring between February 17 and April 18, 2011. Though the events were largely under-reported, some media outlets produced accounts of what transpired (Sly and Qeis 2011; Tawfeeq 2011; Al-Ansary 2011; Human Rights Watch 2011). For sixty-two days, activists in Sulaymaniyah held daily protests calling for reforms in the KRG and an end to corruption, with demonstrations against the KRG also taking place in Halabja, Raniya, and elsewhere in the KRI (Watts 2016). The clashes between protestors and security forces resulted in at least ten deaths and hundreds of injuries before the KRG decided to violently suppress the demonstrations in April. Given the leading role the Kurds played in drafting the 2005 Iraqi constitution, they had historically been satisfied with their administrative arrangement, and demonstrations were uncommon occurrences in the region (Al-Ali 2014; Arato

2009; Jawad 2013). The protests eventually forced the resignation of KRG Prime Minister Barham Salih and led to the creation of a new cabinet headed by Nechirvan Barzani (*Iraq-business News* 2012). Despite this nascent cabinet and strong promises of change and reform by the new prime minister, PUK and KDP domination over key ministries persisted, as debates around cabinet formation focused on the exchange of ministerial posts (UNPO 2012).

The 2013 KRI parliamentary elections further demonstrated the weakening of the two ruling parties, with the KDP winning thirty-eight seats, Gorran winning twenty-four, and the PUK winning eighteen. Nearly eight months passed between the elections held on September 21, 2013 and the announcement of the KRG cabinet on June 18, 2014 (*Iraq-business News* 2014), because debates and discussions around the division of ministerial control superseded a cabinet predicated on governmental strategy (*Rudaw* 2014). The new cabinet faced continued challenges as diplomatic methods of accountability intensified throughout the region's parliament and pressure on two-party rule grew more widespread among the opposition groups. This culminated with the KDP's security forces' preventing the Gorran speaker of parliament from entering Erbil and banning its four other ministers from the KRI capital and, effectively, their offices on October 12, 2015 (*Iraqi Oil Report* 2015). The ministers and speaker of parliament were also Gorran party members, from the Ministries of Finance, Peshmerga Affairs, Trade, and Religious Affairs. The act was condemned by members of the other majority parties, including Gorran, PUK, and smaller Islamic and Christian parties, through a signed statement denouncing the treatment Gorran endured. Yousif Mohammed, the parliamentary speaker who was prevented from entering his office, said the events were an "occupation of Erbil . . . and an attempt to launch a coup d'état against the main source of legitimacy in Kurdistan, which is the parliament. But we, as the parliament, will not accept a coup" (Salih 2015). It seems that democratically winning the second-highest number of seats in the KRG parliamentary elections (*BBC News* 2013) was irrelevant, as the actions of the KDP partisan security forces subverted democratic norms regardless. In 2017, after a meeting between the KDP and the PUK, the KRG announced that the parliament would open again after being closed for almost two years (*Rudaw* 2017).

The 2018 elections saw a momentous KDP victory with forty-five seats, an average performance by the PUK with twenty-one seats, and the relative loss of Gorran, which won only twelve seats (Sulaivany 2018). With the creation of new ministerial posts, the formation of government took nine months, as vicious political battles raged over the region's twenty-two ministries. It was clear from the demands of the PUK—for an equal-partnership sharing of power between the KDP and the PUK—that the trajectory of the KRI is hugely dependent on elite agreements between the ruling parties (Alaaldin 2018). These agreements led to the emergence of a minority elite-serving party of loyalists, friends, and family, as Kurdish elites govern through a system known as *wasta*. It is this *wasta* system—a key societal foundation of the patronage system—that fueled protests, inspired political opposition, and, more importantly, spawned corrupt and discriminatory partisan institutions that became major impediments in the progress of the KRI.

Partisan Institutions

Nawshirwan Mustafa, who was the Gorran leader at the time, outlined the KRI's fundamental issues in a 2012 interview with Ferdinand Hennerbichler, an Austrian historian and former diplomat. Mustafa pointed to "corruption" and "social injustice" because of two political parties: the KDP in Erbil and the PUK in Sulaymaniyah. In the interview, he compared the KRI model to that of the "former Soviet Union," in which single parties rule different areas (Hennerbichler 2017). Mustafa highlighted how democracy is subverted through the KDP and the PUK, which each have their own Peshmerga and Asayish (KRG police) forces along with separate financial ministries. Mustafa explained that the arrangement with Baghdad is not from a unified KRG but from discrete relationships with each political party. Gorran demanded the separation of the dominant political parties and the government, claiming that there was bias in the functions of these parties in what Mustafa called "partisan institutions," which replaced what should be public institutions. Gorran called for either the separation of political parties and the government or the end to "interference" by political parties in the daily duties of the government. In affirming institutional elitism, Mustafa highlighted a major detriment to the ordinary population of KRI: "We want to change the 'partisan institutions for example here in Sulaymaniyah, Asayish, Peshmerga, Police, even the schools' headmasters. If you are not a member of PUK, you have no opportunity to be appointed as an element of the security apparatus, as an element of Peshmerga, as headmaster, as a teacher . . . We want to change the partisan governmental institutions from partisan institutions to national institutions, to be for all the peoples to have the right to be elements in security apparatus in Peshmerga, in everything."

Job Security for Votes

The intricacy of how ruling elites utilize partisan institutions in the KRI is exemplified in the institutions and industries full of civil service jobs where the PUK and KDP have threatened the livelihoods of the electorate to vote freely in elections. There are numerous examples of the dismissal of public servants who do not vote for the party that controls the public institution. Mustafa explained that in the 2009 elections, the PUK dismissed more than two thousand employees and punished more than four thousand governmental employees for voting for Gorran. This example personifies how the KRG's ruling elites operate regardless of the democratic and constitutional rights that are enforced in Iraq's 2005 constitution. Elite rule through partisan institutions where election votes affect employment clearly breaches Iraq's constitution. Section Two, Article 14 of the Constitution of Iraq states that Iraqis are equal before the law without discrimination based on gender, race, ethnicity, nationality, origin, color, religion, sect, belief or opinion, or economic or social status. Article 15 states that "every individual has the right to enjoy life, security, and liberty," while Article 16 makes it clear that "equal opportunities shall be guaranteed to all Iraqis." In demonstrating the nature of unrepresentative elite power in the KRI, the monopolization of institutions by political parties alongside "job security for votes system"—a key element of the patronage system—violate Iraq's constitution and severely undermine democracy.

Democracy in Practice: 2011–2020

Elitist institutions and constitutional violations do not naturally synthesize well with the notion of democracy, which makes representation in the KRI worth examining further. One of the challenges in measuring democracy in the KRI is the lack of transparency in governmental decision-making, making it difficult to gauge insight into how the political system is representative in practice. I tracked and measured the nature of democracy in the KRI since 2011 through the work of NGOs that documented the increasingly frequent violations of Iraq's constitution. Focus on these issues was particularly extensive between 2011 and 2014, when political opposition and civic protests emerged and gained momentum. However, there was a dearth of NGO reporting between 2014 and 2018, because NGOs dedicated their research efforts to the violations of human rights that accompanied the rise of ISIS.

Article 120 states that the KRI, along with any other federal region, can adopt its own constitution as long as it does not contradict the 2005 Iraq

Constitution. It is important to note that the articles of Iraq's 2005 Constitution are binding in the KRI. Article 38 guarantees some fundamental rights:

The state shall guarantee in a way that does not violate public order and morality:
First. Freedom of expression using all means.
Second. Freedom of press, printing, advertisement, media and publication.
Third. Freedom of assembly and peaceful demonstration and this shall be regulated by law (Iraq Constitution 2005).

A 2013 report by Human Rights Watch (HRW) epitomized the nature of KRG elite governance in practice, outlining broad and gross violations of Article 38 of the Iraqi constitution (Human Rights Watch 2013). In 2012, the KRG reportedly engaged in the arbitrary arrest and detention of journalists, critics, and opposition political activists. Additionally, the state prosecuted critics, filing lawsuits concerning the insulting or defamation of public figures. This was based on information obtained by HRW following six different visits to the KRI. One example is Akram Abdulkarim, who was jailed for over a year without trial on national security charges, because he accused leading members of the KDP of illegally pillaging custom revenues at Iraq's border with Turkey. In November and December 2012, HRW interviewed various journalists, political activists, and others who had been arrested—some were released without charge and others prosecuted for defamation and fined or imprisoned. A lawyer named Zana Fatah was among those arrested. Fatah informed HRW that he was arrested in October 2012 in Chamchamal, Iraq, after writing an article accusing the judiciary of lacking independence from the main political parties of KDP and PUK. Unsurprisingly, after meetings with KRG's Department of Foreign Relations and the Asayish, HRW was told that "talk of corruption cannot be tolerated" (Human Rights Watch 2013).

There is no doubt that the application of law and order is biased in favor of ruling elites and, therefore, to the detriment of ordinary citizens who wish to exercise their constitutional and democratic rights. Through the KRI's Press Law of 2007, under Article 2 (Kurdistan Press Law 2008), the protection of rights is awarded to journalists who seek to "obtain information of importance to citizens and relevant to the public interest from diverse sources." The law, according to the fifth point of Article 5, dictates that "anyone who insults or injures a journalist as a result of the performance of his work shall be punished with the punishments decided for those who injure government employees during regular working hours or as a result of the performance of his or her work." The fourth point of Article 8 makes it clear that no crime is committed if a journalist "has published or written about the work of an official or individual entrusted with a public service or a public representative if what he has published does not go beyond the affairs of the profession or of the public or representative service on the condition that he has provided proof supporting what he has ascribed to them." The fifth point of Article 8 confirms that "no legal procedures shall be taken against the journalist after ninety days from the date of publication."

Theoretically, the KRI's Press law makes it unequivocally clear that journalists should be protected from retaliatory arrest and injury as a consequence of their work. Niyaz Abdullah, from the press freedom group Metro Center for Defending Journalists, told HRW that they logged over one hundred complaints regarding breaches of journalistic rights. Abdullah affirmed that the KRG ignores "the laws in place that require it to investigate abuses and harassment of journalists, and to hold the wrongdoers accountable" (Human Rights Watch 2013). In a year-end report, the Metro Center documented twenty-one cases of alleged physical assault against journalists, with one instance of armed assault, as well as fifty arrests, thirty-four cases where security forces confiscated journalists' equipment, and five death threats against journalists for their publications. In March 2012, HRW documented police brutality and detentions targeting journalists who reported on the demonstrations that were eventually dubbed the February 17, 2011 protests, which spread throughout the KRI. That same year, KRI security forces killed ten protestors and injured more than 250. Sarah Leah Whitson, at the time the Middle East director at HRW, commented that the KRG looks "less like the open and thriving democracy it paints itself to be. By undermining legal guarantees for free speech, the KRG is undermining one of the basic pillars of a free society."

Legislative initiatives even attempted to regulate press freedom in June 2012, when a "Draft Law to Protect Sanctities" was submitted to the Kurdish Parliament with the goal of imposing criminal punishments of up to ten years imprisonment for anyone who insults "religious and national symbols." Many civil society activists believed that these vague laws would be repurposed to foster a climate of fear and effectively deter media professionals from publishing freely. The Kurdistan Parliament's Legal, Human Rights, and Civil Affairs Committees rejected the draft law, stating that it would violate Article 38 of the Iraqi Constitution and the KRI's obligations for human rights and other legal statutes. It should be noted that most journalists who are killed or detained were reporting on the corruption of the KDP and PUK and their discriminatory patronage system.

On February 17, 2012, in Sulaymaniyah's Freedom Square, hundreds of peaceful demonstrators and protestors were approached by plainclothes security officers who violently attacked them with batons while official security forces watched without intervening. Metro Center journalists also informed HRW that security forces attacked journalists and photographers who captured the protest, confiscating their equipment. Other journalists reported that media workers from the *KNN* and *NRT* television channels had also been arrested (Abdullah 2012). HRW learned from witnesses that around thirty journalists and protesters were taken to Fermanday prison on the western outskirts of Sulaymaniyah, where they were arrested before being released without charge.

On October 10, 2012, Shawqi Kanabi, who was the director of the *KNN* television channel, interviewed a worker from the Erbil Provincial Council—a public institution—who happened to also be a businessowner. Kanabi learned from the council worker that running companies while publicly employed is legally prohibited. As a result, Kanabi was fined 1.5 million dinars on October 20 for "insulting" a member of the provincial council. The UNAMI Human Rights Office also included this incident in its 2013 report (United Nations Human Rights Office 2013). Kanabi told HRW that "journalists can't gather information legally. When you dig, they have many laws to use against you. The Kurdish government is using unconstitutional means to try to stop free press and political opposition and tries to justify this effort with proper legal procedures. Before, they would kill you; now, they threaten you and arrest you" (Human Rights Watch 2013).

Similarly, Sherwan Sherwani published various articles in *Bashour*, an independent magazine, in April 2012. He reported that around 206 million Iraqi dinars had going missing from Akre City Council's resources due to corruption and fraud. Sherwani wrote another article about the bribes that businessman took, including one instance of a $2-millon bribe as part of a business deal. Sherwani was quickly detained on April 20, without an arrest warrant, and he remained in detention for three days before being released and detained once again for three more days, finally facing charges for defamation. The KRI's Press Law makes it clear that a journalist cannot be penalized after more than ninety days following the publication of reported news. However, Sherwani was charged 170 days after the publication of his article, despite the arrest being unlawful. Additionally, HRW was informed that fourteen journalists from the

Badinan province were forced to promise not to write articles for certain independent journals; the fourteen would not speak to HRW, fearing retaliation from the security services. Asos Hardi, a journalist affiliated with the Sulaymaniyah-based magazine *Awene*, also testified to this, telling HRW, "Talking about politics is a dangerous undertaking . . . Corruption is an especially sensitive issue. The problem is that there is no mentality of accountability. When they want to put someone away, they put them away, and then they look for the excuse." Shwan Saber, the vice-chairman of the Justice Network for Prisoners, confirmed these comments: "When corrupt officials punish free speech, this is what you get. The ruling party is silencing its critics."

Another notable lawsuit targeted Akram Abdulkarim, a former customs officer, who was detained for one week after being arrested at the border for giving media interviews about how leading members of the KDP had been stealing customs revenues generated from the border crossing between the KRI and Turkey. He gave these interviews to *NRT*, *Bashour* magazine, and *Hawlati* magazine, and eventually convinced fifty members of parliament to sign a petition demanding transparency in the accounting records of the revenues generated at the Turkish border crossing. Abdulkarim's lawyer told HRW that he was detained without access to a lawyer for almost three weeks and that, during this period, he was assaulted and eventually charged with jeopardizing national security by publishing an unclassified manual for customs officials that he had developed while working for the Asayish in coordination with the Interior Ministry. The Asayish charged Abdulkarim with violating Article 316 of the 1969 Iraqi Penal Code, a crime that carried a penalty of ten years in prison. On behalf of Abdulkarim, Kamaran Barwany, an activist, told HRW that the case is "not a national security case, this is a case of political dissent and freedom of thought."

Another important case to consider is Sardasht Osman, a twenty-three-year-old in his final year at university who was abducted in Erbil on May 4, 2010. Osman was a freelance journalist who had contributed to the independent newspaper *Ashtiname* and the online news outlets *Sbei, Kurdistan Post, Awene, Hawlati*, and *Livinpress* (Abdulla 2014). Osman generally published articles about the corruption of high-ranking government officials from the PUK and KDP. In one article in the *Kurdistan Post*, he reported on wealth inequality and the possibility of escaping his impoverished roots by marrying into the KDP's family. Immediately after the article was published, Osman received death threats in texts and calls, and, in his final article, he wrote, "I am not afraid of death from torture. I'm here waiting for my appointment with my murderers. I am praying for the most tragic death possible, to match my tragic life" (Abdulla 2014). Osman was eventually found dead on May 4, 2010 on a road near Mosul, with his body exhibiting signs of torture and two bullet wounds in his head (Glenewinkel 2010). Following a tremendous outburst of protests by the people of the KRI, President Masoud Barzani appointed an investigatory committee, which, on September 15, 2010, announced that Ansar al-Islam, an Islamic group connected to Al Qaeda, had murdered Osman. According to the committee, Hisham Mahmood Ismaeel, from Beji, north of Tikrit, had confessed during an interrogation that he had been tasked with blindfolding Osman and taking him to Ansar al-Islam members in Mosul. Controversially, Ansar al-Islam swiftly denied responsibility.

Since the uncovering of evidence regarding corruption, nepotism, and violations of constitutional rights has resulted in heightened political opposition to the KDP and PUK, the KRI's elite parties have responded brutally and violently in order to maintain the iron grip with which they control Iraq's resources. Numerous examples illustrate frequent violations of Article 38 of the Constitution of Iraq, regarding the right to freedom of speech for the press and the general population along with the freedom to peacefully demonstrate. Amnesty International has been relentless in its efforts to report on attacks on journalists and protestors by ruling parties in the KRI and published specific information about these incidents in 2018 (Amnesty International 2018) and 2019 (2019). By 2019, attacks on free speech were no longer limited to journalists and protestors, with Kurdish elites beginning to target the judiciary to maintain their grip on political dominance. On December 2, 2019, Hatsyar Wshyar, an assistant judge from a court in Sulaymaniyah, was sentenced to one year in prison, without being given access to his lawyer and without a fair trial, because he condemned the corruption within the court system (Amnesty International 2020). HRW extensively reported cases involving protestors and journalists being beaten, detained, and shot at by partisan militias in 2017 (Human Rights Watch 2017a, 2017b; Wille 2017) and 2018 (Human Rights Watch 2018a, 2018b). The KRG's partisan security forces embarked on an initiative to close the offices of media outlets that were criticizing the direction and nature of KDP-PUK power structures along with organizations that extensively covered the 2020 protests (Human Rights Watch 2020). HRW specifically asked the KRG to listen to critics rather than arrest them, especially given that the sole demands of protestors were the timely payment of salaries and an end to corruption. This was in the middle of 2020, right at the heart of the COVID-19 pandemic, and it was primarily teachers who detained and arrested (Wille 2020). Amid the consistent violations of constitutional rights is a disregard for law and order by high-ranking officials.

The Presidency: Using Nationalism to Maintain Power

Masoud Barzani was only supposed to serve two four-year terms, as per Article 64 of the KRI's draft constitution, which was created in 2009. According to the constitution, Barzani's term should have ended in 2013, but an agreement—reached behind closed doors between the KDP and PUK elites and rubber-stamped by their majority in the KRI parliament—extended his term by two additional years. This decision was met with resistance from the general population and the opposition parties in the KRI on the grounds that it was unconstitutional (Hassan 2015). After his extended two-year term in office came to an end on August 19, 2015, the KDP and Barzani refused to adhere to the agreement, and he remained president of the KRI until 2017. This provoked heavy objections from the four main parties in the KRI—Gorran, PUK, the Kurdistan Islamic Union, and the Kurdistan Islamic Group—which demanded that Barzani step down and called for respect for the parliamentary system. Barzani, however, was determined to retain his position, as he held more power than the prime minister of the KRG, who, at the time, happened to be his nephew, Nechirvan Barzani (Neuhof 2015). The KRG prime minister stated the president should remain in power until the 2017 election in order to lead the fight against ISIS (Hassan 2015), while Masoud Barzani himself had stated that he would remain in office until his initiative to hold a referendum on independence from Iraq in the KRI had taken place (Wali 2016). In a separate article by the Kurdish newspaper *Rudaw*, Barzani stated that he would not run in the next presidential election and would allow for a new candidate to replace him (*Rudaw* 2016). This new candidate was Nechirvan Barzani, and he was sworn in as president of the KRI on June 10, 2019 (*Rudaw* 2019a), while Masrour Barzani, the son of former President Barzani, was elected prime minister of the KRI on June 11, 2019 (*Rudaw* 2019b).

Given that over 80 percent of the workforce in Iraq receives civil service salaries, incompetence and corruption from elites who control the institutions tasked with budgetary matters can have disastrous effects. One such outcome was a wage crisis, which began in 2015 and has lasted until this chapter was finalized in September 2020. Over a period of five years, there were prolonged periods of unpaid salaries and reduced salary payments. This no doubt led to protests and upheaval, as at one point fifty thousand went on strike in Sulaymaniyah, Iraq (*New Arab* 2016). The reason behind this, according to the KRG Minister of Natural Resources, was a dispute between the GOI in Baghdad and the KRG: "In fact, the current economic crisis is a result of that agreement between Kurdish political parties and Baghdad. Instead of sending $1 billion to the KRG per month, Baghdad sent us $200 [million] to $300 million, which pushed the KRG to seek heavy loans to pay salaries" (*Rudaw* 2015). The GOI's austerity measures followed the declared intentions of President Barzani for a referendum for permanent independence from Iraq and an economic independence policy for the KRG to unilaterally export oil. Iraqi Prime Minister Haider al-Abadi attributed the situation to Kurdish mismanagement, stating "I have a suggestion: Give us the oil and we will give every Kurdish employee a salary like we do for every Iraqi employee" (*Reuters* 2016).

Although low oil prices were blamed for the crisis, Abadi made it clear, in an interview in January 2017, that wages are still paid to all employees working under the authority of Baghdad despite the challenging economic circumstances (*Rudaw* 2017). However, the KRG still blamed the GOI for freezing the portion of its budget allocated to the KRG since February 2014, which, along with low oil prices, made it difficult to pay wages and delayed the salaries of civil servants. Even when wages were paid, these payments amounted to only 25 percent of the typical monthly salary. Abadi noted that "this level of clarity must be exercised in every place, including the Region. We are now calling for transparency and clarity so that we understand where this amount of money is going to. If the Region has some rights withheld by us, we will pay, and if the rest of Iraq has some rights withheld by the Region, they should pay, so that there will be a balance in this issue." Protests have occurred amid the wage crisis every year since 2015, with the situation worsening since 2018 (Rasool 2018). The 2018 protests were momentous in terms of diversity, with teachers, university lecturers, doctors, students, and numerous women in attendance as a result of historic levels of discontent, pushing the KRI to the brink of revolution (Nouri 2018).

Aside from the impacts the dysfunctional KRI had on the public sector, the failure to pay civil salaries on time also affects the private sector, being starved for resources as people have little money to spend. Interestingly, Abadi and Barzani were both quick to set up meetings to secure Iraq's ministries after the 2018 elections despite the very public division and disagreement between them in order to form a governing block in the GOI, and they did so in good spirits and by praising each other (Ali 2018). The elite disagreements over budgets fueled the problems in the civil service as Iraqi Prime Minister Mustafa Al-Kadhimi and KRG Prime Minister Masrour Barzani continued to argue over who is to be held responsible for the region's wage crisis (Ghafuri 2020).

Nationalism and the Referendum

A questionable occurrence was the utilization of nationalism through a referendum which called for the secession of the KRI from Iraq. The move was problematic for a number of reasons. Firstly, it came from President Barzani, who had stayed in office beyond his legitimately sanctified term limit, as opposed to the KRG government, meaning that the initiative lacked consensus among the political parties and contributed to political battles in the KRI (O'Driscoll and Baser 2019). This in turn raised further questions of legitimacy, alongside an extremely risky political maneuver that could have provoked further conflict in the region, since referendums can have catastrophic consequences (Qvortrup 2014). There is significant commonality between the referendum and the KRI's governance in that they are both unrepresentative and respective of the decisions of a minority ruling elite. Instead of inserting a motion for a parliamentary debate—which was put in recess following the banning of the speaker of parliament—Barzani convened a meeting between the unelected heads of the KRI's political parties. The new group of unelected elites were collectively named as the Kurdistan Leadership Council, yet were boycotted by Gorran and both of the Islamic parties. The call for referendum was made at one of these council meetings.

The timing of the referendum could not have been worse, as the KRI was already submerged in crisis and political uncertainty. The referendum undoubtedly was an attempt to distract the public and shift focus away from the mounting political pressure the ruling KDP and PUK elites faced, with their governance style exemplifying a new type of authoritarianism in Iraq (Dodge 2012). This was not the first time that nationalism has been utilized by elites for political gains (Breuilly 1993), but it has done little to legitimize the rule of Kurdish elites, nor has it accomplished anything else to settle the issues in the KRI.

Instead, the referendum exacerbated the implications and repercussions of unrepresentative elite rule. The diverse demands of protesters among the KRI's urban populace and the youth in particular demonstrates the extreme alienation from the governing elite that the civilian population experienced (Dodge 2012).

The decisions of self-serving Kurdish elites have caused substantial decreases in voter turnout numbers in the KRI parliamentary elections between 2009 and 2019. In 2009, voter turnout was 78.5 percent, but this dropped to 74 percent in 2013 and to 51.4 percent in 2018 amid allegations of election fraud, vote rigging, and ballot-box stuffing. This unrepresentative elitist system has shaken voter confidence in the region, as corruption, nepotism, partisan institutions, undemocratic processes, and a lack of protection for constitutional rights have caused voters to become disillusioned with the political process and the democratic pathway to change. Ali Hama Saleh, a politician from Gorran, blamed vote rigging, while Bilal Wahab, a political analyst, blamed the failed referendum and its consequences along with voters' waning confidence in politicians who rule with rigid politics and draw the predominance of their power from "guns and money" (Dri 2018).

Disillusioned Youth

Authoritarian and unrepresentative elites undoubtedly cause collateral damage, yet a main issue facing the KRI is the extent to which this also squanders its future generation of leaders. The importance of youth in politics has significantly decreased in the eyes of the KRI's elites, who once viewed the youth as the "key" to success. In 2005, famous popstar Zakaria was recruited to encourage disgruntled youth to vote in the Iraqi elections (Howard 2005). Even back then, there were protests over corruption, unemployment, and a lack of services. One of the most profound symptoms of elitist KRG rule has been the disillusionment of youth, as competition between the KDP and PUK continues to destroy, neglect, and impede the prospects of KRI youth. The period of legitimate hopefulness among the youth was perhaps in 2011, when groups such as the Youth of Sulaymaniyah and other high school and university students protested for more representation and less corruption in the KRI. As reports suggested then, many of those who were attacked in 2011 were youth. For example, Rezhwan Ali, a fifteen-year-old schoolboy, was shot in the head and killed instantly after security services fired live rounds indiscriminately into a crowd of protestors (Amnesty International 2011a). Additionally, Sardasht Osman, a twenty-three-year-old, fearlessly waved the flag of youth dissent and optimism for change, before his aspirations were cut short because of how he expressed his discontent with the KRI. Osman's and Ali's deaths sparked more NGO coverage, starting with Amnesty International, which began to call for investigations into the deaths of journalists at the hands of the KRG in 2011 (Amnesty International 2011b) and 2013 (Amnesty International 2013).

Additional requests were made to investigate the deaths of journalists and the actions of political party militias in 2015 (Amnesty International 2015) and 2016 (Amnesty International 2016). The Office of the United Nations High Commissioner for Human Rights (OHCHR) also reported recorded unfair imprisonments and killings of journalists in year-end reports published in 2011 (UNAMI 2011), 2012 (UNAMI 2012), and 2013 (UNAMI 2013), which highlighted the prominent death of Kawa Garmyani, a journalist who was gunned down in front of his mother's eyes because of his "anti-corruption" publications (*KNNC* 2013; Mhamad 2016; Rabar 2013). The OHCHR also included details of these incidents in its 2014 annual report (UNAMI 2014).

One of the huge implications of unrepresentative elite rule is the identity crisis amongst the new generation of youth, who, after seeing the coopting of nationalism in political competition, now question the notion of Kurdish patriotism (Saeed 2019). Although patriotism has been a core tenet of the Kurdish identity, especially among the generations of the current leaders of the KRI, it has not received unanimous approval from the youth of the region. In August 2020, the youth took to the streets amid mounting crises relating to the COVID-19 pandemic to protest the never-improving, abysmal standard of public services and rising unemployment, clashing with security services in Sulaymaniyah and Kalar (Oliver 2020). A key theme in the protests was anger at the clientelism between Turkey and the KRI's ruling elites, and the KRG was accused of prioritizing its own interests—allegiance with, and political support from, Turkey—before the security of its people and the protection of its borders. In response to the protests, Prime Minister Barzani issued an ironic statement in which he promised that the perpetrators will be brought to justice. There is no doubt the KRG is out of touch with its youth, who can no longer be pacified through patriotic ideals and sentiments as they grow more doubtful of the authenticity of their own patriotism. Patriotism and nationalism mean little to youth, who have simple demands of fairness, equality, and a right to live freely in securing their futures. This is something for which elitist rule through partisan institutions provides little scope or flexibility, with dissenting voices being targeted and killed.

Diminished Hope

According to a 2018 report released by the Kurdish Region Statistics Office, 20 percent of youth between the ages of eighteen and thirty-four have left the workforce because they "lost hope in finding a job' (Kurdistan Regional Statistics Office 2018). There is a generation of youth who have only experienced KDP-PUK rule, under which hopes for future prosperity have vanished, replaced instead by pessimism (Petkova 2018b). Conversely, it was the youth who led and dominated Iraq's anti-government protests in 2019. But in the KRI, the demoralization of youth has contributed to a historically low morale regarding the capacity to effect change through protest, as traumatic memories of violent repression and murder, such as those of Osman and Ali, still linger (Petkova 2019). As elites in Iraq continue to fight for control over ministries and siphon resources for family and friends with accountability, there is clearly little room for debate about how support youth progress, as Iraq faces a grave mental health crisis. The epitome of youth despondency in the KRI is personified by the 2018 case of Rehat Hama-Aziz, an eighteen-year-old clarinet player from Halabja. Rehat won first place as a solo musician in the prestigious Annual Rwanga Awards, but he took his own life the very next day after performing in his bedroom one last time (Nouri 2019). One in five Iraqis struggle with mental health issues, with youth constituting a significant portion of this growing statistic, indicating how detached Iraqi authorities are from the youth population. It should come as no surprise that many Kurds, especially youth, continue to flee the Kurdish region, risking death, in search of a better life (Petkova 2018a).

The issues mentioned thus far illustrate many of the procedural shortfalls present in KRG governance, as the KRI retrogresses despite the freedoms and rights it has enjoyed under Iraq's constitution. Documented abuses of authority and nepotism by the ruling political parties through political militias and the use of partisan institutions to award public service jobs have discredited and delegitimized the ruling parties and even subverted democracy. The documented evidence makes it clear that political opposition, constitutional rights and universal equality are not being practiced, exemplified by the treatment and rights violations of journalists, protestors, and others expressing political dissent in a manner guaranteed under the constitution. The KRG is conceivably in a period of crisis on almost every level, and supporting this idea are the flagrant constitutional violations, mass protests, violence, and fatal attempts to block political opposition with a forced closure of parliament demonstrating that evokes a regressive democracy. The most substantial indicator of an elitist KRG is how future generations have lost faith to fight for—or work toward—a change they believe in. Instead, many of the region's youth prefer to risk their lives to escape the KRI rather than work to change it.

The disunity between Kurdish elites has a knock-on effect in other areas, as the KRG fails to produce unified progressive policies that can enhance the quality of life for its populace. The repercussions of corruption, nepotism, and incompetence affect the payment of salaries in the public sector, on which the KRI's populace are largely dependent. The ramifications of this ripple through the private sector as well, restricting and even disrupting typical economic flows as consumers have little or no money to spend. These short-term limitations and the illogical and individual decision-making processes among Iraq's ruling elite have triggered instability and prevented investment in the region. Foreign corporations now see the conditions in the KRI as increasing the risk of conducting business in the region, with little or no guarantees for future returns as elite divisions and decision-making continue to poison their reputation. Not only is it imperative that the demands of the youth and other protestors in society are met, but a thorough depoliticization of the region's institutions must take place, starting with the unification of the security forces and public institutions. Until then, short- and long-term prospects in the KRI are bleak.

References

Abdulla, Namo. 2014. "Mountain of impunity looms over Kurdistan journalists A CPJ special report." Committee to Protect Journalists, https://cpj.org/reports/2014/04/mountain-of-impunity-looms-over-kurdistan-journali.php.

Abdullah, Shenah. 2012. "Journalist beaten and arrested by Iraqi Kurdish militia on the anniversary of anti-KRG protests." eKurd, February 18, http://ekurd.net/mismas/articles/misc2012/2/state5897.htm.

Al-Ali, Z. 2014. The Struggle for Iraq's Future. Yale University Press.

Al-Ansary, Khalid. 2011. "Two killed, 47 hurt in Iraq protest violence." Reuters, February 17. http://www.reuters.com/article/us-iraq-protests/two-killed-47-hurt-in-iraq-protest-violence-idUSTRE71G6PF20110217.

Alaaldin, Farhad. 2018. "Government formation in the KRG: a perilously slow process." Washington Institute, https://www.washingtoninstitute.org/fikraforum/view/forming-the-krg-a-perilously-slow-process.

Ali, Sangar. 2018. "Masoud Barzani meets Abadi, leaders across the political spectrum in second-day visit in Baghdad." Kurdistan 24, November 23. https://www.kurdistan24.net/en/news/a26bf7dc-9bed-434d-a3c0-9e8ad963ff71.

Amnesty International. 2011a. "Iraqi authorities must halt attacks on protesters." April 12. https://www.amnesty.org/en/press-releases/2011/04/iraqi-authorities-must-halt-attacks-protesters/.

———. 2011b. "Turkey/Iraq: Investigation needed into killing of civilians in the Kurdistan Region of Iraq." August 26. https://www.amnesty.org/en/documents/reg01/003/2011/en/.

———. 2013. "Iraq: Authorities must investigate killing of journalist." December 6. https://www.amnesty.org/en/documents/mde14/023/2013/en/.

———. 2015. "Iraq: Kurdistan Regional Government Must Rein in Armed Political Party Militias and Investigate Killings During Protests." October 15. https://www.amnesty.org/en/documents/mde14/2711/2015/en/.

———. 2016. "Kurdistan Region of Iraq: Effective Investigation Needed into Killing of Journalist." September 5. https://www.amnesty.org/en/documents/mde14/4764/2016/en/.

———. 2018. "Iraq: Violence against protesters and journalists in Kurdistan Region shows blatant disregard for freedom of expression." March 28. https://www.amnesty.org/en/latest/news/2018/03/iraq-violence-against-protesters-and-journalists-in-kurdistan-region-shows-blatant-disregard-for-freedom-of-expression/.

———. 2019. "Iraq: fist around freedom of expression tightens." March 5. https://www.amnesty.org/en/documents/mde14/9962/2019/en/.

———. 2020. "Iraq: assistant judge convicted in unfair trial: Hatsar Wshyar." February 28. https://www.amnesty.org/en/documents/mde14/1881/2020/en/.

Arato, Andrew. 2009. Constitution Making Under Occupation. Columbia University Press.

BBC News. 2013. "Iraqi Kurdistan opposition party beats PUK in elections." October 2. http://www.bbc.co.uk/news/world-middle-east-24362864.

Breuilly, John. 1993. Nationalism and the State. 2nd ed. Manchester: Manchester University Press.

Dodge, T. 2012. Iraq: From war to a new authoritarianism. Routledge.

Dri, Karwan Faidhi. 2018. "KRG Election: Why such a low turnout?" October 3. http://www.rudaw.net/english/analysis/03102018.

Ghafuri, Lawk. 2020. "Baghdad, Erbil war of words continues over oil-for-budget dispute." Rudaw, August 13. https://www.rudaw.net/english/middleeast/iraq/13082020.

Glenewinkel, Klaas. 2010. "Sardasht Osman: Why was he killed?" Niqash, http://www.niqash.org/en/articles/society/2673/Why-was-he-killed.htm.

Hassan, Kawa. 2015. "Kurdistan's democracy on the brink." EastWest, October 28. https://www.eastwest.ngo/idea/kurdistan%E2%80%99s-democracy-brink.

Hennerbichler, Ferdinand. "NAWSHIRWAN MUSTAFA 1944-2017," YouTube video, 20:21, interview recorded at Newroz 2012 at the "Gorran" headquarters in Sulaymaniyah, Kurdistan Region Iraq, Posted May 25, 2017, https://www.youtube.com/watch?v=YRmV484SYgw.

Hiltermann, Joost. 2010. "Elections in Iraqi Kurdistan: results and implications." Crisis Group, January 1. https://www.crisisgroup.org/middle-east-north-africa/gulf-and-arabian-peninsula/iraq/elections-iraqi-kurdistan-results-and-implications.

Howard, Michael. 2005. "Kurdish youth hold key to power in Iraqi elections." The Guardian, December 12. https://www.theguardian.com/world/2005/dec/12/iraq.michaelhoward.

Human Rights Watch. 2011. "Iraq: Widening Crackdown on Protests." April 21. https://www.hrw.org/news/2011/04/21/iraq-widening-crackdown-protests.

———. 2013. "Iraqi Kurdistan: Free Speech Under Attack Government Critics, Journalists Arbitrarily Detained, Prosecuted for Criticizing Authorities." February 9. https://www.hrw.org/news/2013/02/09/iraqi-kurdistan-free-speech-under-attack.

———. 2017a. "Kurdistan Region of Iraq: 32 arrested at peaceful protest." March 16. https://www.hrw.org/news/2017/03/16/kurdistan-region-iraq-32-arrested-peaceful-protest.

———. 2017b. "Iraq/ Kurdistan Region of Iraq: troops shot at protestors." March 30. https://www.hrw.org/news/2017/03/30/iraq/kurdistan-region-iraq-troops-shot-protesters.

———. 2018a. "Kurdistan Region of Iraq: protestors, journalists detained." February 28. https://www.hrw.org/news/2018/02/28/kurdistan-region-iraq-protesters-journalists-detained.

———. 2018b. "Kurdistan Region of Iraq: Protestors Beaten, Journalists Detained." April 15. https://www.hrw.org/news/2018/04/15/kurdistan-region-iraq-protesters-beaten-journalists-detained.

———. 2020. "Kurdistan Region of Iraq: media offices shut down." October 6. https://www.hrw.org/news/2020/10/06/kurdistan-region-iraq-media-offices-shut-down.

Iraq Constitution. 2005. Article 38. Constitute Project, https://www.constituteproject.org/constitution/Iraq_2005.pdf?lang=en.

Iraq-Business News. 2012. "Kurdistan Parliament approves new KRG cabinet." April 7. https://www.iraq-businessnews.com/2012/04/07/kurdistan-parliament-approves-new-krg-cabinet/.

Iraq-Business News. 2014. "New KRG Cabinet announced." June 20. https://www.iraq-

businessnews.com/2014/06/20/new-krg-cabinet-announced/.
Jawad, Saad. 2013. "The Iraq Constitution: Structural Flaws and Political Implications." LSE Middle East Paper Series.
Kelly, Michael. 2010. "The Kurdish Regional Constitution within the Framework of the Iraqi Federal Constitution: A Struggle for Sovereignty, Oil, Ethnic Identity, and the Prospects for a Reverse Supremacy Clause." Penn State Law Review, http://www.pennstatelawreview.org/articles/114/114%20Penn%20St.%20L.%20Rev.%20707.pdf.
KNNC. 2013. "Kawa Garmyani: Symbol of Glory." http://www.knnc.net/en/full-story-14328-31-False.
Kurdistan Press Law. 2008. http://www.presidency.krd/docs/PressLaw-KRI.pdf.
Kurdistan Regional Statistics Office. 2018. "Demographic survey: Kurdistan Region of Iraq." http://www.krso.net/files/articles/160918035158.pdf
Kurdistan Tribune. 2009. "Draft Constitution of Kurdistan 2009." http://kurdistantribune.com/wp-content/uploads/2012/08/Kurdistan-Draft-Constitution-2009.doc.
Mansour, Renad. 2018. "Rebuilding the Iraqi State: Stabilization, Governance and Reconciliation." European Parliament, Directorate General for External Policies, http://www.europarl.europa.eu/RegData/etudes/STUD/2017/603859/EXPO_STU(2017)603859_EN.pdf.
Mhamad, Aras Ahmed. 2016. "Atrocities against journalists undermine global reputation of the Kurds." New Arab, August 17. https://www.alaraby.co.uk/english/comment/2016/8/17/atrocities-against-journalists-undermine-global-reputation-of-the-kurds.
Mills, C. Wright. 1956. The Power Elite, Oxford U P.
Mosca, Gaetano and Livingston, A. 1896. The ruling class, McGraw-Hill.
Neuhof, Florian. 2015. "Iraq's Kurds, key U.S. ally in Islamic State fight, embroiled in violent political crisis." Washington Times, October 14. http://www.washingtontimes.com/news/2015/oct/14/iraqs-kurds-key-us-ally-in-islamic-state-fight-emb/.
New Arab. 2016. "Thousands of 'unpaid' teachers strike in Iraqi Kurdistan." January 30. https://www.alaraby.co.uk/english/news/2016/1/31/thousands-of-unpaid-teachers-strike-in-iraqi-kurdistan.
Nouri, Bamo. 2018. "Why Iraqi Kurdistan could be on the brink of revolution." The Conversation, April 10. https://theconversation.com/why-iraqi-kurdistan-could-be-on-the-brink-of-revolution-94190.
———. 2019. "After years of conflict, Iraq grapples with a mental health crisis." The Wire, April 9. https://thewire.in/world/after-years-of-conflict-iraq-is-facing-a-severe-mental-health-crisis.
O'Driscoll, Dylan, and Bahar Baser. 2019. "Independence referendums and nationalist rhetoric: the Kurdistan Region of Iraq." Third World Quarterly, 40 (11): 2016–34.
Oliver, Joe. 2020. "Unrest spreads to Iraqi Kurdistan over socioeconomic woes." The Arab Weekly, August 25. https://thearabweekly.com/unrest-spreads-iraqi-kurdistan-over-socioeconomic-woes.
Osgood, Patrick, Rawaz Tahir, and Mohammed Hussein. 2015. "KRG ruling party ejects rivals, escalating political crisis." Iraq Oil Report, October 12. http://www.iraqoilreport.com/news/krg-ruling-party-ejects-rivals-escalating-political-crisis-16709/.
Paasche, Erend. 2016. "The role of corruption in reintegration: experiences of Iraqi Kurds upon return from Europe." Journal of Ethnic and Migration Studies 42(7). 1076–1093.
Pareto. Vilfredo. 1916. The Mind and Society III. New York.
Parry, Geraint. 1986. Political elites. London, Allen and Unwin.
Petkova, Mariya. 2018a. "Why do Kurds continue to flee Iraq's Kurdish region?" Al Jazeera, October 30. https://www.aljazeera.com/indepth/features/kurds-continue-flee-iraq-kurdish-region-181028162624973.html.
———. 2018b. "Anger is simmering among Iraq's Kurdish youth." Al Jazeera, November 12. https://www.aljazeera.com/indepth/features/anger-simmering-iraq-kurdish-youth-181111215952044.html.
———. 2019. "Why are Iraqi Kurds not taking part in protests?" Al Jazeera, November 11.

https://www.aljazeera.com/news/2019/11/iraqi-kurds-part-protests-191111125744569.html.

Prewitt, Kenneth and Allan Stone. 1973. The ruling elites: elite theory, power, and American democracy. Harper and Row, New York, London.

Qvortrup, Matt. 2014. "Referendums on Independence, 1860–2011." The Political Quarterly 85 (1): 57–64.

Rabar, Ruwayda Mustafa. 2013. "Another Journalist murdered in Southern Kurdistan." Alliance for Kurdish Rights, https://kurdishrights.org/2013/12/08/another-journalist-murdered-in-southern-kurdistan/.

Rasool, Mohammed. 2018. "Iraqi Kurdish civil servants protest against salary delays." Al Jazeera, March 29. https://www.aljazeera.com/news/2018/03/iraqi-kurdish-civil-servants-protest-salary-delays-180329194852105.html.

Reuters. 2016. "Iraqi PM offers to pay Kurds' salaries in exchange for oil." February 15. http://www.reuters.com/article/mideast-crisis-iraq-abadi/iraqi-pm-offers-to-pay-kurds-salaries-in-exchange-for-oil-idINKCN0VO2D3.

Rudaw. 2014. "Amid crisis, Kurds form new regional government." June 19. https://www.rudaw.net/english/kurdistan/180620143.

———. 2015. "KRG says delayed salaries to be paid this month." October 20. http://www.rudaw.net/english/kurdistan/201020151.

———. 2016. "Barzani: I will not stand in next presidential elections." June 14. http://www.rudaw.net/english/kurdistan/140720162.

———. 2017a. "Iraqi PM says KRG exports enough oil to pay for its public servants." January 4. http://www.rudaw.net/english/middleeast/iraq/040120175.

———. 2017b. "Kurdistan Parliament to convene on Thursday after KDP-PUK deal." September 10. https://www.rudaw.net/english/kurdistan/100920171.

———. 2019a. "Kurdistan Region swears in Nechirvan Barzani as President." June 10. http://www.rudaw.net/english/kurdistan/100620191.

———. 2019b. "Masrour Barzani elected Prime Minister of Kurdistan Region." June 11. http://www.rudaw.net/english/kurdistan/110620192.

Saeed, Yerevan. 2019. "Without Diversifying its Rentier Economy, Pessimism among Kurdish youth will increase." Washington Institute, September 25. https://www.washingtoninstitute.org/fikraforum/view/without-diversifying-its-rentier-economy-pessimism-among-kurdish-youth-will.

Salih, Mohammed. 2015. "Political turmoil grips Iraqi Kurdistan." Al Jazeera, October 13. http://www.aljazeera.com/news/2015/10/iraqi-kurds-deteriorating-quickly-151013080729534.html.

Sly, Liz and Ali Qeis. 2011. "Two Iraqi protesters killed amid unrest in normally peaceful Kurdistan." Washington Post, February 18. http://www.washingtonpost.com/wp-dyn/content/article/2011/02/17/AR2011021706418.html.

Sulaivany, Karzan. 2018. "Final results: KDP wins Kurdistan's parliamentary elections followed by PUK." Kurdistan 24, October 20. https://www.kurdistan24.net/en/news/f9c62f01-0101-4719-8bb3-c74f7184af88.

Tawfeeq, Mohammed. 2011. "1 killed, 57 injured in Iraqi Kurdish protests." CNN, February 17. http://edition.cnn.com/2011/WORLD/meast/02/17/iraq.protests/index.html.

UNAMI. 2011. "Reports on Human Rights in Iraq: 2011." UNAMI Human Rights Office and Office for the High Commissioner for Human Rights, http://www.ohchr.org/Documents/Countries/IQ/IraqUNAMI-OHCHR_HR_Report2011_en.pdf.

———. 2012. "Reports on Human Rights in Iraq: July–December 2012." UNAMI Human Rights Office and Office for the High Commissioner for Human Rights, http://www.ohchr.org/Documents/Countries/IQ/HRO_July-December2012Report.pdf.

———. 2013. "Reports on Human Rights in Iraq: July–December 2013." UNAMI Human Rights Office and Office for the High Commissioner for Human Rights, http://www.ohchr.org/Documents/Countries/IQ/HRO_July-December2013Report_en.pdf.

———. 2014. "Reports on Human Rights in Iraq: January–June 2014." UNAMI Human Rights Office and Office for the High Commissioner for Human Rights, http://www.ohchr.org/Documents/Countries/IQ/HRO_Jan-Jun2014Report_en.pdf.
United Nations Human Rights Office. 2013. "Report on Human Rights in Iraq: July–December 2012." UNAMI Human Rights Office, http://www.ohchr.org/Documents/Countries/IQ/HRO_July-December2012Report.pdf.
UNPO. 2012. "Iraqi Kurdistan: Parties debate new cabinet options." Kurdish Globe, https://unpo.org/article/13785.
Wali, Zhelwan. 2016. "Barzani: I will step down as president after we declare independence." Rudaw, March 23. http://www.rudaw.net/english/kurdistan/230320161.
Watts, N. 2016. "The Spring in Sulaimani: Kurdish Protest and Political Identities." In Political Identities and Popular Uprisings in the Middle East. Edited by S. Holliday and P. Leech London: Rowman and Littlefield Publishers.
Wille, Belkis. 2017. "Iraq and Kurdistan share bad behavior: Suppressing Media." Human Rights Watch, December 20. https://www.hrw.org/news/2017/12/20/iraq-and-kurdistan-region-share-bad-behavior-suppressing-media.
———. 2020. "The KRG needs to listen to critics, not arrest them." Human Rights Watch, June 15. https://www.hrw.org/news/2020/06/15/krg-needs-listen-critics-not-arrest-them.
Yahya, Maha. 2017. "The summer of our discontents: Sects and Citizens in Lebanon and Iraq." Carnegie Middle East Center, June 30. https://carnegie-mec.org/2017/06/30/summer-of-our-discontent-sects-and-citizens-in-lebanon-and-iraq-pub-71396.

CHAPTER 7

EDUCATIONAL POLICY IN THE KURDISTAN REGION: A CRITICAL DEMOCRATIC RESPONSE

Abdurrahman Ahmad Wahab

Introduction

In this section, I examine the meaning and scope of nationalism and the idea of a nation as a modern social and political construct. I briefly elaborate on the principles and factors of nationalism and illustrate the modernist project of nationalism in constructing the concept of a nation and establishing a modern state through processes such as power, ideology, and hegemony in homogenizing the national culture. I then scrutinize the roles and positions of education as they pertain to nationalism within the process of establishing a modern nation-state.

The most important change that occurred after the Kurds gained control over the administration of their political and cultural affairs in the Kurdish-populated provinces of northern Iraq in 1991, according to Aziz (2009), was a general election and power-sharing arrangement between the main political parties. This political change was largely devoid of substantive transformation in political and sociocultural discourses. In other words, the changes that took place after the 1991 popular uprising in the Kurdistan Region and the formation of the Kurdistan National Assembly and the KRG in 1992 ultimately did not change the political culture that was dominant in contemporary Iraq. Political culture, according to Aziz, is "the dominant pattern of beliefs and values, which are acquired and modify and change as a result of a complex process of socialization and feedback from the political system." He also argues, "If nationalism is about identity and national identity is based on emotional bond, then national identity and political culture in Kurdistan are probably mutually complementary aspects of the same phenomenon. Since nationality is politically shaped, and reflects the national traditions of governance, political culture must be seen as an important aspect of national identity" (Aziz 2009, 94).

Eriksen (2010, 120) posits that, in societies whose political movement is based on the preservation of their cultural identity—meaning their processes of state building is primarily dependent on maintaining their ethnic identity—the force of this identity becomes immense, especially in societies undergoing modernization and "in situations of flux, change, resource competition and threats against boundaries." The persistence of ethnonational identities relates to the political conditions that result in and influence the rise and fall of these identities. While the politicization of Kurdish nationalism in Iraq was a reaction to social injustices and the group's political and ethnic marginalization by successive Iraqi governments, particularly the Ba'thist regime (Bengio 2012; Aziz 2009; Romano 2006; Natali 2005; Stansfield 2003), the Kurdish nationalist discourse has been enacted in the form of a post-colonial reaction. In the Kurdish case, colonial forces have been the dominant source of nationalisms that proliferated in modern Middle Eastern states, since these states have functioned according to models that were unprecedented in the imperial period in the Middle East and that have "imagined a nation without diversity" (Gunter 2013, 35; Natali 2005).

The formal political platform of the Kurdish nationalist movement in Iraq during the second half of the last century developed gradually. The nationalist agenda for an independent Kurdish state had not always been fully envisioned but, rather, was in a dialectical relationship with the political atmosphere of the Iraqi state (Aziz 2009; Natali 2005). A major demand of the Kurdish nationalist movement in Iraq, at least since the 1960s, has been the "administration of education, health and municipal institutions" (Carver 2002, 65). For Kurdish nationalists, establishing a modern Kurdish nation-state not only fulfills this demand but also bestows on the Kurds the status of a distinct, legitimate nation in the face of Iraqi nationalism, which has historically undermined the Kurds as inferior to the Ba'thist pan-Arabist project (Abdullah 2010). The establishment of a modern state is, therefore, significant for a political nationalist project, because it is the most prominent principle of nationalism. Kurdish nationalism is formed, in particular, around the nationalist principle of the congruence between the political boundary and the culture of the ethnonational unit (Gellner 1983). The inclination of Kurdish nationalists has been to challenge the violation of this principle: "If the rulers of the political unit belong to a nation other than that of the majority of the ruled, this, for nationalists, constitutes a quite outstandingly intolerable breech [*sic*] of political propriety" (Gellner 1983, 1). The post-colonial reaction manifests in the Kurdish nationalist sentiment that is galvanized against the violation of this principle. And this reaction is evident in the persistent focus of Kurdish nationalists on the Ba'thist Arab rule in Iraq as the quintessential symbol of evil.

However, the Kurdish reaction to the Ba'thist agenda does not mean that the nationalist elites in the KRG have depended on a state structure that is divergent from that of the Iraqi Ba'thist government. This has implications for the processes of educational policymaking and schooling in Kurdistan. I argue that the issues of education in the Kurdistan Region of Iraq must be understood within, and in relation to, the contingencies of the modern nation-state (Wahab 2017). However, this argument is absent in both the dominant Kurdish nationalist discourse and that of many of Kurdistan's educational critics, who tend to isolate the issues from the overall project of KRG state functionality. Accordingly, the matter of the Iraqi Kurdish nationalist project's maintenance of the Iraqi Ba'thist state structure is twofold, helping to elaborate on the main thesis in this chapter.

First, a critical review of literature on nationalism (Wahab 2017), focusing particularly on Gellner's (1983, 3) analysis of nationalism, indicates that the existence of a state in the form of "politically centralized units" that "possesses the monopoly of legitimate violence" and are "concerned with the enforcement of order" (Gellner 1983, 4) is taken for granted in, and is fundamental to, nationalism. This political philosophy becomes profoundly entrenched in the modern paradigm of the state that it sees, subsequently imagining and creating the nation in the image of that state. The nationalist elites who incubate, consolidate, and disseminate the idea of nation tend to accept the structures of a nationalist state, as long as the nationalist sentiment is fulfilled (Gellner 1983). In the context of the Iraqi Kurdish case, the fulfillment of the nationalist principle is not concerned with what kind of state Kurdish nationalist elite are running as long as they are, in fact, running a state. Following the uprising in 1991, Kurdish forces were compelled to fill in the vacuum created by the withdrawal of the Iraqi government and its administration from the area (Aziz 2009; Ala'Aldeen 2013; Bengio 2012; Natali 2005; Stansfield 2005; Stansfield 2003). Reflecting on the situation until 2002, and contemplating whether the KRG functions as a state, Carver (2002, 73) observed, "Executive, legislative and judicial functions are practiced within the region in principle, by the KRG, the Kurdish National Assembly, and the court institutions. All of these are based upon the Iraqi Government model." In other words, the formation of the KRG in 1992 was not premeditated, nor was it the culmination of extensive planning or previous experiences in governance. As such, the idea of nationalism is concerned not with how but, instead, by whom the nation is governed. In this sense, as long as the Kurds run the KRG and there exists "a moral-political climate in which such centralized units are taken for granted and treated as normative," (Gellner 1983, 4), the Kurdish nationalist discourse does not seem to have fundamental reservations with the structure of the nation-state.

Second, the Kurdish nationalist reaction to the Ba'thist agenda does not mean that the Kurdish nation-state will necessarily be different from the Ba'thist Arab state, in as much as the post-colonial state is not fundamentally different from the colonial state. Nationalism has largely been utilized in post-colonial nations as a reaction to colonization and as a fulfillment of the nationalist principle of self-rule and self-determination (Mehrotra 1998). As Ashcroft, Griffiths, and Tiffin (1998, 154) argue, "the anti-colonial movements of the late nineteenth and early twentieth centuries" used the idea of the nation as a "resistant nationalism" and its formation as a paradigm for self-determination. However, "It was that force of nationalism that had fueled the growth of colonialism in the first place." Similarly, Ahmed (2015, 15) claims, "Postcolonialism itself is derived from Western colonialism." The resistant nationalism of post-colonial nations was, and still is, based on the same paradigm of the difference and distinction of the nation prior to the emergence of the colonial forces. However, it was not the recreation of a social form that existed in the pre-colonization but, rather, a post-colonial state that resembled the preceding colonial power. Thus, the anti-colonial discourse of nationalism reproduces the same discourse propagated by colonialism (Ashcroft, Griffiths, and Tiffin 1998). In other words, post-colonialist national movements have within them the force that enables the perpetuation of colonialism. "The degree to which [advocates of the post-colonial state] incorporated models and institutions based on the European concept of a nation created the continuing linkages that allowed the neo-colonialist control of these states to operate so effectively" (Ashcroft, Griffiths, and Tiffin 1998, 155). In this sense, as Ahmed (2015, 4) contends, "'Postcolonial' nationalism, through its exclusions and inclusions, is colonialism's heir."

Although nationalist arguments occasionally sound enticing and reasonable around the universal rights of nations for statehood, self-determination, and diversity of cultures, "nationalism has often not been so sweetly reasonable, nor so rationally symmetrical" (Gellner 1983, 2). Perhaps this is because the sentiments to which a nation adheres with its own nationalism are not necessarily the same or as prevalent as the nationalism of others. This discrepancy between the sentiments of different nationalisms becomes especially conspicuous when these nationalisms have conflicting political projects, as is evident between and within Middle Eastern nation-states (Ahmed

2015; Vali 2006; Natali 2005). The inconsistency in the nationalist sentiment can create spaces for exclusion and oppression, particularly since nationalism depends so much on the force of the political power, ideology, and hegemony encompassed in the institutions of the modern state. Furthermore, nationalists have a tendency to overlook the flaws in their own nationalisms (Gellner 1983; Soguk 1993), which can lead to the reproduction and perpetuation of oppression and the same injustices against one's nation. According to Mehrotra (1998), self-determination movements in the form of nationalism rarely result in establishing democratic states or the promotion of democratic values in non-democratic states. In fact, the nationalist self-determination discourse may very well destabilize the foundations of democracy. This is particularly relevant when the nation-state of the dominant ethnic group refuses "to grant equal rights to minority ethnic groups residing in its territory" (Mehrotra 1998, 834) and may result in the formation of racial, spatial and social hierarchies (Razack 2002). As a political and ideological doctrine, nationalism, therefore, can present major issues when it comes to upholding democratic principles of equity and inclusion as the foundations of social justice (Wahab 2017).

The KRG Educational System and Its Principal Problems

The above account, concerning the discourse of nationalism, evokes questions regarding the extent to which Kurdish self-governance in the Kurdistan Region has been engaged in imagining a nation without diversity, particularly since the KRG has progressed similarly to the Iraqi model toward building state institutions. In a study on education and nationalism in the Kurdistan Region's educational system, Abdullah[1] (2010) admits that the KRG has not fully departed from the Ba'ath regime's philosophy of undermining other religious and ethnic groups in school curricula, a view also confirmed by Kirmanj (2014). Abdullah (2010) claims that the current system cannot educate a generation that is nationalistic and patriotic, loves Kurdistan, and is aware of the culture of the Kurdish society. The educational system, Abdullah (2010, 201) claims, is not supportive of creating a national identity and sentiment among the Kurdish students. She recommends that the KRG educational system pay more attention to Kurdish nationalism, language, and culture, especially because of the considerable attention placed on foreign languages and cultures.[2] However,

---

[1] Chnar Saad Abdullah is a former MP in the Kurdistan Parliament and former KRG Minister of Martyrs and Anfal Affairs. She is a member of the leadership committee of the Kurdistan Democratic Party (KDP).
[2] Public educational institutions at both the K-12 and higher education levels in the Kurdistan Region are free. Tuition fees for private institutions are capped annually through an agreement between these institutions and the Ministries of Education and Higher Education in the KRG. These ministries implement educational

if we assume that the KRG educational system does not promote Kurdish nationalism and, as Abdullah (2010) suggests, that Kurdish students do not have a strong nationalist sense, it is relevant to ask how non-Kurdish residents, who are not even included in the public educational discourse, feel about their identity in relation to the Kurdistan Region. Aziz's (2009) study reveals that the non-Kurdish university students in the Kurdistan Region do not associate themselves with the Kurdistani identity that is promoted in the formal educational discourse. Abdullah's (2010) recommendation for a new philosophy of education that fits the Kurdistan Region—a proposal that resonates with the philosophy of many Kurdish educational critics and policymakers—is still based on a primordialist view of nationalism that is prevalent in KRG educational policy documents (Wahab 2017). The primordialist nationalist thinking is not very critical of itself, nor is it politically self-conscious. It simply swaps out one nationalism for another without critically examining the systemic implications of nationalism, particularly one that is based on the ethnocentric elements of the nation as the legitimating factor for establishing a nation-state. Kirmanj argues, "Since its creation in 1992, and in particular after 2005, the KRG has endeavored to use school curriculum as a linguistic, ideological, political, and cultural tool in keeping with the modernist interpretation of nation-building" (2014, 368). The modernist interpretation is evident in the pervasive focus on a centralized system of governance and the use of education as a tool to establish a particular national narrative (Wahab 2017).

Discussions of education and educational reform in Kurdistan have two main points of divergence. First is the inherent characteristics of education, schooling, and educational administration and how these characteristics are shaped and must be shaped by modern advances in social, political, and economic contexts and technologies, both globally and within the Kurdistan Region. The second point pertains to how education and schooling could impact the political, social, and economic aspirations of the Kurdistan Region. These two points have become the impetus for considering the nature and role of education in shaping the social, political, and economic realities that constitute the national identity of the Kurdistan Region. These discussions also appear as criticisms of the current schooling system in the Kurdistan Region, both in K-12 and higher education. These criticisms, from independent voices, educational leaders, and politicians, shed light on various issues in the educational system and processes in Kurdistan. Political and educational leaders

---

policies, mandates, and regulations and set standards governing the administration of educational institutions in the region.

as well as critics generally agree that some of these issues have been inherited from the historical development of formal education in Iraq, while some have emerged as a result of recent political, social, and economic developments in the Kurdistan Region (Abdullah 2010; Ala'Aldeen 2013; Saied 2008; Wahab 2014).

The educational issues in the Kurdistan Region of Iraq presented in these discussions can be categorized into (a) issues in the foundation of education, (b) issues in the system of educational administration, and (c) issues in the school practices.

The issues in the foundation of education relate to the theoretical, political, and cultural grounds on which education and schooling are based. Most of the criticism about education in the Kurdistan Region of Iraq associates the issues in the foundation of education with a lack of a Kurdish national educational vision and philosophy and with how this has shaped the course of formal education in the Kurdistan Region. Many critics agree that public education in Kurdistan is not predicated on a Kurdish national social, cultural, political, or economic vision (Abdullah 2010; Ala'Aldeen 2013; Omer 2014; Saied 2008; Shakely 2010). Shakely (2010) and Ala'Aldeen (2013) agree that the developments following the 1991 uprising did not radically impact the quality of social and cultural structures or people's everyday life; neither a radical shift nor a departure from the previous regime transpired. Similarly, radical changes did not take place in the foundations of education and schooling. According to Abdullah (2010) and Saied (2008), the educational system in Kurdistan has only witnessed minor, superficial changes and reforms and has not fundamentally departed from the previous system constructed by the Ba'th regime. This inability to deviate from the previous educational system became apparent once again in 2003 when the US invasion of Iraq led to the toppling of the Ba'th regime and changed the Iraqi governing system. After the invasion and the proclamation of the Kurdistan Region as a federal entity with its own legal administration in the new Iraqi constitution of 2005, an important opportunity for a radical change emerged in different sectors, not only in Iraq but also in the Kurdistan Region and particularly in education. The radical reform that was expected to unfold, however, did not take place. Saied (2008), Abdullah (2010), Shakely (2010), Omer (2014), and Omer (2015) agree that the absence of a national educational and cultural vision and philosophy has been the major reason for the failure of the Kurdish government to initiate radical reform in education and elsewhere in society. This has also prevented the KRG from establishing an inclusive policy that encompasses the foundations on which reform can take place. The criticism for not having a national vision and philosophy of education indicates that the educational system in Kurdistan is not reflective of the social, cultural, and political life in the region. It also accentuates concerns that developments in education represent the continuity of the Ba'thist educational and cultural philosophy, agenda, and system (Abdullah 2010; Ala'Aldeen 2013; Wahab 2013, 2014).

The issues in the administration of the educational system embody the processes, theories, and practices that shape the provision of formal education in the Kurdistan Region. These include problems in the structure, mechanisms, and techniques in the governing and administering of formal educational processes. And they relate to the laws, policies, standards, standardizations, administration, and school systems through which the foundations of education manifest themselves in the public and in formal educational and social discourses. Even though the Kurdistan Region has a democratic governing system in the sense that citizens have the rights to vote and to form political affiliations and political parties to compete in elections, the current education system still resembles those under dictatorships and totalitarian regimes (Abdullah 2010; Wahab 2014), particularly in their design and administration. Saied (2008) believes that the educational system in Kurdistan is a military system, which the Kurdish government has adopted and maintained from the old Iraqi regime without any significant modifications. It is a system that the British imposed on the Iraqis early in the twentieth century. This similarity is also manifest in how schools and universities are designed to look like military bases and prisons and how classroom practices and structures mirror those of military schools and training fields (Saied 2008; Wahab 2012, 2014). This entanglement in the Iraqi system is the result of major issues in the foundation of education indicated earlier as well as political and structural stagnation in Kurdistan. These two factors affecting the state of education are deeply intertwined. In maintaining the educational system, the Kurdish government has not deviated drastically from the previous Iraqi system, because the KRG has depended on the same theoretical foundations and systematic procedures that were utilized by the Iraqi Ba'thist regime.

The issues in the practices of schooling reflect the practices and dispositions that define the realities of education and schooling within educational institutions and society at large. These are the indicators of the society's social, political, cultural, and economic identities as a result of the educational practices, system, and discourse in the Kurdistan Region. These issues are decisive, not only in how schools are defined but also how foundational and systemic issues are cultivated within educational communities. Violence and harassment (Saied 2004, 2008); challenges for human rights, equality, and democracy (Wahab 2012; Osler and Yahya 2013); reliance on indoctrination, rote memorization, and unbalanced power relations between students and teachers (Saied 2008; Kirmanj 2014); and systemic oppression and exclusion from decision-making (Saied 2008; Wahab 2014) are among the principal issues in schooling practices in the Kurdistan Region.

A Framework for Progress

Surveying these issues provides information about the educational system to readers who are not closely involved with, or have not experienced, education in the Kurdistan Region. Critical engagement with educational issues elucidates the high stakes for these arguments and segues into introducing this chapter's primary focus, which is to provide a framework for assessing educational processes in the Kurdistan Region of Iraq more broadly and deeply than has generally taken place. Such a framework is imperative to verify the existence of these educational issues and, more importantly, to illustrate how educational policies and legislation are systemic reflections of the socio-political and socio-historical frameworks that have structured and driven educational communities in schools and society in the Kurdistan Region. In other words, I argue that it is necessary to look critically at the foundational claims of many educational leaders and critics who correlate the educational issues in the Kurdistan Region with the lack of a national educational philosophy and vision. Critical engagement means connecting issues such as the perpetuation of violence, oppression, and exclusion and their depth and complexity in the educational system to their larger socio-political and socio-historical contexts. This requires greater emphasis on the overarching circumstances in which these issues take shape. Critically examining the historical foundations, cultural realities, and political practices that deem the current theoretical foundations and principles indispensable is paramount. It is essential that we move beyond the assumption that these issues are merely isolated educational matters and investigate how people in the Kurdistan Region have established relationships, national identities, and governance within the modern nation-state paradigms.

The main argument that I present in this chapter entails an examination of the educational issues in relation to the processes of building a Kurdish state. This thesis asserts that, contrary to popular belief among educational critics, the KRG *has* a clear vision, which is the establishment of a Kurdish nation-state.

Such a pursuit involves a particular variety of modern state structures and institutions, including, for example, a centralized, top-down educational system. The educational system, particularly when based on an ethno-nationalist framework, inflicts violence and exclusion on society. This violence and exclusion become especially heightened when nationalism, as a political ideology, homogenizes and inculcates a particular identity through its educational system and other institutions so that the people fit into the predetermined modern state structure.

Examining KRG Educational Policy

By considering the Kurdish self-governing experience in the Kurdistan Region since 1992 in relation to the educational issues, I examined the political and systematic support that the KRG has presented in developing and maintaining the current educational system. In other words, I studied the organic relationship between the educational policies that have supported the current educational system and the Kurdish quasi-state in the Kurdistan Region, particularly on the path to independence.

I closely studied fifteen major documents, which consist of over one thousand pages of policy statements, reports, statistics, and charts, and include a variety of legislations, educational conferences, and strategic projects and plans, that the KRG has produced since 1992 (Wahab 2017). I adopted a critical document analysis as a form of textual survey to examine these materials. According to the *Sage Encyclopedia of Qualitative Research Methods*, "Textual analysis is a method of data analysis that closely examines either the content and meaning of texts or their structure and discourse." Textual analysis involves a deconstructive process of various forms of texts, including documents and their discourses, in order to "examine how they operate, the manner in which they are constructed, the ways in which meanings are produced, and the nature of those meanings" (Given 2008, 865). I approached these documents and examined their composition and history from a critical and theoretical perspective (Darder 2005; Darder, Baltodano, and Torres 2003; Peters, Lankshear, and Olssen 2003; Giroux 2003; Kincheloe 1999). A critical analysis ultimately focuses on "the impact of power relationships in human cultures" and exposes the distortions by social and political systems that "create in individuals a false consciousness that keeps them from seeing the real structure of society" (Willis 2007, 81).

While analyzing the policy documents, I did not take policies simply as texts isolated from the overall political and institutional context of the Kurdistan Region. That is why, in my analysis, I considered the political and institutional contexts in which such policies are envisioned and produced. Paying attention to the context and historical development of the documents reflects the critical aspect of my analysis, which includes a deconstructive element. The implication of the deconstructive approach in examining policy is that I consider the policy documents to be ideological products of their particular historical and political contexts rather than "blueprints of political action" (Codd 1988, 244). I also analyzed the areas in which language is used to mask unwanted social realities and political complexities. The analysis of the data focuses on questions of power and hegemony and the ways in which they are produced, maintained, and reinforced. According to Codd (1988), a deconstructive policy analysis means paying attention not only to the importance of contexts in policy processes but also the political nature of policy documents and its effects on those contexts.

Understanding the Educational Policies of the KRG

This analysis of the major educational policy documents highlights three main policy frameworks in the KRG educational system: (a) Kurdish nationalism, (b) democratization and (c) bureaucratization. These policy frameworks have intersected in the Kurdistan Region since 1992 within an overall social and political principle—the process of establishing a Kurdish nation-state in the Kurdistan Region (Wahab 2017).

The analysis of the documents produces two key, interrelated arguments. First, educational policymaking in the Kurdistan Region has perceived nationalism and democracy through the establishment of a modernist structure and submission to modernist tendencies in education. Second, political and educational leaders and policymakers in the Kurdistan Region view the current educational system and bureaucracy as reflective of their nationalist as well as democratic rhetoric. Together, these arguments mean that policymaking and reform initiatives in education have not been launched beyond the established policy frameworks and the current educational system in the Kurdistan Region. The national educational vision in the Kurdistan Region has maintained the institutional status quo mainly because educational leaders have not observed any significant discrepancy between the current educational system and the political project of establishing a nation-state. The analysis indicates that educational policies in the Kurdistan Region are overwhelmingly conceptualized through the establishment of a managerial discourse and economic utilization. The discourses and concepts used in the policies are mostly derived from managerial objectives at the expense of substantive and moral educational objectives. The discourse of school effectiveness, accountability, and standardization along with a minimalist, watered-down notion of democracy has become the bedrock for the dissemination of the Kurdish nationalist agenda in education. However, the discourses of business and management, instrumentalism, utilitarianism, and accountability pose serious challenges, particularly to democratic education. When the discourses of effectiveness, accountability, and "competitive individualism, the superiority of an unregulated market economy…and the necessity of consumption" become widespread, and when the belief in the neutrality of educational institutions "as an objective purveyor of truth" (Kincheloe 1999, 75) is taken for granted, a critical democratic educational discourse becomes necessary and must be used as a counterargument.

An analysis of the conference proceedings, legal documents, and policy statements and visions indicates that educational critics and policymakers in the Kurdistan Region have misconceptions about how the Ba'thist educational agenda has manifested itself in the KRG educational policies and system. Or perhaps the educational and political leaders have understood the power of the educational system in establishing the political agenda of the social, cultural, and economic elite. This approach to governance demonstrates an adherence to a de facto vision, especially since the bottom line of the Kurdish educational reform, particularly during the first decade following the establishment of the KRG, has been to consolidate the discourse of Kurdish ethnonationalism in conjunction with the political parties' control over the Kurdistan Region (Wahab 2017). It would be inaccurate to assume that educational reform processes in the Kurdistan Region do not consider the foundational principles of education. There have been major changes in these principles in the Kurdistan Region, but they have remained within the overarching paradigm of a nationalist education with the purpose of establishing a nation-state under a particular conception of democracy. Hence, the lack of a national comprehensive vision and policy for education in the Kurdistan Region, as many educational critics have assumed, should not mean that the educational process and system work in a theoretical and political vacuum. To the contrary, an analysis of major KRG educational documents reveals that the Region's educational system depends heavily on technical procedures that adherents of realpolitik in the region have favored since 1992. These procedures, nevertheless, have provided temporary, superficial, and ineffective solutions. Attempts at technical reform have not substantively improved the conditions that students, teachers, and their communities face. The foundations for educational and cultural mobilization in the Kurdistan Region have, in fact, been the theories, policies, and practices that have shaped the socio-political and socio-cultural identities and relationships of society and that continue to do so. The existing educational issues are the outcome of larger fundamental issues, such as educational, political, social, and economic frameworks, which deem the current educational system suitable for their own perpetuation.

Therefore, the relationships between issues of nationalism, democratization, and bureaucratization as well as the educational challenges in the Kurdistan Region of Iraq become clear through a critical analysis of the documents. Understanding this dialectic within, and in relation to, the institutional and political context of the Kurdistan Region provides not only a wider lens for exploring the state of the current educational system but also an opportunity to adopt and present a framework that transcends existing models in order to establish a more equitable and just society in the Kurdistan Region.

The Significance of the Critical Framework

The question we must ask regarding the fundamental educational issues is therefore not whether the educational system in the Kurdistan Region is based on a foundational or national vision or whether human rights codes are incorporated into national educational policies. Rather, what questions are most worth answering are under what circumstances we have envisioned our educational foundations and how we must examine these foundations. A critical, theoretical, and anti-oppressive pedagogical framework is paramount to answering these questions and understanding the relationships between the educational issues and the socio-political contexts in the Kurdistan Region. This framework entails a self-conscious critique of established theories and practices in society and a commitment to reveal the often-concealed oppressive tendencies within social and political structures and relationships with the aim of empowering people to transform their oppressive conditions.

However, the critical theoretical framework does not entail a total rejection of nationalism. As such, the critique of nationalism in this chapter is not an orthodox Marxist take, for instance, because it does not completely reject nationalism as a camouflage for the domination and reproduction of the capitalist class. I critically examine, in general, the political reality of nationalism and, in particular, that of Kurdish ethno-nationalism as well as their implications in education. Espousing a critical theoretical framework necessarily dictates focus on the oppressive features and totalitarian tendencies of modern nationalism and its educational system. A critical theoretical approach to education understands schools not only as "capitalist agencies of social, economic, cultural and bureaucratic reproduction" but also as "venues of hope" and "sites of resistance and democratic possibility" (Kincheloe 1999, 71). A critical understanding of democracy involves a critical consciousness of the historical connection between democracy, imperialism, and colonialism. And it uses this consciousness to subvert the oppressive tendencies in liberal democracy, which is thin, institutional, transnational, corporate and market-friendly, for a robust notion of democracy as a way of life, involving the human connections within and among communities and the totality of being. Similarly, the critical theoretical framework in this chapter presents a radical view of nationalism and provides valuable knowledge in this regard. Critical knowledge on nationalism, particularly on Kurdish nationalism in the Kurdistan Region, would resonate with Giroux's (2003, 50) elaboration of "a radical view of knowledge":

> It would be knowledge that would instruct the oppressed about their situation as a group situated within specific relations of domination and subordination. It would be knowledge that would illuminate how the oppressed could develop a discourse free from the distortions of their own partly mangled cultural inheritance. On the other hand, it would be a form of knowledge that instructs the oppressed in how to appropriate the most progressive dimensions of their own cultural histories, as well as how to restructure and appropriate the most radical aspects of bourgeois culture. Finally, such knowledge would have to provide a motivational connection to action itself; it would have to link a radical decoding of history to a vision of the future that not only exploded the reifications of the existing society, but also reached into those pockets of desires and needs that harbored a longing for a new society and new forms of social relations .

Critical theory presents a radical view of knowledge that has profound implications for the oppressed to transform themselves and their situation. In this way, critically understanding the dialectic of nationalism empowers people to act on and transform nationalism. It is with this objective that the concept of "transformative democracy" (Wahab 2017) becomes particularly significant in education.

Transformative democracy focuses on establishing democratic relationships based on robust notions of equity, inclusion, strong participation, and action so that all social and political relationships become opportunities for transformative education. It empowers individuals and communities to transform undemocratic dispositions, attitudes, conditions, and relationships into more democratic ones. At the same time, transformative democracy is fully aware that nationalism and critical democracy can be substantively different in forming people's identities and relationships. It is fundamentally critical of the ideological content and oppressive processes of national identity-formation and the nationalist political projects that reinforce colonial and oppressive attitudes and conditions. With these prominent characteristics, transformative democracy, as a fundamentally educative process, presents a critical understanding of democracy that offers more, rather than less, for individuals and communities to support their endeavors for a fuller and more meaningful life. Unlike political nationalism as an ideology, transformative democracy creates structures based on cultivating and promoting democratic values and relationships rather than appropriating people's identities to conform to predetermined social and political configurations. Education according to the principles of transformative democracy involves theorizing, viewing, and educating beyond the conventional institutions of formal education and represents a radical transformation of modern schooling structures. Therefore, an education that is anti-oppressive, inclusive, and responsive to individual, community, and environmental rights and potentials must rely on the principles of critical democracy. As Dei (2013, 53) aptly elaborates, "Critical democratic education can play a vital role in helping to create, build, and nurture the 'social publics' in terms of sustainable human capacities and capabilities that engage all learners in the political and social processes of schooling and education ." Transformative democracy aims to transform the ideological principles of national belonging and sentiments that are promoted in "nationalism of identities" in order to establish and promote a democratic "nationalism of relationships."

This chapter presents information, knowledge, and critical insights on the state of education and the trajectory of educational processes in the Kurdistan Region since 1992. The perspective from which I presented this critical knowledge is unique considering not only the limited volume of data and information about the KRG educational system in Kurdish and other languages, but also the critical overarching quality in which I analyzed the documents and developed the main arguments. The thesis I presented in this chapter concerns the educational system as well as the political and social systems in the Kurdistan Region. Regional and international interest in the Kurdistan Region of Iraq has recently grown in an unprecedented manner, and the literature on Kurdish nationalism, Kurdish self-governance, and the prospects of an independent Kurdish state has grown considerably. However, many studies on Kurdish nationalism and state-building processes in the Kurdistan Region seem to have underestimated, neglected, or overlooked the role of education in shaping these processes. Such studies usually only consider the history of Kurdish nationalism and the political and economic conditions that have helped shape and direct it.[3] Regarding perspective and scope, these studies adopt pervasive political and economic frameworks in order to understand Kurdish politics. They offer suggestions that are mostly directed to the political elite concerning top-level policy adjustments, technical efficiency in governance, and economic utilization. As such, critical, qualitative research concerning the type of education and its theoretical and political frameworks in the Kurdistan Region are not abundant. By critically examining macro-level educational policies in relation to their social and political implications in schools and society, I not only show and critique the dominant frameworks of policymaking and governance but also suggest that pervasive technical-rationalist approaches to educational, social, and political reform and restructuring can only have limited and rhetorical rather than substantive implications. Although my position as a researcher—situated outside or, at most, at the margins of the educational bureaucracy in the Kurdistan Region—has empowered me with the opportunity to present a more critical analysis, it is less likely that my recommendations in this chapter will impact the immediate policy processes in the Kurdistan Region (Taylor et al. 1997). Nevertheless, this chapter has substantive and long-term implications for educational, social, and political theory as well as for policy and practices in the Kurdistan Region and beyond.

Implications of the Critical Framework

The main argument and findings presented in this chapter can constitute the foundation to rethink education not only in the Kurdistan Region but also in the greater Middle East and elsewhere in the world. Given the main argument, and based on the concluding remarks, which stress the significance of democratic relationships as the main educational framework that could lead to a more equitable and just society in the Kurdistan Region, I present in this

---

[3] Most of the publications referenced in this chapter on Kurdish nationalism, history, and politics in the Kurdistan Region of Iraq are examples that support this claim.

chapter a number of implications for teachers and teacher-education programs.

Implications for Teachers

The main implication for teachers is to reconsider their position as developers and sustainers of the democratic spirit both in schools and society. Teachers must view themselves as democratic agents who are engaged in democratic practices. Democratic practices in education are based on, develop, and promote core democratic values and conditions. The promotion of principles such as justice; moral seriousness; social commitment; critical, coherent and moral reasoning and capacities; choice; fairness; inclusion; and transformation is imperative for a democratic educational process. While the knowledge and skills in any school course is important, it is significant that teachers' overall goals are based on cultivating the democratic moral values in themselves, their students, and their social and institutional environments. For instance, teachers must consider the promotion of justice and moral seriousness as both standard values and principles in their teaching as well as standards for other purposes of schooling, such as training, economic preparation, and the acquisition of skills, as long as they are achieved within the moral purpose of education.

Democratic teachers understand that, while knowledge and skills are basic requirements of democratic processes, they alone cannot uphold the critical democratic spirit without integrating critical thinking as a central feature. By critical thinking, I am referring to a social, political, and cultural disposition, rather than simply a set of technical skills. Critical thinking, as such, entails not only answering questions from different points of view but also asking critical questions about the systemic implications of knowledge in relation to power, authority, and domination. Democratic teachers educate their students based on the conviction that critical thinking turns the knowledge and skills into dynamic processes so that they resist rigidity and stagnation. In an ideal democratic classroom, the critical interaction between students and teachers through the use of knowledge leads to a substantive expansion and transformation of this knowledge. It becomes "a kind of knowledge that is not just propositional but is empathic and based in experience" (Bai 2001, 318). Through a critical transformation, instead of simply reducing it to empirical input for established theories, knowledge also becomes "a standpoint from which to question the validity of the theories themselves" (Graham 2001, 161). Accordingly, a democratic teacher challenges and prevents indoctrination, in its place encourages open and public deliberation, and cooperates with students in conscious action to subvert systemic oppressive environments.

Glickman (1998) refers to a number of studies conducted on the impact of democratic pedagogies on students' learning and achievement, and he concludes that democratic pedagogies positively impact student engagement. According to Glickman (1998, 52), "Those teachers and schools that define democracy as participatory and community-oriented appear to have much greater success with all their students." Democratic educators encourage participatory learning, which not only engages students in understanding the relational nature of critical knowledge but also fosters a growth of knowledge by providing a host of various stimulations. "Diversity of stimulation means novelty, and novelty means challenge to thought," Dewey (1915, 91) argues. "The more activity is restricted to a few definite lines—as it is when there are rigid class lines preventing adequate interplay of experiences—the more action tends to become routine ."

Democratic teachers understand that democratic education is not only concerned with teaching these values but also with teaching them democratically. That is why this form of education depends on democratic pedagogies, which aim for and depend on such values as active, participatory, associative, and mutual learning; choice; responsibility; sharing; contribution; application; and public participation in deliberation and action, on both the individual and collective levels. The transformation of knowledge into critical consciousness is also at the core of critical pedagogy, corresponding to a freeing process of self-reflection and empowerment. Critical consciousness as a moral political objective eventually means that teachers strive to educate themselves, their students, and society in order to critically resist and prevent knowledge from becoming a tool for oppression (Kincheloe 1999).

Implications for Teacher-Education Programs

By upholding the principles of transformative democracy and its implications for teaching, teacher-education programs can become a key element for initiating a transformative educational process in the Kurdistan Region and beyond. Preparing democratic teachers requires a program that can become the environment in which a robust democracy emerges. Educating and preparing teachers in the manner of strong democracy mean focusing on student teachers' creativity and consensus through "common talk, common decision, and common work" (Cunningham 2002, 131). In a democratic teacher-education program, student teacher citizens become active participants in transforming their practice through critical, political awareness of what it means to be a teacher. Such programs are fundamentally opposed to prescribed technique-based teacher-education curricula that are imposed from above and remove teachers from the equation (Thomas 2005).

Teachers should be directly involved in designing teacher-education programs. Dewey (1946) considers the act of teaching as more intellectually demanding than participating in administrative decision-making. Nondemocratic processes of designing teacher-education programs present a contradiction with the assumption that teachers who are deemed unfit to participate in decision-making are, conversely, capable of implementing the result of these decisions.

Educational policies for teacher education in the Kurdistan Region of Iraq do not deviate from the conception of teachers as conveyors of the curriculum content. This is why teacher-education programs in the Kurdistan Region have focused on the knowledge of course content and methods of transferring textbook information to the students. Teacher-education programs should focus not on producing skilled teachers but, instead, on preparing and supporting professional democratic educators. A teacher-education program that aims to prepare democratic teachers must be predicated on the significance of the democratic powers, dispositions, and skills that support transformative social and political action. In other words, the most significant purpose of a democratic teacher-education program is to empower teachers in their endeavors in order to promote social justice, which cannot be fully achieved without encapsulating a robust notion of critical, reflective thinking and action. It is crucial, for a transformative democratic teacher-education program, that critical thinking is not confused with a set of technical-rationalist thinking and teaching skills and methods, which maintain and occur within a positivist, apolitical knowledge paradigm. Rather, critical thinking in a teacher-education program aims to nurture relationships between teachers and their communities in a subject-to-subject manner so that they transform their own circumstances and those of their students in schools and communities.

The implications of a democratic framework in education, as presented in this chapter, underscores the significance of youth in shaping the future of the Kurdistan Region. While educational policies concern the overall social stratification, the role that youth can play in directing educational policy, both as policymakers and policy implementers, demonstrates the need for greater youth involvement in the policy processes. Democratic educational policymaking in the Kurdistan Region requires that youth assume a leading role in manifesting the praxis of democracy in schools and society and reinvigorate their position as both the foundation and the drive of educational reform initiatives. Therefore, the implications presented in this chapter position the youth of the Kurdistan Region, as teachers and teacher educators, at the center of substantive and sustainable educational policymaking for social, political, and economic reform.

References

Abdullah, Chnar Saad. 2010. *Perwerde w Netewayety* [Education and Nationalism]. Aras Publishing.
Ahmed, Hawzhen Rashadaddin. 2015. *"Internal Orients": Literary Representations of Colonial Modernity and the Kurdish "Other" in Turkey, Iran and Iraq*. Leicester: University of Leicester.
Ala'Aldeen, Dlawer. 2013. *Nishtimansazy w Systemy Farmanrewayetyi Khomaly le Haremy Kurdistan* [Nation Building and the System of Self-Governance in the Kurdistan Region]. Aras Publishing.
Ashcroft, Bill, Gareth Griffiths, and Helen Tiffin. 1998. *Key Concepts in Post-Colonial Studies*. London: Routledge.
Aziz, Mahir Abdulwahid. 2009. *Ethno-Nationalism in a De Facto State: An Investigation of National Identity among University Students in the Kurdistan Region of Iraq*. Exeter: University of Exeter.
Bai, Heesoon. 2001. "Cultivating Democratic Citizenship: Towards Intersubjectivity." In *Philosophy of Education: Introductory Readings*, 3rd ed. edited by W. Hare and J. P. Portelli, 307–19. Detselig Enterprises Ltd.
Bengio, Ofra. 2012. *The Kurds of Iraq: Building a State Within a State*. Boulder, CO: Lynne Rienner Publishers, Inc.
Carver, Natasha. 2002. "Is Iraq/Kurdistan a state such that it can be said to operate state systems and thereby offer protection to its 'citizens'?" *International Journal of Refugee Law* 14 (1): 57–84.
Codd, John A. 1988. "The Construction and Deconstruction of Educational Policy Documents." *Journal of Education Policy* 3 (3): 235–47.
Cunningham, Frank. 2002. *Theories of Democracy: A Critical Introduction*. London: Routledge
Darder, Antonia. 2005. "What is Critical Pedagogy?" *Key Questions for Educators*: 90–94.
Darder, Antonia, Marta Baltodano, and Rodolfo D. Torres. 2003. "Critical Pedagogy: An Introduction." In *The Critical Pedagogy Reader*: 1-21.
Dei, George Sefa. 2013. "Democratic education: Thinking out differently." *Educating for Democratic Consciousness: Counter-hegemonic Possibilities*: 50–67.
Dewey, John. 1915. *Democracy and Education: An Introduction to the Philosophy of Education* (Indian Ed.). Aakar Books.
Dewey, John. 1946. *Problems of Men*. New York: Philosophical Library, Inc.
Eriksen, Thomas Hylland. 2010. *Ethnicity and Nationalism: Anthropological Perspectives*. Pluto Press
Gellner, Ernest. 1983. *Nations and Nationalism*. Ithaca: Cornell University Press.
Giroux, Henry A. 2003. "Critical Theory and Educational Practice." *The Critical Pedagogy Reader*: 27–56.
Given, Lisa M., ed. 2008. *The Sage Encyclopedia of Qualitative Research Methods*. Los Angeles: Sage Publications.
Glickman, Carl. 1998. "Educational Leadership for Democratic Purpose: What Do We Mean?" *International Journal of Leadership in Education Theory and Practice* 1 (1): 47–53.
Graham, Kevin. 2001. "Participatory democracy in an age of global capitalism." *The Problems of Resistance: Studies in Alternate Political Cultures*: 155–68.
Gunter, Michael M. 2013. "The contemporary roots of Kurdish nationalism in Iraq." *Kufa Review*, 2 (1): 29–47.
Kincheloe, Joe. 1999. "Critical Democracy and Education." In *Understanding Democratic Curriculum*

Leadership, edited by James G. Henderson and Kathleen R. Kesson, 70–83. New York: Teachers College Press.

Kirmanj, Sherko. 2014. "Kurdish History Textbooks: Building a Nation-State within a Nation-State." *Middle East Journal* 68 (3): 367–384.

Mehrotra, O. N. 1998. "Ethno-Nationalism in the Contemporary World." *Strategic Analysis* 22 (6): 829–840.

Natali, Denise. 2005. *The Kurds and the State: Evolving National Identity in Iraq, Turkey, and Iran*. Syracuse, NY: Syracuse University Press.

Omer, Khalid. 2015. *Zanko Lenewan Naw w Nawerokda* [The University Between Name and Essence]. Karo Publishing .

Omer, Serwer. 2014. *101 Grifty Perwerde* [101 Issues in Education].

Osler, Audrey, and Chalank Yahya. 2013. "Challenges and Complexity in Human Rights Education: Teachers' Understandings of Democratic Participation and Gender Equity in Post-conflict Kurdistan-Iraq." *Education Inquiry* 4 (1): 189–210.

Peters, Michael, Colin Lankshear, and Mark Olssen. 2003. "Introduction: Critical Theory and the Human Condition." *Critical Theory and the Human Condition: Founders and Praxis*: 1–14.

Razack, Sherene. 2002. "When Place Becomes Race." *Race, Space and the Law*: 1–20.

Romano, David. 2006. *The Kurdish Nationalist Movement: Opportunity, Mobilization and Identity*. Cambridge: Cambridge University Press.

Saied, Faiek. 2004. *Tekshkani Behakani Khwendkar* [Destruction of the Pupil's Values]. Ranj Publishing.

———. 2008. *Qutabkhanekan Rwyan le Qibla Niye* [The Schools are not Facing Qibla]. Aras Publishing.

Shakely, Farhad. 2010. *Ke Bazine w Lakeshekan Heldeweshenewe* [When the Circles and Rectangles Dismantle]. Aras Publishing.

Soguk, Nevzat. 1993. "Reflections on the 'Orientalized Orientals.'" *Alternatives: Global, Local, Political* 18 (3): 361–384.

Stansfield, Gareth. 2003. *Iraqi Kurdistan: Political Development and Emergent Democracy*. New York: Routledge.

———. 2005. "Governing Kurdistan: The Strengths of Division." In *The Future of Kurdistan in Iraq*, edited by Brendan O'Leary, John McGarry, and Khaled Salih, 195–218. Philadelphia: University of Pennsylvania Press.

Taylor, Sandra, Fazal Rizvi, Bob Lingard, and Miriam Henry. 1997. *Educational Policy and the Politics of Change*. London: Routledge .

Thomas, Sue. 2005. "Taking Teachers Out of the Equation: Construction of Teachers in Education Policy Documents Over a Ten-year Period." *The Australian Educational Researcher* 32 (3): 45–62.

Vali, Abbas. 2006. "The Kurds and their 'Others': Fragmented Identity and Fragmented Politics." In *The Kurds: Nationalism and Politics* , edited by Faleh A. Jabar and Hosham Dawod, 49–78. London: Saqi.

Wahab, Abdurrahman Ahmad. 2017. "Education in Kurdistan Region at the intersection of nationalism and democracy." PhD diss.

———. 2012. "Literary theory and teaching democracy in a post-dictatorial era." *Radical Teacher* 94: 48–57.

———. 2003. "Helwashandnewey diktatoriyet le prosey perwerdey Kurdistanda" [Dismantling despotism in the Kurdistan educational process]. *Le Monde Deplomatique (Kurdish)*: 4–5.

———. 2014. *Meley Dijerewt: Parwerde le Rwangeyeky Rekhnegranewe* [Swimming Upstream: Education from a Critical Lens]. Karo Publishing .

Willis, Jerry W. 2007. *Foundations of Qualitative Research: Interpretive and Critical Approaches*. Thousand Oaks, CA: SAGE.

CHAPTER 8

MAKING HEAVEN IN A SHITHOLE: CHANGING POLITICAL ENGAGEMENT IN THE AFTERMATH OF THE ISLAMIC STATE

Lana Askari

This chapter draws out how Kurdish youth frame and retain hope for the future through political engagement, despite their ongoing disappointment in Iraqi Kurdish parties. By situating Kobanî and the Rojava Revolution as "critical events" in the Kurdish imagining, this chapter focuses on how, in the aftermath of the fight against the Islamic State (IS), multiple new perspectives on confronting uncertainty emerged through political engagement among youth in the Kurdistan Region of Iraq (KRI). I argue that the war against IS and the mobilization of Kurdish forces created new spaces for young Kurds to imagine and work toward changing social and political structures in KRI that were centered on social inclusion, diversity, and gender equality. Based on fieldwork conducted in the city of Silêmanî between 2015 and 2016, I explore two types of political engagement amongst youth. First, I explore social activism as political engagement in the context of a post-conflict region through the story of Azad, a student who seeks to improve society through the promotion of the multiethnic, multicultural, and multireligious make up of Iraq. Second, through a Kurdish returnee and former guerrilla fighter named Hoshyar, I discuss how the ongoing Kurdish political struggle has changed militarized political engagement among Kurdish youth due to new transnational ties with the diaspora and Western audiences.[1]

> In Rojava, they say that "they made a heaven in a shithole." You see those guys and girls fighting together, you read their laws and rules. You see how they are saving people in this big fight. (Hoshyar, twenty-one-year-old guerrilla fighter)

BANG! A loud boom shook our teacups. "Don't worry, they're at least four kilometers from us," Heval Homer said.[2] Homer, a guerrilla fighter stationed at

---
[1] All the names of interviewees mentioned in this chapter are pseudonyms.
[2] Heval, meaning friend or comrade, is used as a prefix to address someone. It can be used as a standalone address, but when familiar with the person, it is followed by one's first or given nickname. The guerrilla

Makhmour camp, had welcomed us at the entrance and taken us to a small garden outside of the house they used for meetings and teaching—a white one-story building.[3] It was a crisp April morning when we arrived, but the heat was rising as the sun climbed higher in the sky. Commenting on the differences between our tea-drinking rituals, our hosts first poured hot water into the cups and then added the concentrated boiled tea. "Here people put tea and then hot water," Heval Ranj said. "We do it differently." We continued discussing the differences between *Bakur* (Southeast Turkey) and *Bashur* (Kurdistan Region of Iraq) and between the Kurdish dialects of Sorani and Kurmanji. None seemed bothered about the loud bangs, so we resumed our conversation as others handled the IS fighters, who would periodically shell the camp's outskirts. The Hevals showed us their garden filled with pomegranate and fig trees, which were in bloom. The triviality of drinking tea in the garden juxtaposed with the tumultuous shelling seemed to offer everyone some sort of distraction. But the conversation soon turned back to the war, as Heval Homer mentioned that women from the IS territories would often find a way to escape and cross the front line to find shelter with them here. Straight away, Heval Ranj started talking about democratic federalism and Apo's (Öcalan) ideology: "Europe is a mechanical society where people are not close to nature. Here we do it differently."

Earlier that day, we had made it all the way down to Makhmour. We had passed the oilfields and pipelines next to the road from Kirkuk as well as the exit leading to Mosul, which was blocked off at the time. Those manning the many checkpoints set up by the Kurdistan Democratic Party (KDP) all commented laughingly on why we—two academics and a student—were visiting the Makhmour camp for Öcalan's birthday. "Are you going to have a party?" Azad, a student from Silêmanî, invited us to join him as he was going to

---

fighters in this region also address themselves and others in this way.

[3] The Makhmour camp houses about twelve thousand people from Bakur who were expelled from Turkey in the 1990s. The camp is located adjacent to the city of Makhmour, south of Hêwler (Erbil). While the refugee camp originally received aid from the UN, it had become self-ruled when the Kurdistan's Workers Party (PKK) guerrilla took it over when Kurdish Regional Government (KRG) Peshmerga fled from IS in 2014. The PKK is a militant and political organization based in Turkey and Iraq. Established in the 1970s, the PKK has been involved in an armed conflict with the Turkish state. The PKK is listed as a terrorist organization by several states and organizations, including NATO and the EU, but not by the UN. Abdullah Öcalan, the party leader, has been imprisoned in Turkey since 1999 on grounds of leading a terrorist organization, Kurdish uprising, and separatism against the Turkish state. Kurds are not recognized by the Turkish state as an ethnic minority and the suppression of Kurds in Turkey included a ban of the Kurdish language, dress, names, and culture. Some rules were loosened as Turkey made reforms to join the EU in the past decade and peace talks were held between the Turkish state and the PKK (2013–2015). However, following the rise of the Democratic Union Party (PYD) in Rojava, Northern Syria and the coup d'état in Turkey in 2016, relations have deteriorated.

visit his friend, Heval Homer, for the festival on April 4 in celebration of Öcalan's birthday. On the way to the camp, we talked about Azad's troubled relationship with the local Kurdish political parties, which he views as oppressors, and how he wants to overcome this. Anticipating an exchange trip to India to receive training for youth from conflict areas, he said he would get to meet the Dalai Lama and tell him about the Kurds. Questioning that the Dalai Lama might be bad for Tibet, as their nonviolent movement has failed to liberate them, Azad jokingly said he would go there and convince them of armed struggle and Öcalan's ideas.

Image 1. The stage at Makhmour camp with posters commemorating martyred guerrilla fighters. (Photo: Lana Askari 2016).

After we finished our tea with the Hevals, we headed toward the festival area. The houses in the camp were different from usual brick houses in Bashur that were often covered in tiles. Painted white, the homes here formed a labyrinth of small streets that crept up like an old village—a microcosm inside Iraqi Kurdistan. Reaching an amphitheater with a stage in front and rows of sloped seating that sloped upward, we saw children from the local school marching into the square wearing Kurdish clothes and guerrilla outfits and waving different political flags of the PKK and the PYD. Children performed *halparke* or *govend*, traditional circle dancing, in front of posters of martyrs and Öcalan's face. It was well rehearsed, but the militarized performances by children prompted me and a fellow researcher to discuss its problematic nature. Azad, trying not to criticize them, answered jokingly, "Try teaching Bashuri kids this, they have no discipline."

On the drive back after the festival, I asked Azad about his views. If he was visiting the Hevals, does that mean he shares their thoughts and convictions? Azad said he did not like to talk too much or discuss political issues with Heval Ranj, for example, who was very intense on the subject of their ideology during our visit. "Some of them are like that, they just repeat everything exactly from Apo's books. I don't go against them and debate them on these points, but they don't think for themselves. Everything you say, they respond by going back and reciting the exact writings." Azad explained that he was in solidarity with them on a personal level. Azad had brought some Kurdish films that day—illegal copies from the Silêmanî market—that Homer had asked for so that he could listen and practice his Sorani.

We discussed Azad's relationship with the PKK, whose events he frequently attended. He emphasized that when he was in school, people used to tell stories about how the PKK was involved in bestiality and would abduct children at night to train them in their camps. Azad poked fun at these accusations: "Local political parties spread these rumors to keep people attached to them in the 1990s." Through his friend Heval Homer, whom he had met at a political protest the year before, Azad kept in personal contact with the guerrilla fighters located in Bashur. A Sorani speaker, he taught himself Badini, the Iraqi Kurdish dialect of Kurmanji, which was spoken by the Kurdish people in southeast Turkey ("Bakur") and northeast Syria ("Rojava"). This gave him the opportunity to converse easily with speakers of both dialects. What became clear from this day was that while Azad stood in solidarity with this Kurdish movement, he did so by investing in personal ties with the guerrilla fighters and maintaining space to criticize blind adherents of the PKK's ideology.

Critical Events and New Imaginations

In 2015, the liberation of the city of Kobanî, located in Rojava, from IS resonated deeply among the Kurdish population of the KRI and northeastern Syria (NES). Although the political ties between Iraqi Kurdistan and Syrian Kurdistan fluctuate in a struggle for power, the name Kobanî, among others, produced a transnational solidarity movement in different Kurdish cities that appeared in murals, restaurants, hair salons and infants named after the liberated city. The city was soon elevated in status to symbol of hope and Kurdish resistance. When, in 2016, the different parties ruling northern Syria united under the Democratic Federation of Northern Syria (DFNS) and declared themselves as an autonomous region, the news was welcomed in the context of this solidarity movement across Kurdistan, the diaspora, and the wider leftist international community.⁴

The PKK and PYD have in recent years promulgated Öcalan's ideas, with its practical implementation by the PYD in Rojava. The ideology incorporates notions of environmentalism, intra-ethnic and gender equality, and a form of feminism called "jinology" in which women are active participants in both fighting and decision-making bodies (Gunes 2012). Furthermore, the intra-ethnic and multireligious aspects of the ideology have been incorporated into local governmental practices in Rojava, where different ethnic and religious groups are represented. These cross-border relations also increased transnational ties throughout the diaspora, and democratic ties with the EU and NGOs culminated with a newly developed and imagined Kurdish community (Černy 2017; Kardaş and Yesiltaş 2017; Natali 2004; Tekdemir 2018). These ideals are something to which the Kurdistan Regional Government (KRG) has only paid lip service internally. Regionally, but also differing ideologically, the Iraqi Kurdish parties historically incorporated socialist ideas but have abandoned most of these notions in recent years. The Peshmerga forces, its army that fought a guerrilla war in previous decades, are now a state-funded and Western-trained military.⁵

When does an event become critical, and who makes this designation? Few people outside of Rojava had heard of Kobanî, situated on the border between Syria and Turkey. But its liberation was a turning point in terms of conceptualizing the type of future that could exist for greater Kurdistan, a region which encompasses not only Iraqi Kurds but also Syrian Kurds who were amassing greater autonomy in the Middle East. Das and Singh (1995, 5–6) define critical events as those that subsequently create new modes of action or radical social transformation. Within the context of sexual and reproductive violence after the partition of India, they put forward how critical events reveal the contingent nature of the world and make people rethink their own position and how they can assert power over that uncertainty. Following the work of Turner and Gluckman, Kapferer (2015, 10, 18) argues that events should be

---

⁴ Critical of capitalism, ethnic differentiation, and patriarchy, the PYD's democratic confederalism draws inspiration from post-national and feminist discourses that are inspired by Öcalan's writings and understanding of political thinker Murray Bookchin. The ideological basis of this anarchic democratic autonomy and its practical implementation has been questioned by some. Leezenberg (2016), for example, highlights a break from Bookchin on the struggle for militarized self-defense as well as the hierarchical Leninist and Stalinist cult tradition around Öcalan himself as being problematic.

⁵ The Peshmerga, literally translating as "those who face death," were the former Kurdish guerilla fighters who in the past decade have transformed into the military forces of the federal region of Iraqi Kurdistan. While they are ruled by the KRG, in reality, the forces are divided between the Kurdish Democratic Party (KDP) and the Patriotic Union of Kurdistan (PUK).

seen as constructions to which people attach different meanings or significance: They are moments of significance that alter how ongoing events are linked and understood, instead using the phrase "generative moment." While historical events are situated in a common narrative by societies or state actors, events themselves are processual and their interpretations multiple—they change over time. Both terms are useful concepts, but Das and Singh's critical event points to the significance of the event in its own right and point in time, while Kapferer's interpretation compels us to more thoroughly consider the generative aspect of a moment or event. Following both interpretations, I argue that the siege of Kobanî can be seen as a critical event within Rojava and across the other regions of Kurdistan in that it redefined the role of Kurdish forces in the war against IS and traditional categories of Kurdish (female) guerrilla fighters. It was generative in that it opened up new horizons for Kurds to imagine the implementation of progressive social and political systems. It was potent enough to enable new conceptualizations of what the world—or Kurdistan—could look like.

Image 2. Screenshot from "Bridge to Kobane" (dir. Lana Askari, UK, 2016). Rojava Rally in Silêmanî, Iraqi Kurdistan. The rally was covered by more journalists than actual people attending the celebration.

The liberation of Kobanî was appropriated by the wider Kurdish nationalist movement as a symbol of hope and resistance against a common enemy. In following this common narrative, a heightened moment of solidarity, perhaps even unity, existed among different Kurdish populations. The actual situation of Kobanî and the future of its population, obscured by this symbolic narrative and the recent Turkish invasion in Rojava, has perhaps lessened the strength of this symbolism today. However, as a critical event in the Kurdish history, it led people to reimagine the world and the Kurdish region differently, with greater ideas of independence, self-rule, or progress.

Seeing future paths through these "critical" events can be disorienting, and leaving events unexplained can be existentially disruptive when they cause a rupture between what one knows and expects (Irving 2017). Public discourses of anticipating uncertainty (Hermez 2012; Hermez 2017) or conflating various disastrous events with the political (Schäfers 2016) help us to consolidate uncertainty or future insecurity. Crises and periods of precarity have been seen as enabling (Vigh 2008) and productive for rethinking common narratives (Roitman 2013). Scholars have argued that by constructing narratives through storytelling around the precariousness of crisis, one can understand a new situation, enabling forms of agency in oneself (Jackson 2008). As Carr argues, "Narrative is our primary way of organizing our experience of time." Following phenomenological thought on the experience of time, he posits that narrative is unable to represent life—it is a product of imagination and forces events of the past into a particular shape (1991, 45). However, this structuring of time and events into narrative form is one way to live in time by confronting it, to come to terms with change, development, and temporal chaos (181–84). Events can then be understood as processual and multifaceted; they reveal history not as fact but as an ongoing process, and different people put them into myriad narrative forms in an attempt to make sense of their lives. Thus, while I argue that Kobanî and the Rojava Revolution became critical events in that it made space for an alternative way of interpreting how the future will unfold, it also generated discrete interpretations and imaginations of that future for different people.

Sustainable Peace Through Inclusion: The Challenges of Youth Activism

Azad was often fully dressed in traditional Kurdish clothes whenever he would go out. I was having drinks with him one evening at a shisha cafe in Silêmanî's city center when he mentioned his disillusionment with the government and how youth were unable to move on with their lives. "Life in the KRG is boring. After graduating there are no jobs for us, so I'm going to find other things to do, find internships abroad."[6] I asked him how he was spending his time, and he said that he had been actively participating in workshops as well as political and social events at the university, learning more about NGOs and post-conflict issues. The worsening fight against IS and the economic crisis in Iraqi Kurdistan had prompted him to start making friends from different backgrounds in the region and putting what he heard into practice. He saw the fight against IS and the current system in Rojava in relation to his personal goals to consolidate the multiethnic, multicultural, and multireligious make up of society in the region. Originally from the city of Kirkuk himself, Azad linked the Rojava ideals to his personal experiences in the ethnically diverse city. In the aftermath of an ongoing (post-)conflict situation, he wanted to discuss how ruptures between different ethnic groups could be avoided.

Influenced by discourses of peacebuilding, after his graduation in 2016 Azad set up a youth-led peace organization for religious and ethnic minorities in the Middle East. He started organizing cultural events where the multiethnic and multireligious groups in the KRI are represented in different cities across the region. At these events, youth are asked to participate by dressing in their traditional attire and teaching each other about their cultural heritage. More importantly, the organization seeks to create a youth community that can engage in dialogue and be compassionate with others at these events and on social media. For example, one day of the week, one individual receives special recognition from the organization and is praised for their work and engagement in advancing peacebuilding events, which are promoted online. Furthermore, the organization conducts visits with political representatives to promote their cultural events on diversity and holds an annual peace festival.

The study of youth—social individuals involved in social becoming—is contextually defined (Christiansen, Utas, and Vigh 2006) and, as a category, cannot be separated from the postcolonial, industrial, and neoliberal capitalist structures that have shaped understandings of global youth culture (Comaroff and Comaroff 2005). More recently, work on youth culture and male unemployment (Craig 2010; Mains 2007), political engagement (Greenberg 2014), cosmopolitan and future aspirations, and hope within uncertainty

---

[6] In 2015, the heightened presence of IS in Iraq, straining negotiations over the share of the national budget between the KRG and Baghdad and corrupt political structures led to an economic crisis (*qairani aburi*) in Iraqi Kurdistan. The KRG announced a delay in the payment of salaries to public sector workers, who constitute over 40 percent of the workforce in Iraqi Kurdistan. The impact of these austerity measures trickled down to almost all parts of the economy and resulted in a suspension of new governmental hiring that affected recent graduates (World Bank Report 2016).

(Schielke 2015) have gained attention within the field of anthropology. Specific to the Middle East, authors have studied how ordinary and daily practices instill perseverance within young adults during times of uncertainty (Bayat 2013; Khosravi 2017; Schielke 2015). Khosravi (2017) discusses the prolonging of youth in Iran due to unemployment and limited possibilities available to them to become independent. Schielke (2015), examining the frustrating expectations and ambivalent unity of hope in Egypt, highlights how youth must deal with different worlds playing out at the same time. Promises of middle-class prosperity create cosmopolitan longing, for example, to be a part of global fashion trends. However, although Egyptian youth long for these global aspirations, achieving them is more difficult, as nepotism and corruption in Egypt leave these aspirations unfulfilled.

The young adults I worked with during my fieldwork were between the ages of eighteen and thirty-five. Similar to the Iranian case discussed by Khosravi, they were often students or recent graduates who had not yet started families and were struggling to become independent from their parents.[7] Indeed, many of them focused on individual fulfilment and self-making (Zigon 2006; Zigon 2009) by investing in ordinary actions such as dressing fashionably, being active at the gym, and going out with friends. This mode of stabilizing uncertainty focuses on creating hope by seeking spaces in which to express alternative cosmopolitan aspirations outside of existing and restrictive political and social structures. However, this was not all that was happening. While recent literature on youth and waiting has understood their futures as wasted or "on hold," my fieldwork suggests that many Kurdish youth in Iraq were finding hope despite their precarious circumstances. Kurdish youth did become disillusioned with the KRG during the economic crisis in the aftermath of the fight against IS because of a lack of social mobility and deteriorating infrastructure and services. However, some navigated this uncertainty through political engagement and activism that was influenced by events happening in other regions of Kurdistan and elsewhere in the Middle East.

Greenberg's (2014) work on the politics of disappointment in post-revolutionary Serbia discusses how student activists negotiated different

---

[7] The region has a very young population, with the median age being around twenty years old and 25 percent of the population being between the ages of fifteen and twenty-four (KRSO 2014). Iraq has thirty-two million inhabitants, of whom six million live in the KRI. In the KRI, the unemployment rate fluctuates around 13 percent, with this rate being around 27 percent in Iraq. Youth unemployment in the KRI was around 18 percent in the first half of 2018 (CIA factbook, Worldbank 2016). See also Sabr (2018) for an overview of the political and economic events in the region that shaped the experiences of Iraqi Kurdish youth starting in the 1990s.

strategies to pursue present political actions, despite feelings of disappointment with previous expectations. While this condition of a political subjectivity was contingent, Greenberg argues that it is also enabling in that it became a central feature of the students' transformative political action in the present. It gave an enabling force without holding on to any utopian visions for the future. The youth I worked with also exhibited disillusionment and political engagement at the same time, and there was slippage between these modes that held different future visions and would come out at different moments. Cross-border and transnational ties between different Kurdish groups led to new forms of political engagement: political and social activism, and militant fighting that make a return to a communal hope (Graeber 2008; Hauer, Nielsen, and Niewöhner 2018). Certain Kurdish youth engaged in both modes to cultivate their different aspirations for a better future—to maximize their chances, so to speak.

Taking from the PKK and PYD beliefs of cultural and ethnic diversity and inclusion, Azad promoted modernizing and progressive forms of citizenship through social engagement. While these political parties are trying to achieve this through military action and creating new forms of democratic and political structures in Rojava, Azad encouraged inclusion and diversity through social and cultural events for youth, creating a new form of youth citizenship in a post-conflict region. Through this active intervention, he placed some form of hope in a future of inclusivity. The presence and development of the Kurdish nationalist forces opened up a space for him to show acts of solidarity with others and influenced him on several issues, such as inclusion and gender equality, but not without criticism of the full ideology. Rather, Azad adopted parts of their modernization program to improve societal ties in his own environment. This type of political engagement rests on social activism that creates an inclusive society through developing youth citizenship and creating a diverse community of youth from all religious and ethnic backgrounds across the Middle East. While Azad expressed that he was bored and that there was nothing for him to do under the KRG, he was, in fact, actively working to achieve a hopeful future by mobilizing youth and promoting inclusion, thus changing the narrative with which he was disillusioned.

Filling in the Holes: Challenges of Militarized Political Engagement

The context of the fight against IS enabled another form of political engagement, one of militarized action and participation in the Kurdish forces. Having heard about Hoshyar from other university students, I met him at a cafe to discuss his views on the Kurdish movement. A Kurd from the diaspora,

Hoshyar mediated the contingency in Kurdistan and the fight against IS through his participation in social activism in Europe and later through military engagement as a guerrilla fighter. We sat by the window at Cafe Dahlia, where I had become accustomed to holding interviews, as the location was very popular among youth. Hoshyar smoked several cigarettes as he continued to recount the past two years of his life.

Hoshyar grew up in Silêmanî, but his family had migrated to Scandinavia in the late 2000s. Being a "late" migrant to Europe, as most Kurdish migration took place between the late 1980s and the mid-2000s, he had to study in English and learn a new language. Reflecting on his wild life of partying and being rebellious against his parents in Europe, Hoshyar began to change his behavior as IS drew closer to the borders of the KRI in 2014. "In 2014, when DAESH came, I made a discovery. I used to have a very wild life there until two years ago. It was bad, I was rebellious. I hated everything political, but when I turned nineteen, I changed. It was because of DAESH."[8] Visiting the KRI on a trip in 2014, he had dressed up in military clothes and been taken by his uncles to the border, where the fighting against IS took place. This experience led him to become more politically active once he returned to Europe.

Getting to know more people from the Kurdish diaspora and left-wing activists, he joined the many protests in Europe in the aftermath of IS and the fighting in Kobanî. After a while, his volunteering and activism for the Kurdish struggle became a major part of his life:

> I studied fine, but when I started being involved in politics, it took up so much space in my head that I couldn't focus on studying. It was not easy. I was so attached, and it was difficult to let go. It became my new habitus. I wasn't sad about this, because of the work I was doing, with those people. I learned new things—controversial things as well—but with that it had its own joy. You feel like a Kurd. Before I had family, but that had no way of filling in the holes that we [Kurds] have.

The Kurdish forces' fight against IS united the support and solidarity of Kurds from all regions, and the diaspora in particular became mobilized for this cause. Hoshyar was also influenced by what the PKK could offer people in the

---

[8] In most Kurdish discourse, the name DAESH, coming from the Arabic acronym for IS (*al Dawlah al-Islameyah fi Iraq wal-Sham*) is used.

region itself. Becoming disillusioned with the KRG, he felt that the politicians there did not understand or even feel that they should be doing something good for society. "*Amanj yan niya* [They have no goals or hopes]. Apart from the crisis and wage freeze, they have no imagination. So that's why there are so many political issues, we are pulled apart and everyone has trouble with talking to each other," he said. Hoshyar saw this lack of unity and communication differently with the PKK and the YPD. Even though they had many enemies and were involved in controversial issues, Hoshyar felt that their community held on to each other, so he became more involved in the activist networks in Scandinavia.

He started working on a Facebook page in English where he wrote about the issues in the Kurdish region and the fight against IS. Acting as a news page, it started reaching more people even though at first the issues were controversial in nature, including war and guerrilla warfare. After the liberation of Kobanî, these issues also began to be reported by the Western media, and it became less risky to talk about the PKK and the YPD. In this period, Hoshyar was being approached through the Facebook page by people around the word who wanted to join the fight in Syria. He and another woman in Europe started communicating and informing international volunteers on how to join the YPG, both for military involvement and aid work. Hoshyar was becoming so involved in political activism that his studies started to suffer: "I was organizing protests, gatherings, I went to all the events. But I stayed to volunteer all that time, until I decided to return back to Kurdistan. That decision was a change, it was an emotional thing. It was a big change, but I didn't tell my parents."

After a year of being active in Scandinavia, Hoshyar decided to receive military training and travelled back to the KRI to train with the PKK. He told his parents that he was going to a party and took an overnight flight to Silêmanî. In the morning, he called his parents and told them that he was back in Kurdistan to take his *perwerde* (education or training) with the guerrilla fighters in the Qandil mountains. During the six months he spent there, Hoshyar became more aware of the PKK political ideology but also of the boundaries of his part in the armed struggle: "I think that [the PKK/PYD] give *hiwa* (hope). You become part of that hope. There, it says, create something for others. Here [Iraqi Kurdistan], the system is different. Apart from the military and political things that I learned, there I also learned discipline. It was a kind of *hyat* (love) that was very good for me. Physically I am better . . . Their military training is very intense. I have hurt and blackened my hands and fingers, but our minds and hopes were strong because of the ideology."

Irving (2017, 38) argues that "the meaning of an experience or event is only revealed over time through an unfolding of future events and experiences." Some events and their aftermath disrupt the established order of life and expectations of the future, opening up a process of critical reconsidering, a renegotiation of future life. Becoming politically active made Hoshyar rethink his own past and character, from being a rebellious teenager to a political activist and disciplined fighter. Hoshyar placed hope in the PKK and Rojava as an ideal of a better future. This type of hope was both directed at his own self-development into a better person as well as toward a common future horizon.

Hoshyar talked about Rojava as a source of hope for inclusive living and stressed that, through this, he began to think about diversity, "Jewish, Orthodox, Armenian, Kurdish, Azadb, Assyrian, and Ezedi. This diversity is beautiful, you don't have it anywhere else." The ideology extended to ideas about feminism and diversity.

> There was a woman in Qandil who taught us *jineology*. We were sitting and talking about feminism when they said they were opposed to radical feminism because they are not in favor of lesbians. There I was against it, because I grew up abroad. There it is difficult to talk about this, you are in a restricted space. I told them that the People's Democratic Party (HDP) was also fighting for minority lesbian, gay, trans- and bisexual (LGBTI) rights in Turkey, and Abdullah Öcalan didn't oppose it. I said my piece, they replied that they know [LGBTI individuals] exist, but they don't want to oppose or fight for them. I didn't like this point, but at least there I could talk about it and give my own opinion and oppose theirs and even make them understand my way and change their view. Here the Yekety [PUK] maybe doesn't oppose it, but they sure don't talk about it.

Holding this ideology as a yardstick to measure up against the KRG, Hoshyar also reflected on how the educational and political system in the KRI needed to change: "I think that if I had stayed in Bashur, I wouldn't have been so involved. Because of the educational system here and the upbringing, it creates a depoliticized society. You never criticize what you learn. You never question it. Whatever you hear on the TV is reality. This is the problem, but in Europe I changed." Hoshyar saw it as important that within the movement you learned how to speak and argue: a way to learn about the region's history and freely argue and communicate with each other. This was something that he felt was not present in Iraqi Kurdistan. "It is very clear, [in Iraqi Kurdistan] there is no professional communication, it is all bazaar talk."

Hoshyar contrasted the KRI with the endeavor in Rojava and blamed the KRG for not being actively involved as a state, even though they had official and internationally recognized representatives.

> Even if these people in power didn't exist, would anything change in Kurdistan? If they take away the parliament, would anything change? People don't work here anyway, what are they doing? They are not doing anything. They don't work and things are still working, so why do we need them? It is like this thing, you became this official [autonomous government], but you are not doing anything. [In Qandil], it is not like that. If I know something, I share it, and you can criticize me. This is the guerrilla lifestyle. Every evening there we sit in groups of five, you discuss the things that happened today and all the things that went wrong or that you did wrong, you talk about yourself and others . . . *Hiwadarim* (I hope) that the situation doesn't become worse, but maybe it will . . . But the youth and freedom needs another way to get to peace, it is against these ideas. In Europe, it's not just the gatherings, but we talk about these things very easily and in an academic way online as well. These things are needed here, the youth need to learn that they have agency.

When I met him, Hoshyar was planning to return to Europe. His PKK commanders had told him that he would be of most help to them by resuming his former work in Europe. Although he was initially afraid to return to Scandinavia in case he was arrested for his involvement with the PKK, Hoshyar still returned and resumed his studies while continuing his activism on social media. The democratic process in Rojava, where they were "making heaven in a shithole," gave Hoshyar hope for a wider Kurdistan where communication, diversity, and gender equality were celebrated and people would go into meaningful discussion, despite the shortcomings on issues such as LGBTI rights. Political activism and militant engagement in the Kurdish struggle made Hoshyar refigure how to understand himself as a Kurd in the diaspora. He had a role to play within the larger Kurdish struggle, allowing him to actively intervene to shape a different society and future.

Conclusion

In this chapter, I discussed how Kobanî and the aftermath of the fight against IS as a "critical event" in the Kurdish imaginary generated new modes of social and political engagement amongst Iraqi Kurdish youth. While during my fieldwork Iraqi Kurds maintained a stigma of being the least political of all Kurds, as their bellies were filled with "food and money," I argue that the war against IS and the mobilization of Kurdish forces and heightened solidarity and created new spaces for young Kurds to imagine and work toward changing social and political structures in Kurdistan based on social inclusion, diversity, and gender equality. While I only discussed two individuals who partook in social and militarized political engagement, I argued that many individuals had crafted hopeful imaginations about their activism or participation, despite the disillusionment that existed concurrently. Both Hoshyar and Azad both saw the limitations of the political ideologies that inspired them, as well as the limits of the impact they could make inside Iraqi Kurdistan. More importantly, their engagement changed over time as they navigated their own development into adulthood and (foreign) employment.

In the past year there has been a renewed crackdown on protesters in Iraq and the censoring of journalists in Iraqi Kurdistan. Uncertainty around safety due to Turkish bombing in the border areas of Iraqi Kurdistan and political tensions between Kurdish and Iraqi parties have halted aspirations of hope as well as the present-day challenges in containing the COVID-19 outbreak. This leads us to question how Kurdish youth can continue to actively engage in political future-making within an unstable and uncertain context. Existing in a permanent state of uncertainty, in both modern history and as regarded by the states of which it is a part (Taussig 2015), Kurdistan remains an important and understudied place to research how people continue to navigate life in precarious contexts.

References

Bayat, Asef. 2013. Life as Politics: How Ordinary People Change the Middle East. Stanford, CA: Stanford University Press.
Bell, David. 2017. Rethinking Utopia: Place, Power, Affect. London: Routledge.
Carr, David. 1991. Time, Narrative, and History. Bloomington, IN: Indiana University Press.
Černy, Hannes. 2017. Iraqi Kurdistan, the PKK and International Relations: Theory and Ethnic Conflict. London: Routledge.
Christiansen, Catrine, Mats Utas, and Henrik E. Vigh. 2006. Navigating Youth, Generating Adulthood: Social Becoming in an African Context. Nordiska Afrikainstitutet.
Comaroff, Jean and John Comaroff. 2005. "Reflections on Youth, from the Past to the Postcolony." In Makers and Breakers: Children and youth in postcolonial Africa, edited by Alcinda Honwana and Filip De Boeck, 19–30. Oxford: James Currey.

Craig, Jeffrey. 2010. Timepass: Youth, Class, and the Politics of Waiting in India. Stanford, CA: Stanford University Press.
Das, Veena and Bhrigupati Singh. 1995. Critical Events: An Anthropological Perspective on Contemporary India. Vol. 7. Delhi: Oxford University Press.
Graeber, David. 2008. "Hope in Common." https://theanarchistlibrary.org/library/david-graeber-hope-in-common
Greenberg, Jessica. 2014. After the Revolution: Youth, Democracy, and the Politics of Disappointment in Serbia. Stanford, CA: Stanford University Press.
Gunes, Cengiz. 2012. The Kurdish National Movement in Turkey: From Protest to Resistance. London: Routledge.
Hauer, Janine, Jonas Østergaard Nielsen, and Jörg Niewöhner. 2018. "Landscapes of Hoping- urban Expansion and Emerging Futures in Ouagadougou, Burkina Faso." Anthropological Theory 18 (1): 59–80.
Hermez, Sami. 2012. "'The War is Going to Ignite': On the Anticipation of Violence in Lebanon." PoLAR: Political and Legal Anthropology Review 35 (2): 327–344.
Hermez, Sami. 2017. War is Coming: Between Past and Future Violence in Lebanon. Philadelphia, PA: University of Pennsylvania Press.
Irving, Andrew. 2017. "The Art of Turning Left and Right." In Anthropologies and Futures: Researching Emerging and Uncertain Worlds, edited by Juan Francisco Salazar, Sarah Pink, Andrew Irving, and Johannes Sjöberg, 23–42. London: Bloomsbury.
Jackson, Michael. 2008. "The Shock of the New: On Migrant Imaginaries and Critical Transitions." Ethnos 73 (1): 57–72.
Kapferer, Bruce. 2015. "Introduction." In In the Event—Toward an Anthropology of Generic Moments, edited by Lotte Meinert and Bruce Kapferer, 1–28. New York: Berghahn Books.
Kardaş, Tuncay & Murat Yesiltaş. 2017. "Rethinking Kurdish Geopolitical Space: The Politics of Image, Insecurity and Gender." Cambridge Rev. of International Affairs 30 (2-3): 256–82.
Leezenberg, Michiel. 2016. "The Ambiguities of Democratic Autonomy: The Kurdish Movement in Turkey and Rojava." Southeast European and Black Sea Studies 16 (4): 671–90.
Mains, Daniel. 2007. "Neoliberal Times: Progress, Boredom, and Shame Among Young Men in Urban Ethiopia." American Ethnologist 34 (4): 659–73.
Natali, Denise. 2004. "Transnational Networks: New Opportunities and Constraints for Kurdish Statehood." Middle East Policy. 11 (1): 111–14.
Roitman, Janet. 2013. Anti-crisis. Durham, NA: Duke University Press.
Sabr, Shivan Fazil. 2018. "Youth and Generational Divide: Perspectives and Challenges of Young Millennials in the Kurdistan Region of Iraq." MSc diss., 15 September 2018, SOAS, University of London.
Schäfers, Marlene. 2016. "Ruined Futures: Managing Instability in Post-earthquake Van (Turkey)." Social Anthropology 24(2): 228–42.
Schielke, Samuli. 2015. Egypt in the Future Tense: Hope, Frustration, and Ambivalence Before and After 2011. Bloomington, IN: Indiana University Press.
Taussig, Michael. 2015. "The Mastery of Non-mastery." In the Moment, August 19. https://critinq.wordpress.com/2015/08/19/michael-taussig-the-mastery-of-non-mastery/
Tekdemir, Omer. 2018. "The Social Construction of 'Many Kurdishnesses': Mapping Sub-identities of 'EU-ising' Kurdish Politics." Ethnicities: 1–25.
Vigh, Henrik. 2008. "Crisis and Chronicity: Anthropological Perspectives on Continuous Conflict and Decline." Ethnos 73 (1): 5–24.
World Bank. 2016. The Kurdistan Region of Iraq: Reforming the Economy for Shared Prosperity and Protecting the Vulnerable. openknowledge.worldbank.org/handle/10986/24706.
Zigon, Jarrett. 2006. "An Ethics of Hope: Working on the Self in Contemporary Moscow." Anthropology of East Europe Review 24 (2): 71–80.
Zigon, Jarrett. 2009. "Hope Dies Last: Two Aspects of Hope in Contemporary Moscow." Anthropological Theory 9 (3): 253–71.

CHAPTER 9

KURDISH YOUTH AND RELIGIOUS IDENTITY: BETWEEN RELIGIOUS AND NATIONAL TENSIONS

Ibrahim Sadiq

Introduction

According to official figures published by the KRG Ministry of Planning, the percentage of individuals aged thirty and younger in the region constitutes two-thirds of the population. Half of the region's population is under the age of twenty, demonstrating the significant share of the population constituted by young people (KRG 2013). At this susceptible stage of life, youth seek "active engagement in processes of identity formation" (Ryan 2014, 447), and if their energies are not directed and invested in line with a national strategy, the potential repercussions could negatively affect their future and that of the region in general.

Ryan (2014, 447) claims that "religion may replace race as a primary marker of identity." Demonstrating this clash of sectarian identities is the conflict that has raged in Iraq since 2003 between Sunni and Shia Arabs. However, Kurdish citizens are aware of the seriousness of this type of conflict, even if they prioritize religious identity. Owing to the social diversity within Kurdish society, religion has never been an issue between the Kurdish people and other components in the age of the nation-state.

The Kurds have been deprived of basic rights throughout Kurdistan, and with the exception of Iran, which follows a systematic policy of Shi'ism (Tohidi 2009, 305), this is due to national and ethnic differences but not religious issues. Highlighting religious identity, which is characterized by a Sunni or Shiite sectarian tendency, may harm the Kurdish cause and the characteristic tolerance that exists within the Kurdish community. There is also a belief among Kurdish intellectuals and politicians that the countries that have colonized Kurdistan have often used religion to circumvent Kurdish demands. Turkish President Recep Tayyip Erdogan, for example, has mastered the weaponization of religion to achieve his goals in Northern Kurdistan (Kurt 2019, 12) as well as in Eastern Kurdistan, where he is mobilizing Syrian Jihadist mercenaries against the Kurds

(Speckhard 2019). Likewise, Saddam Hussein launched his genocide campaigns against the Kurdish people in Southern Kurdistan in the name of God and Anfal, as a Quranic icon (Black 1993).

It is assumed that young people, the demographic cohort discussed here, are always the group most affected by conflict. This is particularly applicable in psychological and cultural contexts and "the construction of differentiating lifestyles" (Feixa and Nofre 2012, 1), due to the fragility of their own lived experiences, among other reasons. Kurdish youth are not exempt from this equation. The emergence of ISIS was not a purely military phenomenon. Rather, it was accompanied by confusion and shock for the vast majority of people in the Kurdistan region, given the media attention and the Islamic intellectualism that ISIS exhibited in speeches, such as that of "Amirul-Mu'minin (i.e. 'Leader of the Faithful'), the Islamic State, and the Sharia" (Low 2016, 303).

Intellectual debates, as a result of their acquaintance with a new Islam, were not known to the majority of Kurdistan's residents, who were left dealing with the trauma of excessive violence alongside the confusion around their religious legitimacy. These two factors elicit the assumption that there would be a change in people's readiness to confront radicalism on both the intellectual and military level. In addition, the notion of an existent threat that young people would adopt an extremist ideology fuels the sense that they are strangers in society. Relying on isolation leads them to more extremist thoughts and hate toward what the general public does in normal life especially in Kurdish society, which is socially open and tolerant in many regards.

Conversely, the move by ISIS out of Baghdad and toward the borders of the Kurdistan Region (Hamasaeed and Nada 2020) shocked many political and public circles and divided people into two different understandings of the situation. The majority of the Kurds believed that Islam had been disowned by this organization, which had become a weaponized political tool against the Kurdish people in the hands of neighboring countries, particularly Turkey (Kurt 2019, 12). Others believed that the Kurds were the weakest link as well as open to extermination and access to the Turkish frontiers, especially when ISIS attacked and massacred the Yazidi Kurds, relying on some religious heritage standards that are inconsistent with modern values and charters. There are also those who believe that this violence is proprietary to Islam. A sharp debate began in the media and on social networks between several religious and secular parties, including Islamists, and those who condemned Islam, which they perceived as being responsible for ISIS' crimes.

The fundamental questions here are what the actual changes were that accompanied the emergence of ISIS and what the repercussions were that have endured even after the advent of COVID-19, which, like ISIS, has resulted in a significant loss of life. The virus precipitated numerous religious controversies, especially among the youth. What, as a result of these issues, is the extent to which these events influence youth regarding their connections with religion?

Obtaining satisfactory results in this research was not an easy endeavor. I concluded that using a single method or only a questionnaire form would be insufficient. I therefore decided to follow a bimodal method, including a questionnaire component to which I received 385 responses. This is a relatively sizable number of responses when considering the number of youth in Kurdish society in the Kurdistan Region. A series of interviews were conducted in addition to the questionnaire in order to engage in more fruitful discussion, to probe further into the responses given on the questionnaire, and to obtain more accurate results. These interviews were conducted in July 2020 through WhatsApp, Messenger, and Google Meet. Within the group of interviewees were young people, most of whom were university students, from the four provinces of Southern Kurdistan.

Theoretical Framework

The conditions experienced by the Kurdish community in the Kurdistan Region have led to turmoil in many social areas due to the type of conflict that has occurred. It was marked by bloody and ideological violence that provoked sharp arguments between Islamists on the one hand and secularists, nationalists and leftists on the other. Under these circumstances, the emergence of ISIS presented both a physical threat and an ideological danger that was effective in its ability to divide society. At first, the militant group gained the admiration of many Islamists as well as non-Islamist religious individuals due to its use of a religious language that is prevalent in Islamic traditions. These opposing movements may have spawned some degree of uncertainty—a crisis of religious identity—among young people that has had lasting consequences for society. It is important to explain what identity crisis means in this context.

Identity, in its primitive concept, is what distinguishes the self from others by acquiring a kind of privacy, differentiating "us" from "them" (Wodak 2008, 57), "the established" and "the outsiders" (Elias and Scotson 1994, 37). It may be reflected psychologically and emotionally in regard to human relationships. Accordingly, these relationships can take on dimensions that are unusual or characterized by compulsion and may result in violence (Sen 2007, 1). In other words, it is a "dilemma in the meaning and content of identity for groups and societies in various social, political and cultural contexts" (McGarry and Jasper 2015). This distinction of identity in its human dimension can perform certain functions, negative or positive, among "which is to protect the individual and collective self from the erosion and dissolution factor" (Aziz and Hamdaoui 2011).

The emergence of identity could represent a range of symbolic or expressive forms. It could be reflected in clothes or in the practice of a certain behavior. It is "the set of meanings that define who one is when one is an occupant of a particular role in society, a member of a particular group, or claims particular characteristics that identify him or her as a unique person." And it is important to know "how their identities influence their behaviour, thoughts, and feelings or emotions; and how their identities tie them in to society at large" (Stets and Burke 2000, 3).

Identity Crisis

Through the confusion of identity that afflicts the human existence, youth in particular may feel conflicted between religious, ethnic, or national affiliations as well as various secondary affiliations. In the context of this uncertainty youth experience regarding their identity, it is useful to explore whether or not they are afflicted with a profound crisis of identity. From this notion, Erikson formulated the term "identity crisis" (Erikson 1968, 18). This identity confusion is due to a complex process that many young people may not experience, due to their instability and the complex and exciting ideas around them, especially Kurdish youth, who were facing two crises. The first is the widespread criticism of the Kurdish authority about the rampant corruption in institutions, unemployment, and poor services, and the second is the war that ISIS waged against the region's borders in intellectual and military terms. Kurdish society is, by nature, a religious society. Thus, the discourse that was propagated by ISIS is that of ideology and religion, which may have convinced many of the extremist vision for the implementation of Sharia law. This was conceived as if, with its application, the world would be free of problems, and social justice would take its course in contrast to a reality that was unable to attract the attention of young people from a social, religious, and economic standpoint.

Thus, in relation to the impact of identity on one's life and its complexities, people's awareness of dealing with these ideas may be more important. We are confronted with a generation that is aware of the social changes and political fluctuations that accompanied the conditions that brought about ISIS. Here, a sense of identity occurs, according to Erickson, that is not limited merely to the teenage years. But this formation and growth that changes and evolves throughout life as people face new challenges and deal with different experiences (Cherry 2019).

Thus, religious identity or its strengthening among the youth may have emerged during this period, a time when society groaned from myriad economic and political problems. The crises themselves laid the foundation for such a division between the traditional parties that fought the Ba'athist regime and the regimes that preceded it for independence. Moreover, the new generation did not see those tragedies, as it is believed to be characterized by a weak belonging to the homeland and a lacking of a sense of conscious responsibility for the future and later generations. This is all within the framework of traditional identities, such as Kurdishness.

Therefore, the importance of knowing the reasons for that religiosity lies in three points:

1. The extent of believing the assumption that in crises people return to religion and adhere to it more than before.
2. The depth of religiosity in Kurdish society, especially among its youth.
3. The issue of attributing youth to identity, whether primary or secondary.

From here, it is necessary to explore the reasons that led to the emergence of a religious identity rather than other identities.

Socio-political Background

The Kurdistan Region of Iraq (KRI) is constitutionally recognized as a federal region. This region is formed of four major cities, including the capital, Erbil, Sulaymaniyah, Dohuk, and the governorate of Halabja, which was recently formed as a new governorate.[1] Since 1991, it has been administered by two Kurdish parties—the Kurdistan Democratic Party (KDP) and the Patriotic

---

[1] The area of this region constitutes only half of the area of Iraqi Kurdistan, which is inhabited by the Kurdish majority. The Kurdish areas outside the Kurdistan Region, which are controlled by the Baghdad government, are known in the Iraqi constitution as disputed areas, which must be administered jointly by the government of Baghdad and the regional government pending the holding of the referendum in them in order to find out whether their residents want to stay in Iraq or join the Kurdistan Region.

Union of Kurdistan (PUK)—as well as some other smaller, marginal parties. The Kurdish people in the Kurdistan Region were subjected to genocide by the Iraqi Ba'ath Party starting in the 1960s, followed by the implementation of the Anfal operations in 1988 in which religion was mobilized to further these genocidal actions. This was in addition to the policies of exclusion, displacement, marginalization, and Arabization that took place in Iraq.

These types of politics continued, even after the fall of Saddam Hussein's regime, with a new political organization led by Shiite and Sunni Islamic parties and the establishment of a new government in Baghdad with the participation of the Kurdish political parties. Moreover, the provisions of the Iraqi constitution that were agreed upon between the components of Iraq—especially those relating to the Kurdistan Region's relationship with Iraq—have not been implemented.

Conversely, the region's two Kurdish parties have never successfully governed the region due to the lack of a political strategy and a clear vision for a successful administration. They quickly divided the region into two zones of influence (Abdullah and Hama 2020, 7) and attempted to control the sources of the three authorities of the executive, the legislative, and the judiciary as well as the wealth of the region. A distinct political reality was formed despite the limited scope of democracy, press freedom, and parliamentary elections. However, it failed to match the ambitions of various segments in Kurdish society, particularly the youth, as unemployment spread among them before and during the coming of ISIS in 2014. According to a United Nations report, unemployment in 2014 reached 10.1 percent among young men and 37.6 percent among young women in the Kurdistan region (UNDP 2016).

The conditions that confront the Kurdistan Region's youth, being an important segment of human societies, are, in one way or another, linked to those that society faces in general. Thus, young people, given their vitality and the beginning of their social and economic lives, seek to build relationships that may be typical social, economic, political, and cultural in nature or may be exceptional and ideological. All these relationships are cultivated or created under circumstances that may be normal or exceptional and characterized by some kind of controversy. Moreover, identity formation in abnormal circumstances may be tinged with a host of anxious formalities. One of the manifestations of human societies, especially developing societies, including the Kurdistan Region, is that religion plays a major role in social relations.

Religion in these societies may represent a condition for building balanced relationships that are not imbued with social tensions. A religious dispute may lead to the termination of these relations or to other major problems, such as those created in recent years by extremist groups in Islamic countries and by ISIS. In this context, one youth whom I interviewed and who preferred to be named Azad (2020, pers. comm.) said, "I no longer feel safe even inside my house, because almost all of my relatives, including cousins, are boycotting me, even my relationship with my father is critical. The only reason is I am no longer convinced in prayer."

Among the spread of the religious phenomenon is the intense presence of Islamists in Iraqi Kurdistan, including the Muslim Brotherhood represented by the Islamic Union of Kurdistan. Groups that believe in jihad as a method of change, including the Kurdistan Islamic Jama'a (*Komelî Îslamî Kurdistan*), the Islamic Movement, and Salafi groups, enjoy complete independence in their mission. They have headquarters and gathering centers as well as mosques and sermons in which they interpret Islam according to the policies they pursue. The Islamic Union, the Islamic Jama'a, and the Islamic Movement have members in the Kurdistan Parliament, and they participated in previous regional governments. This was reflected in their intense presence and their influence on bringing young people to their mosques. With regard to this aspect, Shawkat (2020, pers. comm.), a twenty-four-year-old, told me, "My younger brother [twenty-two years old] used to go to the mosque with my father, and there he was recruited to one of the Islamic parties. Since that time, the comfort and stability has been lifted from our home. Every day he is bringing something new to us, we are not familiar with either from my very religious parents, nor from my grandparents. This new religion is demolishing, not building; dividing, not uniting. It is a political religion with a strange interpretation that has nothing to do with the Kurdish community."

This religious and Islamic dimension in the Kurdistan Region is reflected in the strengthening of religious institutions, which are represented by the Ministry of Endowments (KRG-MERA 2007) and the Union of Muslim Scholars (KRG-UIRCK 2020), including five colleges of Sharia and Islamic studies under the Ministry of Higher Education (MHESR 2018). There are also five religious institutes affiliated with the Ministry of Endowments (*Rudaw* 2015) at which more than 3,616 students between the ages of eighteen and twenty study. Additionally, according to the latest statement by the spokesperson of the Ministry of Endowments in 2016, the number of mosques in the Kurdistan

Region has grown to 5,473 mosques (*SpeeMedia* 2016). A new mosque is built every ten days in the region (*Rudaw* 2016). If we divide the population of the region—an estimated five million residents (Kirmanj 2013)—by the number of mosques, there is one mosque for every thousand men, women, and children (*SpeeMedia* 2016).

Demography of the Participants

The gender makeup of those who participated in the questionnaire reflects the reality throughout the Kurdistan Region, as we can see that the participation of male youth corresponds to two-thirds of female youth. Here, we know that unemployment among male youth is 10 percent, while it exceeds 37 percent among female youth. When comparing this questionnaire with the UNDP 2016 report, the percentage difference in unemployment is very similar. The percentage of female students who study at universities is nearly equal to that of male students: "50.3 percent male students and 49.7 percent female students" (Salam, Hamadameen, and Showani 2015, 10).

Figure 1 A: respondents by gender   **Figure 1B**: respondents by age

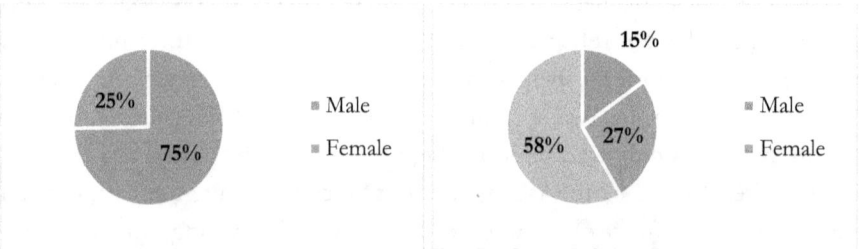

Figure 1 C: respondents by education   **Figure 1 D**: respondents by locality

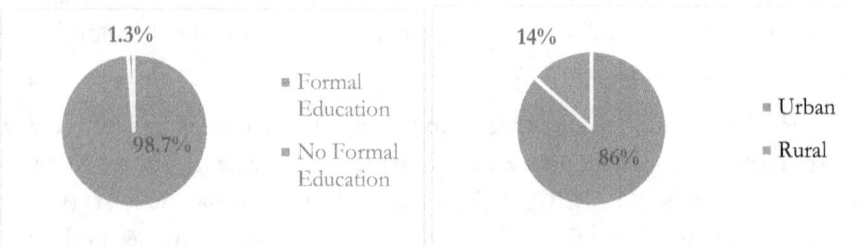

The overwhelming majority of the participants are educated, and most reside in urban areas. Their ages, as shown in the chart, range between eighteen and twenty-seven, but most individuals in the group are between the ages of twenty-four and twenty-seven. Age has a major role in intellectual stability, which increases over time. Here, the results are more realistic and permanent.

In order to find out about religiosity and its influence on the youth, I interviewed Avesta (2020, pers. comm.), a twenty-six-year-old who is studying to receive a bachelor's degree in biology. I asked her if she attempted to find a job after graduation, and she bitterly answered, "The labor market, particularly the private sector, is male, and many of them are watching girls with an inappropriate sexual view. Many families are reluctant to send their daughters to the market, either because they know about some man's morals, or because they do not believe that girls will enter the field of work." The reason for that, she answered, is due to "the inferior view of women by many mosque preachers and their advice not to allow women outside the home."

The issue of gender identity among young people raises major questions, as many of them are still under the influence of the prevailing culture and religion, even though they are university graduates.

Hajar (2020, pers. comm.), a twenty-three-year-old with a bachelor's degree in sociology, was asked about his opinions as a religious individual in the participation of women in the labor market. He replied, "I do not like my future wife to be a university graduate and to enter the labor market, even in the public sector, because they were created to raise children and serve the husband." A twenty-four-year-old with a bachelor's degree in sociology, Hiwa (2020, pers. comm.), is also religious, and his opinion deviated from that of Hajar. He stated, "I do not want my wife to be a housemaid, and I hope that her degree will be higher than mine, and that she will have a respectable job." When I asked the same question to Barzan (2020, pers. comm.), another twenty-three-year-old with a bachelor's degree in sociology but who is not religious, he replied, "I do not see a difference between young males and females, and they have the same right to work as men. For that gender discrimination in our society, we need a real revolution against the prevailing culture." Thus, the view of many religious youth regarding the opposite sex is still confined to the dominant Islamic culture, while others expressed an alternative view.

Identity Anxiety

This study struggled to discover what happened to the thinking of the Kurdish youth during the emergence of ISIS, which appeared as a shock to the Muslim community in several ways. Has there been a major change in people's perceptions of religion or of the prevailing Islamic culture in society? It is true that debates were intense among the public and between the critics of an intellectual system that could not differentiate between Islamic heritage, which is the product of human thinking and jurisprudence, and religious texts that must be reinterpreted according to the requirements of modernity.

Hence, a chasm developed between the ideological system that modernity has brought and the ideology of ISIS as a variant product of modernity. Furthermore, an element of uncertainty was added by conspiratorial thinking that the Great Powers sought to exert control over the region—a widespread belief among Muslims, especially with regard to the emergence of ISIS. "The more recent allegations of CIA and Mossad involvement behind the rise of ISIS in the Middle East show the persisting popularity of secret government conspiracy narratives" (Harambam 2017, 96). Youth have been involved in this debate, but with a kind of simplification fluctuating between seriousness and mockery and between a negligible minority sympathizing with all or some of ISIS' tendencies and those who reject these notions outright.

The questionnaire in this study suggests that the religious nature of the youth is mainly dominant, at around 50 percent of the participants, in addition to some exceptions, which are also worth mentioning. If the data from respondents who reject religion or do not care about it are collected by adding Option F, the percentage of those who are not interested in religion increases to 49 percent. This is a sizable percentage that encompasses almost half of the participants. The important question here is whether the identity of religious youth in the region is in crisis. Participation seemed normal, given that the change due to the emergence of ISIS was not significant and did not exceed 8 percent.

On closely examining the hypothesis that people in crisis turn to religion, there was an increase in religiosity with the emergence of ISIS, but there were also elements of decline in religiosity, which were one degree higher than the turn to religion. This indicates that there is a concern around religious identity among a segment of young people, but it does not reach the level of a serious crisis.

Challenging economic and social circumstances within social ranks can exert "broad influences on thought, emotion, and social behaviour independently of the substance of objective social class" (Manstead 2018, 6) in the sense that it creates an unusual psychological state for certain classes or segments of society. This can apply to all human societies, because the psychological impact of social conditions is a comprehensive human condition, and youth can be more affected than other generations, particularly the war that was imposed by ISIS and the controversy that it brought about concerning religious heritage and

Sharia law that was implemented by them. This is in addition to what has been confirmed by many studies that "members of low-status social groups are more likely to be religious" (Brandt and Henry 2012, 321).

Figure 2. religious identity after the emergence of ISIS

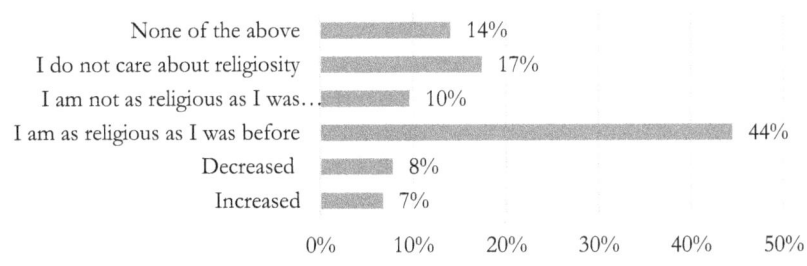

What we notice in the answers to this second question is that the psychological position of the participants was not particularly inconsistent or unstable, because the percentage affected by economic circumstances and the war was small, not exceeding 7 or 9 percent. The natural state that reflects the reality of Kurdish society, including the youth, is concentrated in answer E, which links religious and national identity, even though those who consider themselves religious without concern for their national identity reached 29 percent, which could warrant further study.

Shivan (2020, pers. comm.), a twenty-one-year-old engineering student, was one of the respondents. I contacted him again, and he agreed to have a discussion with me. When responding to the question about interest in religious and national identity, he said, "The only identity that I am proud of is my religious identity." Regarding his living situation, he confirmed, "It depends on the salary of my retired father, which does not exceed six hundred dollars per month. I am living with my parents and three sisters."

Jiyar (2020, pers. comm.) is a twenty-year-old education student, and his income is very good. In his answer to those who differentiate between religious and national identity, he confirmed, "Those who differentiate between national and religious identity do not understand the religion or the homeland." Therefore, we do not have a unified understanding of religious issues, and this is what we see in the Islamic arena, from extremists and moderates of all classes according to their understanding of religious texts, or the influence of religious heritage, which may give rise to such ideas as those of ISIS. In this regard, Ashna

(2020, pers. comm.), a nineteen-year-old art student whose living conditions are good, claimed, "Since 2012, I have been praying—before the arrival of the ISIS terrorist group. But we are an open family, and I am shaking hands with men and go out freely. I am proud of my Kurdishness, and I consider religion to be just a state of sentiment only."

Figure 3. Socio-economic conditions and religious identity after the emergence of ISIS

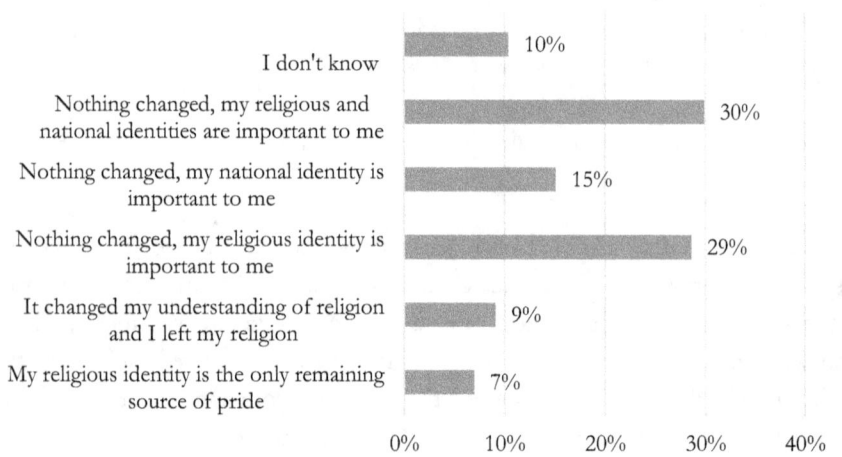

Kurdish society, in addition to being subjected to genocide, has been constantly marginalized, starved, and faced unjust and exceptional policies. These policies targeted Kurdish infrastructure at a time when the Iraqi government controlled the Kurdistan Region until 1991, and nearly all of the rural areas were demolished—a region that contained more than 4,500 villages and towns. Citizens were gathered in forcible compounds and besieged by the Iraqi security forces (Sadiq 2017, 71). This policy constituted a severe blow to the psychological state of the Kurdish individual, and it produced immense levels of unemployment among peasant citizens, who had been wholly dependent on work in the agricultural sector. Despite this situation, Kurdish citizens did not resort to revenge or terrorist activities. The negative repercussions of the genocide of Kurdish citizens persists in all regions , and the survivors of the genocide as well as those who were affected by the arbitrary policies have not been compensated. A large percentage of young people in Kurdistan are from rural areas, and their families are genocide survivors or have been impacted severely by these policies. Despite this exceptional situation in Kurdish society and the instability of material and security conditions, it is still relatively stable from a psychological point of view.

The answers here confirm a state of relative psychological stability. Likewise, "Identity achievement is a crucial developmental milestone, as it enables a young person to make positive contributions to society and to avert identity diffusion and despair" (Furrow, King, and White 2004, 17). Thus, trends in the number of participants who expressed disbelief in extremist trends is clear, as are the trends in the strengthening of religious identity among youth. If we add the element of religiosity, a segment comprising 67 percent of respondents who do not believe in the ISIS ideology, and if we also add the element of non-religiosity, which comprises 21 percent, the total becomes 88 percent.

What is striking here is that only one participant believes that ISIS has returned hope and whose religiosity has increased as a result. But no respondents declared their adherence to the Islamic movement. This result for the Islamic movement, if any conclusions are to be drawn from this, is the curtailment of the Islamic movement in Kurdistan among the youth. Conversely, the Islamic movement succeeded in socializing its ideology and relegating it to segments of society. Many religious people defend a set of values or, rather, a group of ideological positions that did not exist before the advent of political Islam in Kurdistan. From here, we see the depth of religiosity among youth and among the broader segments of society.

Figure 4. what is strengthening your religious identity?

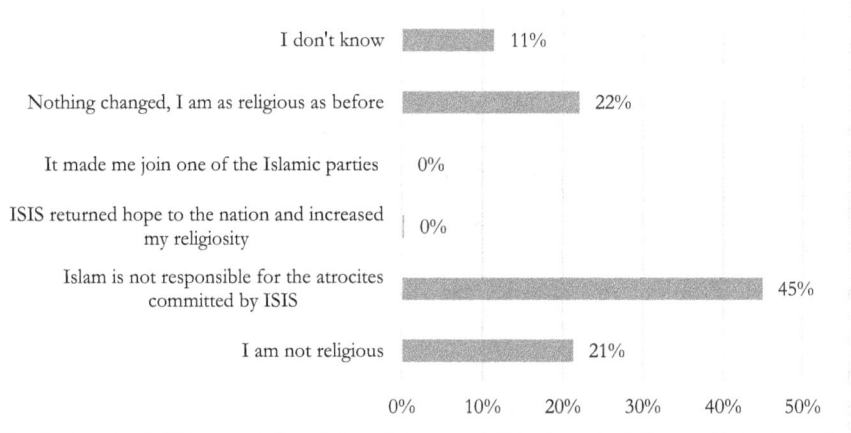

The percentage of respondents who considered themselves non-religious before the emergence of ISIS is significant, and if we add to it the other answers, except for A and F, it becomes 50 percent. Among those I interviewed, five non-religious youth confirmed that they had abandoned religion when they saw the massacres committed by ISIS in the name of Islam. And 7 percent of the respondents believe that ISIS represents the true Islam. Here, we see the level of anxiety and retreat from religious identity among youth. The hypothesis reflects the belief that people in crisis tend to be religious (Goodman 2020). In addition to the role of crises in shaping identity, "Identity formation includes growing self-awareness, which often involves negotiation of conflicts around attitudes, values, and goals within close relationships" (Kerpelman and Pittman 2018, 1).

Figure 5. what is weakening your religious identity?

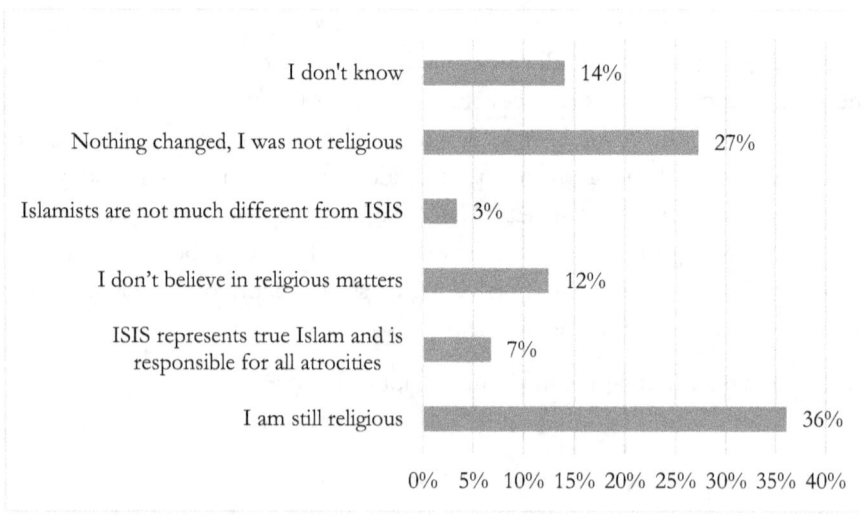

Strengthening identity, as stated above, "includes growing self-awareness" (Kerpelman and Pittman 2018, 1). Here we face an important question regarding self-awareness. The process of socialization may be separate from that of self-awareness or human desire, because "socialization continues as people learn how to behave in relation to new areas of social life, such as work environments and political beliefs" (Giddens and Sutton 2017, 373). Thus, upbringing begins with childhood and continues and accompanies individuals until the end of their lives. From here, we see that social environment is the expected answer for the majority of the participants, and ISIS did not have a direct effect in repelling the participants away from religion or in making them more religious. Also, visiting mosques or friends is not an action that lies outside the social environment. However, 6 percent of the participants turned to religiosity under the influence of social networks. This effect may be negative, because we may face extremist sources that bring the youth to religion but then convert them into extremists (Sharma 2016, 9).

Figure 6. How did your religious identity become strong?

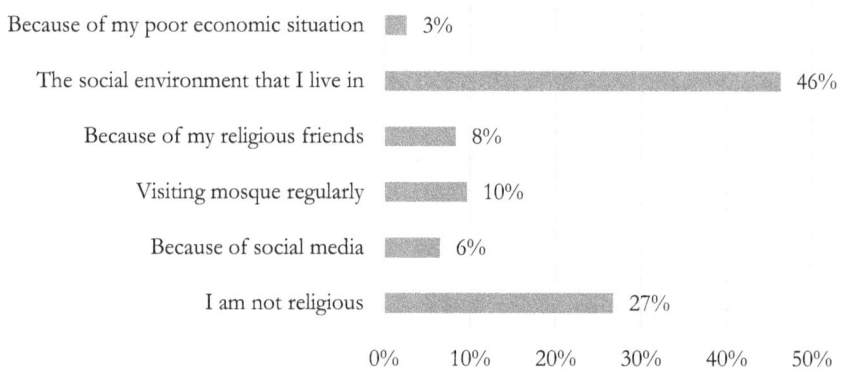

If the strengthening of identity is as above and "includes growing self-awareness" (Kerpelman and Pittman 2018, 1), does the weakness of a certain identity indicate an increase in self-awareness, or are there external factors that push the person in a certain direction? "The processes of development and identity formation are not fixed and . . . identity varies in its emergence with relational factors" (Kerpelman and Pittman 2018, 2). This indicates that self-awareness may weaken external influences in the formation of an identity and that the choice in deciding on an identity is stronger than all social relations in the issue of forming an identity. When asked about why his religious identity was weakened, Sherdil, who is twenty-four, responded with a degree of bitterness and pain: "Now I know the extent of the injustice I suffered from my father. When they taught me the prayer, fasting, and a lot of religious obligations, I became a ready-made template within Islam. Islam as an identity I was proud of, without knowing that I was just a mold without a soul within the molds of family and society. I was not me, I was 'everyone.' I was an obedient slave of family and society. I was the property of everyone, except for myself" (2020, pers. comm.).

From here, we face a pattern of social education that may not be compulsory in a technical sense, but it is certainly weak in its structure, as it is not based on conviction or rational standards and creates unreal happiness. Happiness is based on fear of what is beyond nature, from the grave and arithmetic. This means building a lean psyche that may collapse at any moment and when tested. Religious faith may, at times, face insurmountable crises at times, because it does not have convincing questions for many theological issues. Its result is a retreat toward other principles, or it may be the delinquency to vices. Sherdil continued:

> Suddenly, I met the author of a novel which I had read previously, and I asked him some questions. When I met him, I saw an opportunity to ask my questions and get answers. The answers were like a thunderbolt. What my father and the entire family, the community including to my school and the mosque, and all its social and political centers had built collapsed before my eyes. I used to see myself liberated from a bondage that was not long, but I felt at the time that it was tough. I was running away, and the molds that my family and my community built were collapsing around me one by one. I was able to save myself before the debris of collapsing molds crushing me. I was liberated, my soul was liberated. My soul was freed from the illusion of religions. I am now more committed to my relationships with others, and have more sense of my responsibility to others, because I do not do this for the sake of satisfying the goddess or for the sake of social control.

This young man is lucky to have found his conviction, and he feels happiness that may not be real, but it is a choice on his own, and no one forced him to adopt it. The result is, in his own words, "liberation." Emancipation is not from the principles of religion but from the fear that was implanted in the psyche of the young man, and the accompanying anxiety was a result of his lack of convictions in matters of faith.

This is the instability of identity. Self-awareness may create a realistic fluctuation toward the self, not society. This statement indicates that ethical issues are not linked to religious matters. It refrains from the idea that religion increases a person's commitment to society. Rather, what increases this commitment is self-awareness. Creating awareness among young people —and not imposing a specific religious education or indoctrination—may be the most important basis for educational institutions. Because as Vian (2020, pers. comm.), a twenty-three-year-old, assured me, "The sense of moral obligations toward society stems from my personal belief and conviction, and not because it is a religious duty or something like that." She added, "It means not to lie. If the Qur'an does not say it, is lying permissible? This is what makes religious people wrong toward those who are freed from the illusion of religion" (Vian 2020).

Thus, personal efforts to understand the phenomenon of religiosity and emancipation from it, as illustrated by the 24 percent of respondents who chose answer D, exceed the social environment. This denies not the direct influence on the formation of an identity but, rather, the success in escaping this influence and learning to alleviate societal restrictions, as 16 percent of the participants are not religious despite the effects of the social environment. All this disproves the first point that people in crisis return to religiosity, because, as previously mentioned, self-awareness has a pivotal role in a person choosing an appropriate identity.

Figure 7. How did your religious identity become weak?

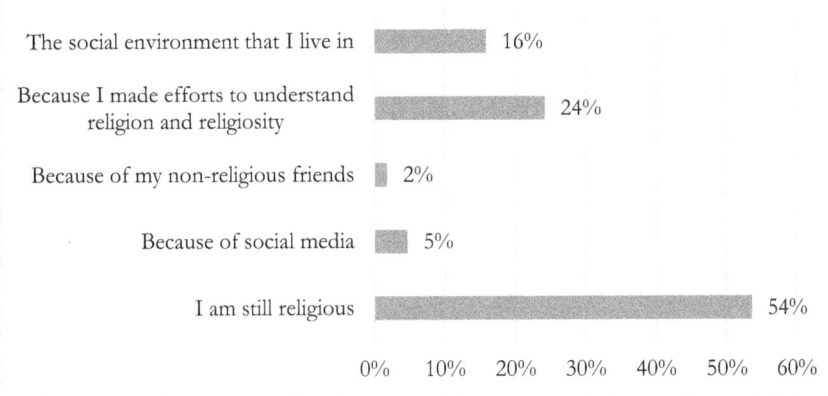

COVID-19 and Youth

People could hardly believe that the ISIS militants had been defeated and the situation would return to what it was before 2014, or that the economic and political situation would improve. However, "an invisible ISIS" appeared. People could not see it with the naked eye, and it forced members of society, including the youth who make up the majority, to return to their homes without a source of livelihood or a suitable means, even to study via networks of communication.

In some developed countries, the affected people were compensated, and those who lost their livelihoods were taken care of. But in the Kurdistan Region due to the financial distress and the consequences of the ISIS war, among other reasons, young people did not receive such support. This includes those who lost their jobs and those who were dependent on family members who lost their jobs as well. However, the purpose in this study, by highlighting this aspect of the post-ISIS phase, is to complement the first section and further explore the relationship between youth and religion. The goal was to understand the impact of COVID-19 on the stability of religious identity. It is striking, here, that 29 percent of young people consider COVID-19 to be a divine test, therefore making them proud of their religious identity.

This pride may result from the fear of this hidden enemy at a time of considerable controversy about the life-threatening danger of the virus. Viruses have appeared throughout many stages in history, and millions have died in absence of treatment or health awareness in some countries. Today, the virus emerged at a time when there was no direct treatment for it, and the psychological factor was—and still is—one of the most important elements that played a role in confronting such threats. It is known that religiosity may strengthen this psychological factor even though the virus has no link to religion. If this result is from the psychological point of view, it is a good factor. On the other hand, it is a reflection of a religiosity that cannot be rational, as COVID-19 is a divine test. In addition to all this, it is a validation of the hypothesis of strengthening religiosity during times of crisis and of strengthening identity.

Figure 8. Has the COVID-19 pandemic affected your religious identity?

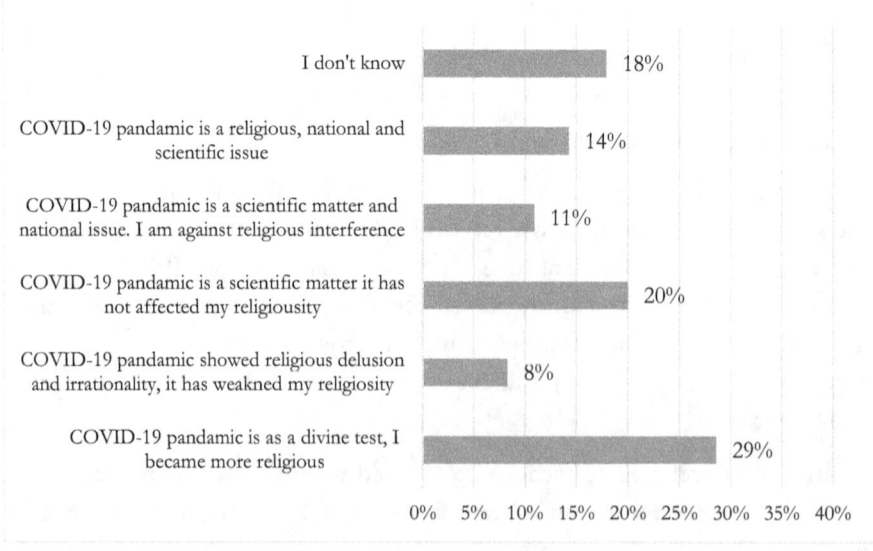

In return, the proportion of youth, whether religious, patriotic, or both, who responded with answers C, D, and E would be 45 percent, and an additional 18 percent of the respondents stated that they do not know anything about the virus, and they do not like to discuss it. The two answers demonstrate positive indicators from the respondents that there is stability in opinion regarding major issues that have arisen due to COVID-19.

Conclusion

Religion may be an important aspect of young people's lives, starting with the specificity of religious identity and ending with the influence and tendency to depart from this identity. From here, we seek to understand that identity faces numerous crises, and it is important to examine the effects of these on human relations, particularly among youth. In addition to religious affiliation, there are other competing affiliations, and multiple crises in society may affect the strengthening of any one identity. Here, we confront the identity crisis that is afflicting young people as a result of greater problems that are prevalent in society.

The emergence of ISIS came as an extension of the Islamic movements that believe in violence as a means of effecting societal change and in imposing a certain approach and thought on the human components, relations, and political systems. Its emergence had a direct impact on the stability of the Kurdish community in the Kurdistan Region in terms of security, politics, and economics. This study confirms the effects of these influences on the youth as a particularly important segment of society, including the trends around religious identity after the advent of ISIS and the extent of creating an identity crisis among youth. Accordingly, several hypotheses have been put forward regarding the assumption that people will never return to adhering to religion: the depth of religiosity among young people, the issue of youth attributing religion to their own identity, and whether it is a primary or secondary identity.

The geopolitical background of the region's citizens, the growing number of youth, and a political map that divides more than it unites has affected youth attitudes and culminated with their detachment from the political arena. This includes the economic crisis and rampant unemployment among youth, and it directly reflects on the orientation of youth identities. Likewise, the issue of gender has added another burden to girls who are unable to express or participate in societal changes due to the traditions prevailing in society, including the religious influence that distinguishes between the male and the female position in terms of human relations. Thus, unemployment has doubled among girls, and they are much less likely to attain levels of education than boys.

The issue of religious identity has been studied and researched through a questionnaire form, which 385 young men and women completed. Some of the youths who participated in the questionnaire were interviewed. The results revealed a suitable rate of stability and a lack of significant impact due to the emergence of ISIS. The prevailing state of religiosity has remained the same, with the exception of about 7 percent of respondents who became religious converts because of ISIS. On the other hand, between 8 and 9 percent of religious youth abandoned their religion due to the atrocities committed by ISIS.

In general, we can say that religious identity among youth in Kurdistan tended to be stable and that there has been no significant change in the religious tendencies of young people. However, while it was discovered that 50 percent of the youth are religious, there is also a trend toward non-religiosity, which is present in as many as half of the respondents. The study also shows that the trend of Islamism is declining, and there is no evidence of the existence of Islamism related to the emergence of ISIS. There was a question about the impact of the COVID-19, but the youth respondents were divided over how to deal with the disease. It shows the strengthening of religious identity, as 29 percent of young people consider it to be a divine test for society.

References

Abdullah, Farhad Hassan, and Hawre Hasan Hama. 2020. "The Nature of the Political System in the Kurdistan Region of Iraq." *Asian Journal of Comparative Politics* 5 (3): 300–15.
Bekdil, Burak. 2015. "Turkey's Double Game with ISIS: Dateline." *Middle East Quarterly*.
Black, Georgte. 1993. *Genocide in Iraq: The Anfal Campaign Against the Kurds*. Human Rights Watch.
Brandt, Mark J. and P. J. Henry. 2012. "Psychological Defensiveness as a Mechanism Explaining the Relationship Between Low Socioeconomic Status and Religiosity." *International Journal for the Psychology of Religion* 22 (4): 321–32.
Cherry, Kendra. 2019. "Could You Be Experiencing an Identity Crisis?" *Very Well Mind*, October 31. https://www.verywellmind.com/what-is-an-identity-crisis-2795948.
Elias, Norbert and John L. Scotson. 1994. *The Established and the Outsiders*. Vol. 32. Sage.
Erikson, Erik H. 1968. *Identity: Youth and Crisis*. No. 7. WW Norton & Company.
Feixa, Carles and Jordi Nofre. 2012. "Youth Cultures." *Sociopedia*. London: SAGE & ISA. DOI: 10.1177/2056846012822.
Furrow, James L., Pamela Ebstyne King, and Krystal White. 2004. "Religion and Positive Youth Development: Identity, Meaning, and Prosocial concerns." *Applied Developmental Science* 8 (1): 17–26.
Giddens, Anthony and Philip W. Sutton. 2017. *Essential Concepts in Sociology*. John Wiley & Sons.
Goodman, Bryan. 2020. "Faith in a Time of Crisis." American Psychological Association, May 11. https://www.apa.org/topics/covid-19/faith-crisis.
Hamasaeed, Sarhang and Garrett Nada. 2020. "Iraq Timeline: Since the 2003 War ." United States Institute of Peace, August 19. https://www.usip.org/iraq-timeline-2003-war.

Harambam, J. 2017. "'The Truth Is Out There': Conspiracy culture in an age of epistemic instability." Erasmus University Rotterdam. http://hdl.handle.net/1765/102423

Kerpelman, Jennifer L. and Joe F. Pittman. 2018. "Erikson and the Relational Context of Identity: Strengthening Connections with Attachment Theory." *Identity* 18 (4): 306–14.

Kirmanj, Sherko. 2013. "Kurdistan Region: A Country Profile." *Journal of International Studies* 9: 145-58.

KRG, M. 2013. Kurdistan Region of Iraq 2020: A Vision for the Future. Minister of Planning, Erbil. https://us.gov.krd/media/1286/krg_2020_last_english.pdf

KRG-MERA. 2007. Law No. 11: Yasaî Wezaretî Ewqaf u Karubarî Ayinî le Herêmî Kurdistan. Erbil: Kurdistan Parliament.

KRG-UIRCK. 2020. "Man Nahnu?" Erbil: YZAK. http://zanayan.org/arabic/sites.php?section=6

Kurt, Mehmet. 2019. "'My Muslim Kurdish brother': colonial rule and Islamist governmentality in the Kurdish region of Turkey." *Journal of Balkan and Near Eastern Studies* 21 (3): 350–65.

Low, Remy. 2016. "Making Up the Ummah: The Rhetoric of ISIS as Public Pedagogy." *Review of Education, Pedagogy, and Cultural Studies* 38 (4): 297–316.

Sadiq Malazada, Ibrahim. 2017. "Forced Displacement and Concentration Camps as a Civilizing Offensive: A Case Study on the Mass Deportation of the Kurdish People Between 1976 and 1986." In *Iraqi Kurdistan Region: A Path Forward*, edited by Sasha Toperich, Tea Ivanovic, and Nahro Zagros, 63–77. Center for Transatlantic Relations.

Manstead, Antony S.R. "The Psychology of Social Class: How Socioeconomic Status Impacts Thought, Feelings, and Behaviour ." *British Journal of Social Psychology* 57 (2): 267– 91.

McGarry, Aidan and James Jasper. 2015. *The Identity Dilemma: Social Movements and Collective Identity*. Temple University Press.

MHESR. 2018. Hiç Bešêkî Zaniste Îslamiyekan Danexirawe. Erbil: MHESR. http://archive.gov.krd/mohe/mhe-krg.org/index.php/ku/node/3844.html

Ryan, Louise. 2014. "'Islam Does Not Change': Young People Narrating Negotiations of Religion and Identity." *Journal of Youth Studies* 17 (4): 446–60.

Rudaw. 2015. "Increasing monitoring of Islamic schools and institutes," February 9. https://www.rudaw.net/arabic/kurdistan/090220151.

Rudaw. 2016. "The number of mosques in the Kurdistan Region," March 2. https://www.facebook.com/watch/?v=986854324743704.

Salam, Dana, Saeed Hamadameen, and Dana Showani. 2015. "The Gender Equality Situation in Kurdistan Region Education and Higher Education Policy: A Field Analytic Research About Women's Role in Phrasing Education and Higher Education Policy." MHE-KRG. http://emmaorg.me/wp-content/uploads/2016/08/gender-equality-in-education-sector.pdf.

Samia Aziz, and Omar Hamdaoui. 2011 "Dawr almujtama' almadani fi almuhafadza ala alhawiya althaqafiya." *Mujalat Albahith fi alulum alijtima'iya* 2011 (6): 707 –22.

Sen, Amartya. 2007. *Identity and Violence: The Illusion of Destiny*. 1st ed. Penguin Books India.

Sharma, Kunaal. 2016. "What Causes Extremist Attitudes Among Sunni and Shia Youth? Evidence from Northern India." *Program on Extremism*. George Washington University.

Speckhard, Anne. 2019. "Is Turkey Fueling a New Jihad in Northeast Syria?" International Center for the Study of Violent Extremism, November 11 .

SpeeMedia. July 30, 2016. "Le Šeš Mang da, 130 Mizgewit Kirawnetewe, Jimareî Mizgewtekan le Herê 5473 Mizgewte. http://www.speemedia.com/dreja.aspx?=hewal&jmare=35673&Jor=34.

Stets, Jan E., and Peter J. Burke. 2000. "Identity Theory and Social Identity Theory." *Social Psychology Quarterly*: 224–37.

Tohidi, Nayereh. 2009. "Ethnicity and Religious Minority Politics in Iran." In *Contemporary Iran: Economy, Society, Politics*, edited by Ali Gheissari, 299–323. New York: Oxford University Press.

UNDP (United Nations Development Programme). 2016. "Iraq Human Development Report 2014." http://hdr.undp.org/en/content/iraq-human-development-report-2014.

Wodak, Ruth. 2008. "'Us' and 'Them': Inclusion and Exclusion—Discrimination via Discourse."

In *Identity, Belonging and Migration*, edited by Gerard Delanty, Ruth Wodak, and Paul Jones, 54–77. Liverpool: Liverpool University Press.

CHAPTER 10

YOUTH RADICALIZATION IN KURDISTAN: THE GOVERNMENT RESPONSE

Kamaran Palani

Iraqi Kurdistan has become increasingly polarized in recent years, fueled by rising youth dissatisfaction and disillusionment with the authorities. Some factors to explain the tremendous pressures youth are facing (see Said 2019) include the post-2014 financial crisis, a lack of effective anti-corruption government reforms, insufficient policies to empower youth (see Jiyad, Küçükkeles, and Schillings 2020, 40–44), and widening political divisions. It is not the historical struggle for independence from the Iraqi state that defines the priorities and dreams of the people of Kurdistan today but, rather, youth dissatisfaction and anger toward the Kurdish authorities. A new identity is thus emerging among young Kurds within which the political class is viewed as "the other" (Palani 2021, 4). This anti-authority sentiment translates into different manifestations of resistance against, and disengagement with, political processes, ranging from emigration to Europe (*NRT* 2020), protest movements (Costantini 2020, 6), and potential youth radicalization, which is the main concern of this chapter.

Youth disillusionment with the Kurdistan Region of Iraq's (KRI) heavily politicized system of governance is not a novel phenomenon. What is new, however, is that the anger boiling among youth today poses a serious challenge to Kurdistan's internal legitimacy, which has been a pillar of the region's de facto autonomy for nearly thirty years. A recent study by the Dutch organization SPARK indicates a well-founded concern that the polarization of Kurdish society and its dissatisfied youth fosters an environment conducive for future youth radicalization and violent extremism (VE).[1]

The Kurdistan Regional Government (KRG) is presently overwhelmed with financial problems, internal political rivalry, preventing youth radicalization, and VE, and as a result, key initiatives such as educational and

---

[1] SPARK has been operating in the KRI since 2014 to develop higher education and entrepreneurship to empower young people.

religious reforms do not receive the warranted prioritization. However, KRI authorities are rather complacent in their belief that they possess the effective hard security tools to stave off terrorism and exert strong control over the KRI's territory and borders. There is also a perception that the people's adherence to *Kurdayati* (Kurdishness) (see Yousif and Muhammad 2020, 11) as well as the dominant spiritual rather than politicized practices of religion among the Kurds (Gharib 2017; Mamakani 2016) create resilience against extremism, especially religious extremism. Though these perceptions are prevalent among various stakeholders, recent developments indicate a diminishing sense of *Kurdayati* among youth and have contributed to the erosion of an element that for many years, had constrained religiously motivated extremism and violence in the KRI (Palani 2021, 4). Therefore, without the engagement of international actors in comprehensive assessments and discussions regarding the prevention of VE among Kurdistan's youth, the factors fueling violence and extremism may only increase.

In addition to explaining and contextualizing the factors that may contribute to the cultivation of an environment that enables youth radicalization and VE in the KRI, this chapter also seeks to present how KRI authorities have understood and reacted to such developments. This approach allows us to identify gaps in the government's approach. Inhibiting the effectiveness of some previous research, the terminology around VE is confusing and problematic. Terms are politicized and used interchangeably, often without clear definitions, thus resulting in the same terms being used to illustrate discrete approaches (UNDP 2018, 15). The 2015 United Nations Plan of Action on Preventing Violent Extremism states, "Violent extremism is a diverse phenomenon, without clear definition. It is neither new nor exclusive to any region, nationality or system of belief" (United Nations General Assembly 2015). I adopt the United States Agency for International Development (USAID) definition of VE: "advocating, engaging in, preparing, or otherwise supporting ideologically motivated or justified violence to further social, economic or political objectives" (USAID 2011, 2).

Methodology

This chapter utilizes qualitative data I gathered between 2016 and 2020 as part of (1) a joint research project countering violent extremism through a human security approach in Iraq and (2) a baseline research project on preventing violent extremism (PVE) that studied the empowerment of youth in order to prevent radicalization in Iraqi Kurdistan.

I also conducted eleven face-to-face telephone interviews with representatives of the KRI security forces, journalists, and civil society activists in the KRI governorates of Erbil and Sulaimaniyah between October 2019 and July 2020. The interviewees preferred to remain anonymous.

The next section provides a contextual analysis of the concerns regarding youth radicalization, beginning in 2014 with the rise of the so-called Islamic State (IS) and the financial crisis in the same year, before examining the KRG approach to youth radicalization and the issue of VE. The following sections are dedicated to an analysis of how the government and security institutions engaged with youth as well as their perspectives on the sources of youth radicalization.

Knowledge Gaps

Salahaddin University's Centre for Political and Strategic Studies published one of the few studies published in English on VE in Iraq and the Kurdistan as part of a broader research project entitled "Testing the Feasibility of a Human Security Approach to Combat Violent Extremism in Palestine, Egypt, and Iraq" (Shiera 2019, 29–46). The study provides valuable insights for the analysis of VE in Iraq, including in the Kurdistan Region, and is guided by a specific research question: Can a human security approach effectively address the drivers of VE? While the study provides offers a unique look into the political and social context of VE in the country, its main limitation is that it is rooted in a research hypothesis that allows no specific focus on the process of youth radicalization.

A study conducted in 2020 by a local NGO, the Peace and Freedom Organization, investigated the causes of VE and strategies to prevent its emergence, adopting a methodology of qualitative analysis that utilized interviews and document analysis. The study's main findings indicate a wide range of factors that contribute to VE, including poor governance, extremist political Islam and the lack—or frailty—of alternative narratives, poor prison conditions, and the KRG's weak education system (Yousif and Muhammad 2020). Nevertheless, as with the study above, it neglects to incorporate the conditions and concerns of youth into the discussion on radicalization and VE in Kurdistan.

Adel Bakawan's (2017, 11) study provides a good explanation and mapping of changes and transformations that have occurred in Kurdish extremist movements since the 1980s. The study concluded that, unlike previous generations of Kurdish extremists, the recent generation of jihadists had limited knowledge of Arabic and, interestingly, limited or no affiliation with the existing Kurdish Islamist parties. Bakawan found that 27 percent were unemployed, 41 percent were laborers, 25 percent were students, and only 7 percent were government employees, with 75 percent between the ages of fourteen and twenty-nine. The study, however, lacks a robust methodology and analysis of the root causes and drivers of youth VE beyond religious extremism. Bakawan's methodology for collecting information on IS members and his methods of data analysis are also unclear.

Alexander Meleagrou-Hitchens and Ranj Alaaldin (Meleagrou-Hitchens and Alaaldin 2016) conducted a policy analysis entitled "The Kurds of ISIS: Why Some Join the Terrorist Group." The study contextualizes the phenomenon of IS Kurds within the broader history of Kurdish jihadists, beginning in the 1980s. It utilized interviews with Kurdish security officials, Peshmerga commanders, intelligence officers, and Kurdish prisoners who had joined IS. Similarly to Bakawan, Meleagrou-Hitchens and Alaaldin also find that the existing Islamist parties did not have a role in the radicalization of Kurdish youth, nor were they instrumental in their decision to join IS. The authors instead highlighted the internet as a key source of radicalization and recruitment .

The main limitation in all the studies mentioned above is their lack of focus on how the growing frustration and disappointment of youth may exacerbate the factors compelling them to engage in violence and extremism, and on how the government understands and responds to youth radicalization.

Why We Should Be Worried

Concerns over surging youth inclinations for VE have been growing since 2014 in Iraqi Kurdistan. Two key factors may explain these concerns: the rise of the Islamic State and increasing youth dissatisfaction. The main focus of this section is the cultivation of an environment that is conducive for youth radicalization and violent radicalization in the KRI. In addition, this section seeks to explain and map the factors that have the potential to lead the youth toward radicalization and the use of violence.

The Rise of the Islamic State

The dramatic rise of IS in Syria and Iraq attracted many youth in the region and across the world, including some Kurds. Kurdistan suddenly had a new, extremely aggressive neighbor festering only a couple hundred kilometers across its border. In 2014, IS seized control of large swathes of territory in northern

Iraq, including parts of the Kurdistan Region, and in August of that year, the KRI capital Erbil was plagued by an acute crisis when IS besieged residents of Shingal, the Nineveh Plain, and Makhmour. On August 7, 2014, IS militants advanced as close as twenty-five miles from Erbil, before US President Barack Obama ordered airstrikes against the group to drive them out of the Kurdish-controlled territory (Palani et al., 2019, 2273).

IS represented both an external and domestic security threat. No research can state with absolute certainty how many Kurdish youth joined IS, but KRG officials estimate this number to be around 530 young Iraqi Kurds. The majority—300 to 330—of this group died in Syria and Iraq between 2014 and 2017, while around 150 ultimately returned and surrendered themselves to the KRI authorities (Shilani 2019). The number of young Kurds who joined the organization is low considering the geographical proximity of Iraqi Kurdistan, especially in the early months of the group's emergence in Iraq. However, this number would have been significantly higher if the Kurdish security forces (Asayesh) had not arrested over eight hundred individuals wishing to join IS before they could achieve their goal (Anonymous. 2019. Interview with a security official by the author. December 22). Nearly all research studying the Kurds of IS has neglected to report on the success of these efforts.

In addition to the movement of some young Kurds to areas controlled by IS, there was also concern over how established Kurdish Islamist parties and groups would respond to these new circumstances. Tensions escalated on social media and at conferences, with individuals and groups opposed to the Islamists attempting to undermine their legitimacy by calling them a "soft version of IS" or "IS on hold." However, all the Kurdish parties, including the Islamic Union, Islamic Group, and Islamic Movement—the three Islamist parties in Kurdistan—officially denounced IS and supported the Peshmerga's fight against the group.

While Islamic movements and parties believe that they have a significant role in preventing radicalization and extremism among Kurdish youth, the KRI's security institutions are deeply distrustful of them, maintaining that these parties are among the key sources of youth radicalization in Kurdistan. In this context, it is important to highlight that security institutions in Kurdistan, including the police, are controlled exclusively by the KRI's two leading parties, the Kurdistan Democratic Party (KDP) and the Patriotic Union of Kurdistan (PUK). Islamist parties view the police and other security forces as tools for political manipulation under the control of the KDP and PUK (Anonymous 2020.

Interview with Islamic Union official by the author. June 4). This suspicion has resulted in a limited degree of cooperation between Islamists and security institutions.

Increasing Youth Dissatisfaction

Over the past six years, beginning with the 2014 financial crisis in the KRI, Kurdistan has witnessed an astonishing magnitude of youth disengagement and discontent with the authorities. The amount of frustration with the party-led division of the region is also proliferating (Jiyad, Küçükkeles, and Schillings 2020, 6). Over a quarter of the population in the Kurdish region is between the ages of eighteen and thirty-four, and many suffer the effects of high unemployment and increasing disillusionment (IOM 2018). Youth unemployment and migration to Europe have increased significantly since 2014. And according to a 2018 statement by Sirwan Mohammad, the head of KRG's Statistics Office, the unemployment rate stood at 9 percent (*Rudaw* 2020b). However, KRG Minister for Labor and Social Affairs Kwestan Mohammed stated, "Different rates have been published claiming unemployment in the Kurdistan Region stands at 11 percent, some others say 14 or 18 percent . . . I cannot rely on any of them because we still do not know the Kurdistan Region's population, or how much of the population has reached standard working age" (*Rudaw* 2020a). High rates of unemployment and economic deprivation pose structural barriers to youth participation and empowerment, condemning many youth in Kurdistan to a subsistence bracket in which they are forced to direct their energy to meet their basic needs. Like to the unemployment rate, there is no accurate or official statistics for the number of the young Kurds who left Kurdistan hoping for asylum in a European country. Between 2014 and 2017, youth migration to Europe became a widespread phenomenon, with thousands crossing borders illegally.

The fight against IS and the financial crisis, both of which erupted in early 2014, put an end to the economic growth and progress Kurdistan had experienced in the decade after the 2003 US-led invasion of Iraq. A collapse in oil prices, Baghdad's decision to freeze the KRI's budget to the effect of a nearly one billion dollar monthly shortfall, and an influx of 250,000 Syrian refugees and 1.5 million internally displaced people fleeing IS further overwhelmed Kurdistan. This has since effected significant implications for the wellbeing of its population, especially for youth. The KRG has been unable to pay its government employees, who constitute about 20 percent of the population, in a timely manner, nor can it provide job opportunities for thousands of university graduates. High unemployment and economic deprivation pose structural barriers to youth empowerment and mean that many of Kurdistan's youth are preoccupied with accessing the most basic needs (Palani 2021, 7). The lack of systematic reform to address the root causes of the KRI's fragility and mismanagement has created further disappointment and disengagement.

Overall, the circumstances of youth across the KRI remain precarious. Without viable recourse to the mechanisms that might allow them to alleviate their situation, the region's youth are growing increasingly hopeless and eager to migrate in search of a better life. In the case of Kurdistan, there is no evidence as yet demonstrating clearly how youth disengagement and feelings of powerlessness can transform into support for VE. But the general literature on youth radicalization and VE illustrates that young people's mistrust of the authorities as well as perceptions of illegitimacy and corruption constitute major drivers pushing some toward VE. As the literature demonstrates, repeated negative encounters experienced by themselves, a family member, or a peer with, for example, a member of the security forces, a civil servant, or judge produces feelings of anger and alienation and fuels the susceptibility of young people toward radicalization (UNDP 2017, 5). When societies fail to meaningfully integrate youth, they are more likely to engage in political violence (UNDP 2016, 30).

The KRG Reaction to Youth Radicalization and VE

In this section, we address how the KRI authorities have understood and reacted to youth radicalization and VE as well as the sources and factors contributing to radicalization and violence. Importantly, this will also allow us to identify gaps in how the government approaches these issues. At the outset, it is critical to highlight that, although the KRI has two decades of experience with fighting terrorist and extremist groups, the government has not adopted clear definitions of extremism, radicalization, or VE. The current cabinet in Iraqi Kurdistan has no dedicated position for countering VE (Sheira 2019, 28). In the KRI, both authorities and the public tend to define extremism almost entirely from a religious perspective; the authorities also do not differentiate between "extremism" and "terrorism." While the concepts of terrorism and VE have much in common, they require different approaches (Erstad 2018). In terms of tackling these complex challenges, terrorism demands a short-term and hard security-driven approach, whereas the phenomenon of VE requires a long-term and soft security-driven approach (Erstad 2018). Kurdistan has effectively countered terrorism but has failed to develop a national policy that clearly defines and successfully prevents and counters VE and its drivers.

One illustration of the KRI authorities' limited conceptualization of VE appears in the tendencies of authorities and security institutions to view Islamic movements with suspicion, regardless of statements of peaceful aims, and to perceive them as varieties of Islamist extremism. Moreover, other Kurdish political parties, such as the Kurdistan Workers' Party (*Partîya Karkerên Kurdistanê*, PKK) and its affiliate organizations, have adopted violence at varying times and places. This is viewed not as "extremism" but as a "legitimate" response to attacks on Kurds by the states in the region, such as Turkey. Ethnically motivated violence is thus not subject to "genuine" criticism. Islamist parties do not—or cannot—label the violence used by the PKK and its affiliates as "violent extremism" due to fears of a public backlash.

Nevertheless, with the threat of IS and the attempts of hundreds of young Kurds to join the group since 2014, there has been a growing interest in extremism and radicalization in Kurdistan. In this context, the KRG's Ministry of Education initiated reforms in school curricula, introducing in 2019 a new area of study called "life skills" for primary schools and preaching tolerance and teaching students to respect other ethno-religious identities in society, among neighbors and friends. This program was piloted in two hundred schools across the Kurdistan Region (Anonymous 2020. Interview with official from the KRG Ministry of Education by the author. July 2). The Ministry of Endowments and Religious Affairs has pursued a similar approach toward regulating religious education by, for example, establishing an institute for training imams that included seminars on the principles of coexistence and tolerance (Skare et al. 2021, 14).

Lack of a Unified Security Approach for Youth Engagement

Beneath the façade of the KRG's state-like institutions, the KDP and PUK maintain parallel systems of governance, each controlling economic resources, different branches of the security and military apparatuses, and components of the administration. A defining feature of this system has been a two-party duopoly, constraining the region's democratization and state-building efforts. The private and public sectors, access to government contracts, and positions in the security forces, are all tightly controlled in the hands of the two parties. The excessive influence the two parties wield over governance forms a structural and administrative barrier, effectively precluding the participation of an increasingly unaffiliated and independent youth constituency (Petkova 2018).

Security Institutions' Engagement with Youth

The key informant interviewees (KII) who participated in the gathering of this research reveal that the KRI's security institutions have not directly established a relationship with the youth in society. Unlike the involvement of Kurdistan's imams, for example, there have been no initiatives to engage with youth in the context of the government's anti-radicalization or counterextremism measures, though youth are the main target of such policies and are an essential part of their implementation and success. Their burgeoning dissatisfaction makes them particularly vulnerable in this regard. Nevertheless, there are overlapping elements between accessing youth and engaging with imams: The government considers engagement with imams essential for creating a link with youth due to the degree of influence religious leaders maintain over this segment of the population.

In general, the development and evolution of both security and non-security institutions in Kurdistan have constrained attempts at engaging the youth in the formulation and implementation of counter-radicalization and VE policies. Efforts to cultivate security and political engagement with youth largely utilize partisan methods and channels, such as student unions at universities and neighborhood youth centers. This necessitates a greater degree of cognizance when partnerships with these centers and union are proposed and attempted. To reach a wider community of youth, it is important to carefully identify the existing channels available for youth engagement in Kurdistani society, which are primarily based on political party networks. Engagement with these elements is still critical, as they maintain grassroots operations, but the most glaring risk is that such engagement will fortify a structure that is not designed to embody genuine representation for youth.

A solution may lie in (1) working to establish an independent and nonpartisan space for youth, (2) fostering a more inclusive social media environment that can provide a broader space beyond the available party-based channels, and (3) coordinating with youth as effective partners, which should be viewed as a key priority in PVE programming.

Security Institutions' Perspectives on the Combatting and Origins of Youth Radicalization

Security institutions such as Kurdistan's Directorate General of Asayesh, which has departments in both Erbil and Sulaimaniyah that are dominated by the KDP and PUK, respectively, are concerned with home-grown youth radicalization in Kurdistan. A critical detail in this issue is that nearly all attempted and successful terrorist attacks in Kurdistan have been perpetrated in connection with local sympathizers or contacts (see van Wilgenburg 2018a). The threat of violent extremism is local, compelling security institutions and the government to combine both hard and soft security measures.

As mentioned above, when security institutions and personnel in Kurdistan refer to radicalization and extremism, they primarily emphasize religious and Islamist radicalization and terrorism. A similar perspective is also prevalent in non-security institutions, such as the Ministries of Education and of Endowment and Religious Affairs. However, we have recently witnessed a striking change in the government's discourse and work in this regard. Security institutions claim that their ultimate objective is the rehabilitation and reintegration of radicalized individuals into society, but they have been unable to develop the skills and tools necessary to accomplish this. A security official commented on this situation in a private interview: "Radicalization is an outcome of isolation in society. When we arrest radicalized young people, we do not want them to feel isolated. Sometimes it happens that I personally want to hit them, but I am not authorized" (Anonymous 2020. Interview with security official by the author. November 11).

Members of Kurdistan's Asayesh are aware of the need to weaken the factors that produce extremism and radicalization, and strengthen the factors that prevent them. The question remains as to whether institutions have the capacity to address the root causes of VE and radicalization. They are designed to fight terrorism, not address the factors that lead to extremism, and their work is also deeply influenced by the country's lack of unified security institutions and unstable political dynamics, which prevent long-term and comprehensive planning.

Kurdistan's PVE campaign falls within the framework of its counterterrorism policy, as mentioned above, and there is a limited engagement with youth and civil society. However, there are some encouraging signs. Security forces do not arrest extremists or people who hold radical views; instead, they try to monitor their movements on the ground and seek to deradicalize them through informal and indirect social channels, such as parents and imams. A KII in security stated, "If individuals are arrested, security forces attempt to rehabilitate them with their limited resources and capacity"

(Anonymous 2020. Interview with security official by the author. November 12).

Here emerges the critical need to differentiate between genuine extremists and individuals suffering from psychological disorders. According to the KIIs, there are cases where young people have been arrested and accused of Islamist extremism but were in fact mentally ill, and there was no effective mechanism available for identifying their problems. Prison staff and the Asayesh do not have the capacity necessary to identify and diagnose these cases. To address this challenge, it is believed that the support of the European countries, international actors, and NGOs that do have the necessary capacity and experience may be helpful. This is, therefore, an area in which countries and INGOs can support Kurdistan's institutions in its attempt to improve the youth radicalization and rehabilitation programs.

Sources of Youth Radicalization in Kurdistan

Kurdistan's security institutions prioritize four potential sources of youth radicalization in Kurdish society. They have already made significant investments in the context of addressing these sources to prevent youth radicalization, but they require greater cooperation with various stakeholders in the identified categories. These four sources are:

Mullahs/Imams. It is worth noting that it is not mosques themselves that are sources of youth radicalization but, rather, imams, demonstrating the need to adjust the prevalent terminology. Some imams have the power and charisma to influence and radicalize youth. As explained above, the Asayesh has closely monitored imams, has established amicable relationships with many, and has stopped the activities of others. However, the challenge lies in the idea that the excessive centralization and regulation of Islamic institutions and mosques will engender problems in the legitimacy of these centers, as trust in, and perceptions of, the legitimacy of government institutions is low.

Families. The Asayesh has identified certain families in Kurdistan that have long provided a space for youth radicalization and from which are drawn a significant proportion of extremists. The Asayesh closely monitors these families.

Islamist parties. Security institutions see Islamist parties as sources that contribute significantly to youth radicalization. For the political reasons discussed previously, the Asayesh has not established a good relationship with

Islamist parties. With the elements of political calculation and competition between the ruling parties and Islamist parties, especially the Islamic Group and the Islamic Movement, cooperation has not been favorable. But there have been some constructive developments, such as when the Islamic Group warned the Asayesh of the threat of radicalization in an Islamist party when two of its members joined IS in 2014 (Anonymous 2020. Interview with security official by the author. November 11).

Social media. The Asayesh also sees social media as an effective source of youth radicalization and are engaged in monitoring social media accounts. However, they lack expertise and capacity in this domain, compared to their activity regarding the other three sources that they see as possessing potential for the radicalization of Kurdish youth.

To summarize, how the KRG and its security institutions understand sources of youth radicalization include both hard and soft security measures. Hard security measures entail arrests, interrogations, and imprisonment, whereas soft measures include engaging with imams and monitoring individuals suspected of extremism. Nevertheless, their understanding still relies on heavy-handed securitized approaches and the assumption that the drivers are primarily religious. Security responses are essential in such an unstable and dangerous region but will not tackle the underlying conditions that push the youth toward radicalization.

As this chapter has argued, there should be a greater focus on long-term prevention-related factors and measures, such as resolving political polarization and perceptions of corruption and injustice among youth. For this reason, handling youth radicalization and VE should not only be placed under the volition of security actors. Other government institutions should play a larger role in formulating the government's understanding and vision toward both identifying push and pull factors driving youth radicalization and preventing these from occurring.

Conclusion

This chapter has sought to show how growing youth frustration and the government's securitized approach constitute a significant cause for concern, and the government's orthodox short-term securitization efforts to prevent youth radicalization and VE may be insufficient in the future. Though Kurdistan's traditional securitized approach to terrorism has so far been largely effective, it is hard to predict if this approach will continue to be so in the face of the emerging domestic environment of the polarization of youth. What is currently lacking is a charismatic Kurdish religious leader or movement that can mobilize and radicalize youth. The absence of such an element has not been the function of an existing PVE policy, but certain religious and ethnic factors that have been bulwarks against extremism are now eroding.

A successful initiative requires the implementation of certain elements and circumstances. The key to effectively preventing VE in Iraqi Kurdistan is empowering youth and addressing their concerns. A dissatisfied and angry population of youth is a major barrier to the success of prevention policies. The second element is the development and implementation of a coherent national PVE policy. The rationale for this is that various government sectors including educational and religious institutions currently lack the comprehensive guidance necessary to cooperate in their capacity and expertise. The main challenge to youth empowerment and the development of national PVE policy is that the KRG is currently overwhelmed by financial difficulties and internal political rivalry, with very limited focus being placed on long-term plans to empower youth and prevent VE.

Another important element is the need for coordination mechanisms at all levels. For example, coordination between teachers and parents, especially in detecting changes in behavior in students, is currently lacking. Similarly, the lack of clear conceptualization and definition of radicalization and VE is also an issue across government institutions and ministries. To improve coordination and communication, international development and peace-building actors should establish multi-sector and coordination mechanisms between governmental and non-governmental actors, delineating roles and responsibilities in both developing and implementing PVE.

References

Bakawan, Adel. 2017. "Three generations of jihadism in Iraqi Kurdistan." Notes de l'Ifri. https://www.ifri.org/sites/default/files/atoms/files/bakawan_jihadism_iraqi_kurdistan_2017.pdf

Costantini, Irene. 2020. "The Iraqi protest movement: social mobilization amidst violence and instability." *British Journal of Middle Eastern Studies*: 1–18.

Erstad, Henriette Ullavik. 2018. "The EU in the Middle East - how to prevent terrorism and violent extremism?" Norwegian Institute of International Affairs, November 13. https://www.nupi.no/nupi_eng/News/The-EU-in-the-Middle-East-how-to-prevent-terrorism-and-violent-extremism

Gharib, Tahsin. 2017. "ئیسلامی کوردی گۆڕانکارییە یان تێگەیشتنێکی دروستە لە ئایینی ئیسلام؟" [Is Kurdish Islam a Change or a Correct Understanding of Islam?] *Rudaw*, June 7. https://www.rudaw.net/sorani/onair/tv/episodes/episode/islam_u_jyan_07062018

IOM (International Organization for Migration). 2018. "Demographic Survey Kurdistan Region of Iraq." http://www.krso.net/files/articles/160918035158.pdf.

Jiyad, Sajad, Müjge Küçükkeleş, and Tobias Schillings. 2020. "Economic Drivers of Youth Political Discontent in Iraq: The Voice of Young People in Kurdistan, Baghdad, Basra and Thi-Qar." Global Partners Governance.

Mamakani, Ehsan. 2016. "KRG official: Kurdish Islam, not extremism." *Kurdistan24,* January 6. https://www.kurdistan24.net/en/story/1741-KRG-official:-Kurdish-Islam,-not-extremism.

Meleagrou-Hitchens, Alexander and Ranj Alaaldin. 2016. "The Kurds of ISIS: Why Some Join the Terrorist Group." *Foreign Affairs*, August 8. https://www.foreignaffairs.com/articles/syria/2016-08-08/kurds-isis

NRT. 2020. "More than 32,000 people, mostly youths, migrate from Kurdistan region, Iraq in 2020: advocacy organization." October 23. https://www.nrttv.com/en/News.aspx?id=24690&MapID=1

Palani, Kamaran, Jaafar Khidir, Mark Dechesne, and Edwin Bakker. 2019. "The Development of Kurdistan's De Facto Statehood: Kurdistan's September 2017 Referendum for Independence." *Third World Quarterly* 40 (12): 2270–88.

Palani, Kamaran. 2021. "Youthful anger and the crisis of legitimacy in Iraqi Kurdistan." Al Sharq Strategic Research, January 5. https://research.sharqforum.org/2021/01/06/youthful-anger-and-the-crisis-of-legitimacy-in-iraqi-kurdistan/

Petkova, Mariya. 2018. "Anger is simmering among Iraq's Kurdish youth." *Al Jazeera*, November 12. https://www.aljazeera.com/features/2018/11/12/anger-is-simmering-among-iraqs-kurdish-youth

Rudaw. 2020a. "Tackling unemployment is a job for the whole cabinet: KRG labor minister." January 23. https://www.rudaw.net/english/interview/23012020

———. 2020b. "9%یە لە کوردستان هەرێمی لە بێکاری ڕێژەی ئاماری دەستەی" [Statistics Office: the unemployment rate in the Kurdistan Region is 9 percent]. March 25. https://www.rudaw.net/sorani/kurdistan/2503202016

Said, Yerevan. 2019. "Without Diversifying its Rentier Economy, Pessimism Among Kurdish Youth Will Increase." *Washington Institute for Near East Policy*, September 25 https://www.washingtoninstitute.org/policy-analysis/without-diversifying-its-rentier-economy-pessimism-among-kurdish-youth-will.

Salafi, Abdullatif. 2019. "Kurdistan24's interview with Dr. Abdullatif Salafi." *Kurdistan24*, June 3. https://www.kurdistan24.net/ckb/tv_episode/4458-

Sheira, Omar, Rabha Allam, and Ziad Akl. 2019. "Testing the feasibility of a human security approach to combat violent extremism in Palestine, Egypt, and Iraq." Human Security to Counter Extremism. http://www.humansecurity2cve.org/wp-content/uploads/2020/02/NWO-WOTRO_CVE-final-report.pdf

Shilani, Hiwa. 2019. "150 Kurdish ISIS militants who surrendered to Kurdistan Region authorities are in prison: Official." *Kurdistan24*, May 23. https://www.kurdistan24.net/en/news/fe5cb55d-9871-4692-ae29-67f2e4d5be7c

Skare, Erik, Kamaran Palani, Stéphane Lacroix, Tine Gade, Dlawer Ala'Aldeen, Kjetil Selvik and Olivier Roy. 2021. "Preventing violent extremism: The Middle East". https://www.prevex-balkan-mena.eu/wp-content/uploads/2020/12/PREVEX-D7.1-Policy-Brief-the-Middle-East_FINAL.pdf?fbclid=IwAR2VTtwzAEDutJSt3ygIGiLC65qXxnVuWf0LUYzHhIuAgK_tevzYN2trSCk

UNDP (United Nations Development ProgramP). 2016. "Preventing violent extremism through promoting inclusive development, tolerance and respect for diversity."

———. 2017. "Journey to extremism in Africa: Drivers, incentives and the tipping point for recruitment."

———. 2018. Improving the impact of preventing violent extremism programming: A toolkit for design, monitoring and evaluation."

United Nations General Assembly. 2015. "Plan of action to prevent violent extremism: Report of the Secretary General," A/70/674.

USAID (United States Agency for International Development). 2011. "The development

response to violent extremism and insurgency: Putting principles into practice."
van Wilgenburg, Wladimir. 2018. "The threat from within: Erbil attack exposes radicalization in Kurdistan." *Kurdistan24*, July 25. https://www.kurdistan24.net/en/news/12af610a-b0be-4ef1-9b06-cb9fb8ae31bb
———. 2018b. "New Kurdistan survey shows high youth unemployment, low income." *Kurdistan24*, Sep 13. https://www.kurdistan24.net/en/news/12af610a-b0be-4ef1-9b06-cb9fb8ae31bb
Yousif, Sanger and Abdulsamih Muhammad. 2020. "Violent extremism: Factors and approaches to prevention in the Kurdistan Region-Iraq." Peace and Freedom Organization within the Iraqi Observatory for the Prevention of Violent Extremism (OPEV-Iraq).